AWE

Other Books by Paul Pearsall, Ph.D.

The Last Self-Help Book You'll Ever Need

The Beethoven Factor

Toxic Success

Partners in Pleasure

Wishing Well

The Heart's Code

The Pleasure Prescription

Write Your Own Pleasure Prescription

The Pleasure Principle (audio series)

Sexual Healing

The Ten Laws of Lasting Love

Making Miracles

The Power of the Family

Super Immunity

Super Marital Sex

Super Joy

AWE

THE DELIGHTS AND DANGERS OF OUR ELEVENTH EMOTION

Paul Pearsall, Ph.D.

Health Communications, Inc.

Deerfield Beach, Florida

www.hcibooks.com

Library of Congress Cataloging-in-Publication Data

Pearsall, Paul.
  Awe : the delights and dangers of our eleventh emotion / Paul Pearsall.
    p. cm.
  Includes index.
  ISBN-13: 978-0-7573-0585-6 (hardcover)
  ISBN-10: 0-7573-0585-7 (hardcover)
  1. Awe. I. Title.
BF575.A9P43 2007
152.4–dc22

2007020434

Publisher: Health Communications, Inc.
        3201 S.W. 15th Street
        Deerfield Beach, FL 33442-8190

Cover design by Larissa Hise Henoch
Inside book design and formatting by Dawn Von Strolley Grove

For our son Scott,
who leaves us in awe.

CONTENTS

ACKNOWLEDGMENTS...ix

INTRODUCTION: *The Awe of Understanding* xi

CHAPTER 1: *The Choice of a Lifetime* 1

CHAPTER 2: *To Heaven and Back*...31

CHAPTER 3: *Awe Full Moments* 61

CHAPTER 4: *The Case for an Eleventh Emotion* 91

CHAPTER 5: *The Real Secret*...115

CHAPTER 6: *The Flourishing Factor* 145

CHAPTER 7: *Elated by Life* 169

CHAPTER 8: *Awful Awe*...195

CHAPTER 9: *Your Awe-Inspired Life* 223

CHAPTER 10: *Left in Awe*..243

ENDNOTES..259

INDEX 279

ACKNOWLEDGMENTS

In Hawaiian, the word *ho`omaika`i* means to express one's most sincere loving appreciation. After you have finished reading this book, you will understand why my appreciation for the persons named here is so deep and profound.

My wife of forty-three years, Celest, is my life. She has helped me write every one of my twenty books by advising, criticizing, encouraging, and editing. She is the most patient and strongest person I know and has endured decades of my insecure repetitive author's question, "But what do you *really* think?" As you will read, her strength at this time in our life is the core of our survival.

Because that's all they had, my deceased parents, Carol and Frank, taught my brother Dennis and me how to find awe in the simple things. Through their struggles dealing with their serious disabilities and the discrimination that they too often elicited, my sons, Roger and Scott, showed me the dark and light sides of awe and what happens when people respond with "awe lite," the kind of awe that lacks understanding.

My extended Hawaiian family, *Kuhai Halau O Kawaikapuokalani Pa Olapa Kahiko,* continues to provide the aloha that sustains us, and we are in awe of the loving wisdom of the *kumu* (teacher) of this *halau* Kawaikapuokalani Hewett. Without them now, I don't know how we would be carrying on.

I owe so much to my agent, Michael Bourret, for his faith in the concept of this book even when no one seemed interested and for his persistence, caring, and guidance. Mahalo, Michael, for never giving up on me. My editor at HCI Books, Michele Matrisciani, is truly a jack-of-all publishing trades and master of all of them. She grasped the idea of awe right away, and beyond her always gentle but excellent editorial guidance, she has shown loving caring not often found in the competitive world of publishing.

As always, I owe a huge debt to all the scientists and writers quoted in these pages, particularly psychologist Dr. Jonathan Haidt, who, to the best of my knowledge, was the first to discuss the awe response from a scientific perspective. I express my aloha to psychologist Dr. Gary Schwartz not only for being my friend but for finding such awe in the mysteries of the world that he just can't stop researching what few scientists dare to study.

Ho`omaika`i to the hundreds of persons who shared the experiences of awe. I hope I have not let any of the persons named here down in my efforts to share what I consider to be our most elevating, transformative, and instructive eleventh emotion.

THE AWE OF UNDERSTANDING

"I'd take the awe of understanding over the awe of ignorance any day."

—DOUGLAS ADAMS[1]

A PROMISE TO MY SON

I sat in awe as my newborn son struggled to stay alive. He looked so frail and vulnerable, and it seemed that after each labored breath he would not have the strength to take another. His tiny fingers were curled in tight fists that encased his thumbs, and I pulled them gently open so I could feel his grip with my index fingers. But there wasn't strength in his hands to grab onto me. His eyes looked directly up and into mine as if asking me to help him, and I was in the most profound state of awe I have ever known—an awe for him, for life, for death, and for the love my wife and I shared that gave us this child and would now have to sustain us as we fought to keep him alive.

I can never know the pain our baby must have felt as his body lay rigid while a tube pumping air into his lungs caused his tiny chest to heave grotesquely. I could see his every heartbeat making his entire body quiver, and I panicked each time there was a long delay before another beat. A doctor's mistake had delayed our son's birth, and when I noticed his distress after the emergency cesarean delivery that saved his life, I insisted he be rushed to an emergency neonatal intensive care unit at a local children's hospital. There he lay alone in a huge glass incubator. I leaned over that incubator with my arms widespread, trying to embrace my son through the glass, and I sobbed harder than I had ever sobbed in my life.

I still remember my wife and me crying bitterly after his birth. As other parents looked fondly at their new babies, we went to the window to see the ambulance below taking our son from us—perhaps forever. At that terrible moment, as the siren blared and the ambulance rushed our baby to the other hospital, our collective breath seemed to be taken away from us; we gasped for air and held one another. We both felt an overwhelming chill and goose bumps as the worst dread a person could feel spread over us. But it was a fear strangely mixed with an exciting, childlike, confusing, joyful hope that our son might be allowed to live. We later spoke of the unique kind of sadness we felt then, one related not just to the possibility that our child would die and the horror of the moment, but also to a failure to treasure more, and spend even more moments than we had, savoring and celebrating together the miracle of our son's growing in my wife's body. We admitted feeling that we should have relished his existence when we still had him, and the grief over the lost opportunities to cherish life was as strong as our fear that our son's life would be snuffed out. At this most terrible moment in our young lives, and despite our fears, we felt a strangely overwhelming sense that something magnificent was taking place, that we were being immersed together in something—some process—that was infinitely beyond what we could ever understand, but that we were destined to keep trying. I know now that what we felt was the most intense, wonderful, upsetting, and transcendently terrible of all human emotions: awe.

As you will read in this book, *awe* is our eleventh emotion, the one least studied but yet more powerful than the other ten basic feelings that psychologists recognize. As I look back now after my research on awe (which you will be reading about) and reflect on the emotions my wife and I experienced during our baby's fight and—we felt—our fight as well for his life, I am convinced that awe is our most unique emotion. Unlike all the other emotions, it's all of our feelings rolled up into one intense one. You can't peg it as just happy, sad, afraid, angry, or hopeful. Instead, it's a matter of experiencing all of these feelings and yet, paradoxically, experiencing no clearly identifiable, or at least any easily describable, emotion. Awe overwhelms and drains the power out of any other singular emotion we may have had before it took hold, and the best description I've been able to give it so far is that—no matter how good or bad our brain considers whatever is happening to be—it is feeling more totally and completely alive than we thought possible before we were in awe. It's feeling numbed yet totally alert at the same time. These are some of awe's mysteries that are explored in the chapters you are about to read.

Because my wife was still weak from her surgery, I rushed alone to the intensive care unit, where I sat for hours watching my son fight for his life. Again, that strange sense of awe came over me. I saw blue letters on a strip of bandage stuck on my son's incubator that said, "Baby Boy Pearsall." We had already named him Scott, but a nurse told me that the staff wanted parents to avoid "too much attachment" in case "things don't go well." Of course, it was far too late to "not become attached." As any new parent, my wife and I already loved our son—a love made even stronger by our awe for his eerily silent struggle to live. Babies are supposed to cry, but he was silent and seemed so alone. So I demanded that Scott be taken out of the incubator and with tubes dangling from his body, I held him against my chest and rocked him.

For hour after hour, and pausing only when hospital staff had to apply treatment or give medicine, I held my son and felt in total awe of him and his refusal to leave us. How could someone so new and little be so strong? I could feel his heart beating with mine and, despite the doctors' negative prognosis, I felt him getting stronger, which made me stronger—a gift Scott would give me throughout our lives, despite his cerebral palsy (CP).

When Scott's eyes opened one morning, seeming to radiate more life energy than I had seen before and to be saying "Hi, Dad" and not "Help me," I felt goose bumps again, struggled to get my breath, and began to sob. I was scared to death and thrilled beyond measure at the same time. What was this mysterious miracle unfolding before me? I was in total awe of Scott's healing energy, his refusal to give up, his reaching out to me beyond words, and the frightening blend of the power and fragility of the life force that seems to so quickly come and go, offer such joy and sorrow, and promise so much while causing such despair and desperate yearning. Somehow, in some confusing way, my awe was allowing me a frightening, fascinating, overwhelming glimpse into the infinite wonder of life that seemed so far beyond my understanding, yet was demanding my effort to try.

Scott continues to awe his mother and me and anyone who is open to the understanding kind of awe that allows us to see, experience, and react not only to overwhelming beauty and perfection, but also to unique differences and imperfect variations on life that reveal a little more about its infinite mysterious ways. When he is asked about the cerebral palsy that leaves him limping, expending immense effort to speak, and enduring constant gazes—and even mocking and taunting by those who show the ignorant kind of awe and its narrow limits of what is beautiful and even sacred—Scott often says, "You know, Dad, it's not how I feel but how others seem to feel about my CP that's my problem. So many are so ignorant and just don't try to understand, and they stare but they never see. I haven't been given what you might call a really good life, but it sure is an incredible one. Too bad for me, and for them, that so many people can't, or won't, ever share that with me."

Throughout my research on awe, I have never known a person who is more in awe of life itself than my son. He graduated with honors from college, became a financial advisor, designed and built his own home, cared for me when I nearly died of cancer, and achieved many other accomplishments, including becoming a police aide and a student pilot. He is one of the most loving and brilliant persons I have ever known, and those who can be in understanding awe of his heart and spirit tell us their lives and their appreciation of life are enhanced by knowing Scott. They don't see how he moves but feel how he moves them emotionally by how he leads his life, despite his chronic severe pain. We, and all who know him, experience awe and sense his awe whenever we are with him.

I promised myself when I was rocking my new son so long ago that someday I would try to learn more about the strange, confusing awe Scott inspired within me and between us as we moved rhythmically together in the dim light of that intensive care unit. As I told my son recently just before I sent the manuscript of this book to my editor, this book is my fulfillment of that promise to him.

THE STUDY OF THE AWE INSPIRED

How many times in your life have you been awestruck? What caused it? How did it feel and what were you thinking before it happened? How did it affect you? What did you learn from it? How did being in awe influence your religious beliefs, your view of your work, and how you spend your time? How did it affect your relationships? These were some of the questions I asked in the Study of the Awe Inspired (SAI). The more answers I collected, the more questions I had and more confident I became that psychology had neglected our most transformative emotion.

More than twenty years ago, I began collecting as much information I could about awe. I audiotape-recorded over 100 lengthy descriptions of awe as provided by men, women, and children from around the world; made more than 20 videotapes of persons talking about their awe responses; and collected more than 400 additional written descriptions of awe-inspired people. You will read more about this study in the following pages and read the true stories of people who shared what it was like for them to be in awe.

My Study of the Awe Inspired continues today as people send me their stories about awe in their lives. (Some of the participants in my early research began to refer to my work as the "SAI," because they said it captured the sound many people make when they are in awe.) I recorded what the SAI respondents said about the emotional, physical, and spiritual aspects of what they experienced as awe and asked them how it influenced their lives. Because I spent several years as a neuropsychologist and eventually director of a psychological clinic at Sinai Hospital of Detroit, I was also able to obtain some direct physiological measures of some persons as they described awe they had felt long ago. Although it is not enough to meet the criteria for scientific publication, I also collected a few physical records from persons while they said they were in awe. I found that, for some people, just talking about their awe experience leads to more awe, and that response was reflected in changes in heart and breathing rhythm and other measures like skin conductivity.

Combined with what I learned from my reading and studying about awe, the SAI provides much of the support for what I have come to understand as our *neglected eleventh emotion,* but I fully acknowledge that personal stories and reports are only a beginning to a scientific study of awe. I don't think they are enough to prove as fact what you will read in this book about awe, but I do assert that they are sufficient to support the need for more scientific study of what may be our most powerful human response.

My intent is to encourage and promote more interest in, and research on, the awe response, and I don't have nearly all the answers to the questions I raise about awe in this book. It may be that my many years studying awe have caused my own awe to render me biased and lose the objectivity necessary for good science. However, I agree with sociologist/philosopher Thorstein Veblen, who wrote, "The outcome of any serious research can only be to make two questions grow where only one grew before."

The more I learn about awe, the more questions I have, but I've become more certain of one thing: Despite its neglect, it is by all scientific criteria a basic and powerful emotion that influences every aspect of our lives as none of the other basic ten can. To leave it out of scientific scrutiny is to ignore a major dimension of what makes life meaningful. To not have much of it in our daily lives squanders one of our most precious gifts.

I offer this book to encourage you to reflect on, and learn from, the periods of awe in your life and the lives of others. I offer it to help differentiate between what I call the *ignorant awe* of confirmed beliefs and ideas (or the simple, excited interest so frequently described as "awesome") and the awe of understanding through which whatever demands our profound attention causes us to think in new and different ways about life. I also offer this book as a warning against the increasing silent epidemic of languishing that now exceeds anxiety and depression as the most frequent negative emotional state and is related to what seems to be our newest ADD—Awe Deficiency Disorder.

Languishing is not being sad or happy. It's not being mentally healthy or mentally ill, perhaps because it's more a state of chronic doing than engaged being. Because it is mistaking a busy life for a meaningful one, it's generally awe-deficient. It's living in a state of often unacknowledged quiet despair, unrecognized because we mistake a busy personal life for a meaningfully connected one.[2] Languishing is going through the motions without a lot of any kind of emotion. I suggest that, because of its unique blend of delight, dread, depression, elation, confusion, and sense of profound and troubling awareness of a "something more" that comes with awe, it's this emotion that most often allows us to flourish and not languish.

You may be a reader who feels that life is difficult and confusing enough; that ignorance can be bliss; or that you already have all the meaning, faith, and purpose in your life and don't need to think deeply—at least right now—about things that might awe you and how awe can cause you to think. True awe raises more questions than it does answers and challenges faith more than confirms it, so you may feel that awe in the form of temporarily focused attention or confirmation of a prior firm belief is enough for you, but I hope you will still take the time to consider what the SAI participants had to say about awe in their lives, just in case you might be failing to benefit from awe's full power. And if you're prone to constantly pursuing the mysteries of life even if you never find the answers, I hope you will find inspiration and guidelines in the following pages for continuing your journey.

This is not a book about how to be happy, but I hope it helps you more fully be. As you will read, you can choose to make yourself more available to be awed, but you can't will it to happen. It suddenly takes you under its spell, and you can't achieve it by going through prescribed steps, a positive attitude, or more self-awareness achieved through a self-help program. In fact, because awe is first and foremost our most connective emotion, the more you think about yourself, the less likely it is you will be in awe. Awe is an emotion designed to help us experience and learn from the paradox that life is as dreadful as it is divine, better than we can imagine and worse than we fear, and as short as it is magnificent.

BEYOND THE ARROGANCE OF CERTAINTY

Awe makes us feel powerless and insignificant yet at the same time also strangely empowered, because we feel we've been uniquely blessed by being given a brief challenging glimpse of a deeper significance to life that we may never understand but must keep trying. It's as if the universe has given us a special privilege—that it sees us as worthy and deserving enough to trust us with a look at its secret, whatever that may be. Awe is when life grants us the chance to think differently and deeper about itself, so that we are not left squandering its gift by languishing it away.

Being in awe can make a real mess of our lives by disrupting our certainty about ourselves and the world, but it also enlivens and invigorates our living and can change how we decide to live. Ultimately, the decision between an easier, fascinating life and a harder, tremendously mysterious one is a choice between the solace of certitude and the aggravating invigoration of unending inscrutability.

With the fuller, deeper awareness and total engagement with all of life that awe brings, the highs are higher, the lows lower, and the sadness will be as deep as the moments of rapture are profound. There will be far more doubt than certainty, so what happens after life's end will always be a part of the tremendous mystery—the mystery that, bit by bit, is revealed with each awe experience. It will be as much a struggle as a celebration and as filled with tears of grief as tears of pure joy.

I saw my son Scott fly today. I saw him just above the Koholau mountains on the island of O`ahu. I saw him dip the wings of his airplane from side to side in the pilot's signal of hello, and I felt the same goose bumps, thrill, fear, hope, and confusion about life's mysterious ways that I felt when Scott was born. There he was, soaring in the heavens above, inspiring awe again and no doubt feeling it himself as he was momentarily free of the ignorant awe of insignificant things that causes so many people to miss out on the awe he could inspire within them.

I hope that, in the following pages, you might become more aware of your own awe response and how it may be intended as the one human emotion designed for helping us deal with and grow through the unavoidable, infinite, baffling, great, and horrible complexities of life. I hope you will consider that it's true awe that helps us continue to seek the understanding that provides the only two things philosophers say all of us really need: something worth living for and something worth dying for. I hope what you will learn about our neglected eleventh emotion can help you reawaken the kind of awe that comes only with a life fully engaged in the search for a meaning—meaning that none of us may ever fully discover, but the frighteningly fascinating and unending quest for what might be the "secret of life" that so many of us hope to find.

1

THE CHOICE OF A LIFETIME

"Awe: Mysterium tremendium et facinas"

—RUDOLF OTTO

FAITH IN THE MYSTERIOUS

Imagine that you were given the choice of a lifetime—the choice between an easy life and a difficult life. The easy life would be interesting; moreover, it would be relatively stress free and calmly predictable. An unshakable explanatory system would provide a safety net when crisis happened, and nothing astonishingly and perplexingly wonderful would ever mess up your thinking. Horrible and/or challenging life events would not keep defying how you see and understood life. The other, more difficult life would be vastly more enthralling, but also full of tremendous mysteries and would sometimes send you down into the depths of confused depression, even as it lifted you to the strange elation that life can be so magnificent and powerfully confusing. This difficult life would consist of constantly searching for the meaning of life and how life should be lived and understood, and would prompt you to totally rearrange your life and how you view it. Which would you

1

choose? This is a book about what happens if you could make the second choice or, as often happens, have that kind of life imposed upon you by events that lead to undeniably true and deep awe. It's about a life full of moments of powerful and transformative emotions that frequently send chills down our spines, fill our eyes with tears, cause our hearts to race, make the hair on the backs of our necks stand on end, boggle the mind, and literally take our breath away—in other words, a life full of awe.

This book makes the case for the valuable irresistible fascination, the highest elation, and sometimes a most profound sadness that leaves us in a state of puzzled apprehension, perplexing dread, yet appreciative wonder and hope regarding the vast mysteries of life that is known as awe. But be warned: Choosing or having imposed upon you the more difficult, challenging, awe-inspired life won't always be what most people might call "a good life," even though it is guaranteed to be a *full* life. It will be far from an easy life, but it will be an unimaginably intense one that may not leave you feeling better but will leave you *feeling* in ways that you may never have imagined possible.

What is so difficult about living a life filled with awe? The kind of awe, as experienced by hundreds of people who describe their experiences with this most unique of human responses in the following pages, is much more than appreciating beauty found in nature, having a temporarily reverent religious experience, or experiencing what is being described by the increasingly ubiquitous word "awesome." It is a mystical feeling that seems to be capable of incorporating almost all of our other emotions. It's as "real" as our experience of life ever gets—so real, in fact, that it overwhelms you like no other emotion and, like passionate love-making, can leave you feeling drained as much as inspired.

Although intense contemplation of its meaning can end up deepening it, awe often shakes our faith and disturbs the solace of our spiritual certitude. When we're in awe, life ceases to make sense, or at least to comply with the sense we've made of it so far. It doesn't make the kind of sense we thought it made before we were awed by something that seems beyond our understanding of what makes (or can make) sense. Awe results in a sense of fear and submission to things, events, people, and ideas that are experienced as being much greater than the self, and that can make us feel wonderful or terrible, or even both ways at the same time.

Choosing a life full of awe means that we are frequently anxious and uncertain and are never self-confident, because awe is the ultimate "ism" breaker. Being in the kind of awe you will be reading about upsets any firm conviction we may hold—that our personal version of monotheism, polytheism, pantheism, agnosticism, or atheism is the one and only right belief. Because it so suddenly puts an end to our sense of self—and offers only mystery rather than answers, and a need to know more rather than a sense that we finally know it all—awe is more like feeling repeatedly "dead again" than the experience of being "born again" (comfortably and safely converted to the certainty of having finally found the answer).

If you choose a life of awe, you will surrender the solace of certitude. You will live with more "open-ture" than closure and, unless you can learn to find a strange, exciting comfort in being presented with and grappling with the tremendous mysteries life offers, you will seldom feel calm or at ease for very long. Awe offers far more stress and aggravation than comfort or relief, more self-doubt and agitation than assured self-confidence, and often more contemplative sadness than relieved joy. You might not end up having faith in anything other than the fact that life and the universe are not only beyond what you even imagined, but also transcend what anyone can or will ever be able to imagine. One woman from my Study of the Awe Inspired (SAI) described her awe response by saying, "When I was in awe, I felt like I had suddenly discovered the secret of life, but I didn't know what it was. I just suddenly felt that there was this immense, scary, wonderfully overwhelming secret that made me feel afraid, sad, and strangely invigorated all at the same time. I don't think I've ever felt more messed up or more alive in my whole life."

Another person I interviewed in SAI expressed her experience of awe by saying, "When you have a lot of awe in your life, I mean the real deep kind of life-altering awe that makes you rethink everything, you're not born again. It's more like you keep dying again and again, until there's almost no more you. You're not 'born again' in any single religious sense because you don't end up converted or suddenly finding one answer or one idea that you have unshakable faith in. I guess the faith you do end up with, after you've thought a lot about whatever awed you, is a faith in the fact that there is an endless mystery of life that we're privileged to have the chance to grapple with, and that's a very big and fascinating thing to have faith in—that's there's more than we do or can know. I agree now with Helen Keller when she said that life is a daring adventure or it is nothing at all."

AN INCREDIBLE JOURNEY

Awe is experienced as the sudden awareness that life is, as the famous biologist J. B. S. Haldane put it in his essay "Possible Worlds," "not only queerer than we suppose [which relates to a *facinas,* or fascinating life] but queerer than we can suppose [which relates to *mysterium tremendium,* or a tremendously mysterious life]."[1] When we're in awe, Hamlet's challenge to Horatio that there are more things in heaven and earth than his philosophy could dream is experienced as is the even more disarming sense that there may be no philosophy sufficient to create a dream bizarre or outlandish enough to incorporate whatever it was that inspired our awe. Awe renders us dumbstruck, and it's up to us whether we want to take it from there and start thinking deeper and differently about life or experience a brief spiritual buzz that leaves our life's explanatory system unperturbed.

Awe can make us feel strange, because it's the emotion we feel when we're most in touch with the unfathomable eeriness that is the universe we live in. It wakes us from the languishing sleeplike state we've fallen into that results in taking so much of life for granted. If we think long and hard enough about whatever inspired it, awe can turn things we've gotten used to into revelations that make us wonder how we could have ever taken them for granted. Awe can turn what we seldom allow ourselves to pay attention to into astonishing new questions about our place in the universe—questions that can take considerable mental effort to keep ignoring. But if you're the kind of person who's looking for answers, the choice of an awe-filled life isn't for you.

If you take a few moments to reflect on the following facts—even though a very narrow band of imagination and understanding limits humans to sensing such a very small part of the world around us—you might experience the blend of unbounded delight, humbling dread, and excited incredulousness that characterizes the awe response. It's difficult to imagine a race of beings taking the following facts for granted and considering them ordinary, but they describe how we're all traveling every second of our life: We seldom think about it (our senses are so limited that we don't feel it, and our narrow band of belief seldom allows us to accept it), but we're all riding around together on one of the universe's billion fragile, cracking, exploding rocks, on which even our existence is a statistical fluke beyond one in billions. Sucked to our gas-covered rock by an invisible force, we're being spun around at 17 miles per second while at the same time whizzing at 19 miles per second around a nuclear exploding fireball that, even though it's 90 million miles away, holds our rock in its orbit with its invisible force, and, if our rock got too close, could cook us all in a nanosecond.

If thinking about those numbers isn't enough to tease at least a little awe out of you, consider these additional facts: The rock spinning us around, the fireball that keeps life on our rock alive, and the entire solar system that contains these speeding objects are also spinning together at 140 miles per second as one huge mass. This mass is spinning around the center of a galaxy called the Milky Way, and even at this unfathomable speed, this galaxy is so vast in size that it still takes about 200 million years for the rock and its fireball to complete one orbit around it.

If you've chosen the easier, busier, interesting, less mentally bothersome life over the harder, awesome kind that gets you more easily and deeply personally involved in tremendous mysteries suggested by those numbers, you may have already thought, "Wow, that's kind of interesting," and like a distracted business traveler on a jet plane, sat back and ignored how fast you are traveling, dismissed the perils of such a warp-speed trip, and preferred not to contemplate why or how this galactic race is happening in the first place. On the other hand, if you tend to have a lower awe threshold and are in the midst of the difficult mysterious life that comes with it, you may not only be thinking about what these numbers mean, but also even trying to feel the speed they describe.

If I still haven't gotten you to reflect on the fact of just how fast you're going and the paradox that you could be going so unbelievably fast and still feel that you're sitting perfectly still reading this book, maybe just a few more facts will engage your awe response. The Earth, Sun, and Milky Way are also speeding through the nothingness of space at 25 miles per hour, and, together with a few other neighboring galactic systems, this entire cosmic collection itself is also hurtling at 375 miles per second toward some of the other 100 billion-plus galaxies that are also spinning and whizzing around.

If thinking about all this for even a minute still doesn't boggle your mind to be awed enough to want to think about what this all means, consider that all of this speed is ultimately generated by the influence of invisible stuff called *dark matter*. That's a phrase similar to the old term *terra incognita* used by ancient cartographers, who were also in awe of the world they were trying to represent but couldn't find the words to describe undocumented mysterious territories.

Dark matter is something we can't see, but scientists have proven it has to be there because, whatever it is, its ghostly presence and energy keep pulling and tugging on the galaxies and the small amount of matter we can see, like the rock we're riding on. In fact astrophysicists tell us that the matter we see makes up only 4 percent of the universe, and based on what you are about to read about our awe response, that might serve as a reasonable estimate of about how much of our life we allow ourselves to be in awe of.

Because awe is so mind-boggling and perturbing to our mental and emotional status quo, you may have already said to yourself by now, "Enough already! I get the point." But *do* you? You will read in the following pages that awe can be so powerfully disruptive to our thinking that it tires it out, and we want to quickly try to get past it and move on. I encourage you not to bail out and instead to keep reflecting about the fantastic voyage you're on.

The harder life, one characterized by frequently being in awe and not being frightened by the time-consuming and often upsetting contemplation and reflection that awe offers, is the most fully lived life of all. But the choice is yours. You could decide to just be inspired for a few moments by the wonderfully puzzling events that happen in life, and then return quickly back to a more comfortable daily routine. Just as we're often told to "keep busy" or "keep going" or even take medication to numb our feelings to get us through our grief and despair, we can choose to be awed and let the terrible things pass or explain them away with old ideas seldom challenged or indoctrinated in us during childhood. The current incidence of languishing—the psychological diagnosis for mistaking an intensely busy life for a meaningfully connected one—is related to diminishing awe to a brief high that has little lasting impact on our lives.

Consider the fact that, in addition to the 22 percent of the universe made up of the mysterious dark matter, the rest of whatever "is" in the universe is an even stranger something called *dark energy.* No one can see it, but it's pushing everything away from everything else. It makes up the remaining 74 percent of the universe and gives off a repulsive invisible energy totally resistant to gravity and that is causing the vast nothingness in which all the travel described in this chapter is taking place to constantly expand.

It seems worthy of our attention to reflect on the idea that nothingness can keep expanding as the after-effect of an as-yet-unexplained, sudden "big bang" that took place 13 billion years ago, when time is assumed to have begun. I haven't had enough time yet to try to figure out where time was before it began, but some scientists now suggest that the nothingness of space may be breathing in a 20-billion-year cycle of an exhale-like, post-bang expansion, followed eventually by a reactive contraction in a big-crunch cosmic inhale, and so on and so on for infinity—whatever that is.

You're probably suffering from severe awe fatigue by now, because the brain just doesn't want to deal with all this information and is more interested in its usual fixation on the four f's of fighting, fleeing, feeding, or fornicating. That's because we've allowed our awe response to atrophy from disuse. The easy life choosers might call the facts you've just read "fascinating" or even say they knew them already—and so what? But choosers of a difficult life who are open to awe's challenges are willing to go the next step to contemplating the tremendous mystery they represent.

A DEBT TO THE UNBORN

Awe is an overwhelming and bewildering sense of connection with a startling universe that is usually far beyond the narrow band of our consciousness. For many of us, a little awe once in a while in the form of brief, attentive fascination is enough, and the time and effort of reflective awe and all the mental and emotional upheaval it causes isn't something we want or have time for in our daily lives. Our awe response is made even more intense and bothersome because it comes with the frightening, increased awareness of how small and powerless we are and how briefly we live—ideas and feelings that are distracting in our current "don't worry, me first, be happy, quick fix" culture.

Any feeling of being more alive that comes from awe derives from the mysterious energy we sense from our connection with whatever it is that inspires our awe. It's not our individual self that's coming more alive but our deepened sense, as one of my interviewees put it, "of the essence of Being itself, and you can't feel that when you're just feeling yourself." Awe offers the invitation to leave our state of languishing and to flourish, but the choice is ultimately ours as to what we do with this most delightful and dangerous eleventh emotion. Awe is the emotion we experience when something causes us to feel supremely lucky—lucky to be the beneficiary of being given one out of the trillions of chances to having a life at all. These are the odds of winning at what author Richard Dawkins describes as the "combinatorial lottery of DNA," a stunningly rare opportunity to live, when trillions of others who theoretically could have had a life will never get that chance.[2] Awe may be such an intense emotion because it awakens—somewhere deep in our evolutionary consciousness—our sense of responsibility and obligation to the trillions of the never-to-be born losers of the DNA lottery who, as Dawkins put it, "will never even be offered life in the first place."[3]

Maybe awe is so intense and disrupting an emotion because it can cause us to feel at least a little guilty about wasting or complaining about a gift billions of the never-lived never received. Maybe our awe response is an occasional reminder that we've been squandering the most miraculous gift in the universe.

Perhaps it's because awe is so closely associated with our worst dread—the expiration of the gift of life—that it leads to some of our most introspective moments. As you will read, true awe always comes with a sense of terror of the vast nothingness that also makes awe so exciting. It's an anxiety of non-being that's an unavoidable requirement of the experience of being itself.[4] Awe is our most intense emotion because it brings us closer to a sense of being in its most infinite and profound sense, and closer to death at the same time. Perhaps because awe makes us realize we will eventually lose the existence that allows us awe's profound awareness of being, it must almost come with sadness and a sense of shame for our ingratitude for the gift of life.

A CONSCIOUSNESS COPERNICAN REVOLUTION

Awe is unique in that, unlike our other basic emotions, it can be experienced in combination with any of those other basic emotions. It's not physiologically possible to feel intensely joyful and extremely sad or angry and loving at exactly the same time, but we can experience awe during any of these states. Awe can deepen and intensify any other emotion and can even cause them to blend together, as when the awe we feel for nature's beauty is made more intense by feelings of anger at humankind's disrespect for it, joy that we can still experience it, and anxiety that we had better get to it and start savoring and protecting it. The loving awe we feel for another person can come not only with joy and amorous feelings, but also with the anxiety that we must continue to earn its reciprocity and sadness that we cannot be physically with that person forever.

Awe is a responsibility as much as a gift. As Buddhist thinkers have taught for more than 2,000 years, and as Western philosophers like Hegel, Schopenhauer, Paré, Llinás, and Kant have pointed out, awe happens not because your mind involuntarily reacts to the outside world, but because our understanding and experience of the outside world is transformed by how we think about it. If we want to

immerse ourselves in the profound mysteries of life and the great
and horrible things that happen as a part of being alive in a chaotic
world, we have to make the choice to be open to awe and willing
to reflect about what experiencing it means and suggests about our
humanness.

Awe's risk factor is the constant mental and spiritual upheaval it
can cause, and it often results in as much sadness as delight. But
the reward is an intensely connected life made as meaningful as it
is difficult, because we have taken the time and had the courage to
struggle with mysteries we sense but will never ultimately solve.
We may not end up feeling happier, but we will surely end up feeling much more than we have ever felt by becoming fully engaged
with all of life—and somehow become more of a crucial part of its
ultimately inexplicable essence.

Comparing his ideas about awe to Copernicus's discovery that the
Earth is not the center of the universe, Immanuel Kant referred to
his view of our emotional experience of life as a "Copernican
Revolution." He asserted that it is the representation that makes
the object possible rather than the object that makes the representation possible. We are the ones who do the representing, and
it is we who must choose between being just interested in life and
being totally engaged in it. It's up to us as to whether we allow
allow ourselves to see life as full of tremendous mysteries far
beyond enjoyment and nice little surprises.

Life can feel busy and interesting (and a lot easier) when we automatically and quickly react to our world, but it becomes an awe-
inspiring, tremendous mystery when we take responsibility for the
fact that how we see, think about, and experience our world is
largely a matter of our own conscious choice to embrace and think
longer and more deeply about its mystifying grandeur. We can go

through the ten basic human emotions or be open to the unique eleventh by becoming more deeply aware of nature, a person, or even ideas—like the fact that we are finite beings speeding at inconceivable speeds through a mostly invisible world or each a one-in-a-billion occurrence of the gift of life. Being aware is much more than reacting. It's experiencing that we are experiencing and applying our full and deepest consciousness to where, with whom, and why we are, and that's what can inspire profound awe.

When Kant wrote, "Two things awe me most, the starry sky above me and the moral law within me," he was referring to the perplexing connection between the world and how we experience it, and that's the exact juncture where awe happens.[5] Kant believed that unless we fully perceive and try to process and understand what happens to us, even though it upsets us and we may never fully succeed, life becomes, in his words, "less than even a dream." It's interesting to look up at the starry nights, but those same nights become tremendous mysteries when we choose to think about what it means that the same stuff that makes up those stars is in our bodies. We can choose to go through life busy with all it has to offer or struggle to be fully aware that we are experiencing what we're experiencing. In an increasingly languishing world full of busy people having lots of experiences, there is less and less time for the full awareness that leads to awe.

AN EMOTIONAL BOMBSHELL

Choosing a more ordinary easy life can result in interesting, wonderful memories, but choosing the extraordinarily difficult life of awe can cause even these memories to become upsetting, tremendous mysteries. Looking at photos of our family can be an interesting family activity or lead to thoughts that the images we are looking at no longer exist and how moments in time are so brief and gone so quickly. I remember being in awe when I tried to answer author Steve Grand's challenge to his readers to think about a wonderful childhood experience that they could feel and even smell.[6] I could do it immediately and felt my grandmother's touch on my shoulder as she poked so caringly at the Christmas turkey. I could smell that turkey roasting and could hear again the chatter of my family happily gathering around the table, and tears filled my eyes as I recalled that wonderful time.

But then Grand dropped what he called "the bombshell," and that's what awe feels like when it causes our fixed ideas about life to explode and shatter: Grand correctly pointed out that the "I" at this moment was never and could never have actually been there for the Christmas at Grandma's house! He described the science that shows that there wasn't a single atom in my body today—the one that was reacting so strongly to my memory of that magical Christmas day— that was present that day. With complete scientific validity, he said that whatever we are, we're not the stuff we are made of, and for me it was an awe-inspiring concept that the "me" doing the remembering wasn't the person present at the memory-making.

Grand discussed how our "self stuff" is the temporary dynamic arrangement of matter that comes and goes, constantly rearranging itself to be what we consider to be our current "me" at any given moment. It scatters and rearranges in other forms at another place and in another time. Alive or dead now, all the people who were the main characters of my memory are all gone and their "matter" or energy somewhere else, yet I could feel that memory as if it were happening right now and as if I were again the person who "wasn't there."

Grand asks whether the idea that we were not, in fact, "there" for such profound moments in the history of our lives "doesn't make the hair stand up on the back of your neck." Mine sure did, but his challenge didn't diminish my memory. It expanded it and turned it into something I could think about in new ways—in terms of how I could understand my life, its meaning, and even the meaning of a memory and how one is made. This new knowledge caused what awe always causes if you elect to think hard enough about it and not just be halfheartedly interested in it—a major shift in consciousness and awareness. Grand's idea transformed what had always been a reassuring memory into a tremendous mystery that, at the same time, messed up and yet strangely deepened my thinking and feeling about the place, time, and people that formed the template of my memory and the content of my consciousness.

As awe so often does, Grand's challenging idea caused me to wonder where Grandma, Grandpa, and my deceased relatives were now, where the "me" who was there is now, and if I could actually be "with" those who have died when I die, all questions that sound bizarre even as I write them—but that's what awe does. Awe makes us feel and think in strange and disconcerting ways about life's large and small concepts, about our fondest memories and greatest fears, and about the paradox that these issues are all manifestations of the same mysterious forces of our speeding lives. One of my interviewees described awe's "weird" involvement in the mysterious as it contrasts with the choice for just the interesting "normal kind" of life in which we mistake intensity for meaning by saying, "I'm the weird one in our marriage. For me, everything's a big mystery, and I talk in ways and about things that my husband says are goofy or far out. When I wanted to talk about how mysterious it was that waves are part of the ocean, break, but don't end, he thought I was nuts. He said a wave is a wave and he always just

takes things as they are, but I'm always so much into why and how
they are and what it all means. He's so much calmer, steadier, and
normal than I am, so I have 'to talk to my weird friends' when I get
in awe of something that my husband thinks is no big deal. Almost
everything to me is getting to be a big deal."

To this day, I'm still trying to deal with the mystery of how I wasn't
"there" for the best or the worst times in my life and won't eventually be after the ones in the future. The "me" who's writing the
words you're reading won't exist by the time you read this, and the
"you" who's reading them won't exist when you're done reading.
Grand's bombshell still causes me to wonder where in the heck we
are, where we were, and where we will be. Despite the confusion it
causes me, I would still choose ideas that cause me to be in awe,
because it feels as invigorating as it does upsetting.

Our other ten basic emotions are how we experience and express
our life, but awe is how we ultimately transform it. Awe can be
inspired by a person, place, thing, or—as in Grand's challenge—
even an idea, but like the speeding galaxy we're riding, these cata-
lysts for an awe-inspired life are always there. They're waiting for
us to "represent them," so that they can come to life in our lives.
As Kant suggests, it's our frame of mind or our own consciousness
that puts us more deeply and intensely in touch with these ideas
and allows us to contemplate them over and over again in different ways. It is through this decision of how we will consciously
engage with the world that we make the choice every day between
an ordinary and more soothing life and an extraordinary one full
of inspiring turmoil.

OUR AMAZING ELEVENTH EMOTION

Even though awe meets all the criteria to be considered a fundamental emotion, it has been left off psychologists' accepted lists of the basic ten emotions. Psychologists have been trying to come up with a definition of an emotion for over 100 years, but consistent in all the differing definitions is that an emotion is something that's triggered by our interpretation of events (such as thinking about not "being there" for our most cherished memories), involves most if not all of our physical systems (awe's goose bumps, racing heart, chills, and so on), somehow communicates our experience to others (the gasping look of confused shock that comes with awe), and can be disruptive and adaptive to our lives at the same time (awe's delightful dread).[7] Although awe hasn't made it into the big ten, awe fits all these criteria, and this book makes the case that it deserves to be there. Awe offers the hope that, by choosing to make it a more frequent part of your emotional repertoire and learning more about it and what inspires it, your life may not end up being wonderful but it will be amazing.

There are many versions of lists of the basic emotions. A statistical technique called *factor analysis* that looked at most of the lists of emotions from the perspective of our autonomic nervous system reaction yielded emotions that generally fell into one of the following categories: love, fear, sadness, embarrassment, curiosity, pride, enjoyment, despair, guilt, and anger. Some lists replace sadness with loneliness, and others include words like joy instead of enjoyment, disgust instead of shame, and contempt instead of anger, but the basic ten I've listed have generally been accepted by most psychologists as the basic ten human emotions.[8] One of the most respected researchers in the field of human emotion is psychologist Carroll Izard, and his work suggests that the ten emotions listed above or terms close to them are in fact the fundamental emotions from which all the others derive.[9] They're the ten ways we react to what life gives us, but awe, as our eleventh emotion, is how we constantly create and re-create our lives. It's unique not only in its capacity to create more consciousness chaos for us than the others, but to blend and intensify all the others so that we can find new and deeper meaning in all of them.

How many times do you experience one of the basic ten emotions? If you're like most people, you've probably experienced them far more often than you've experienced awe. When you were in awe, you may have noticed that it was very much unlike the other ten in that it lasts a much shorter time than the others, but when it does happen, it tends to leave an imprint on your consciousness that is hard to ignore or deny.

Awe can't be managed or controlled, and no matter how hard we try, we can't sustain it for long. We can stay angry or sad, but we can't stay in awe for more than a few moments. Awe is an emotion we seem able to tolerate only in short, small doses, but thinking about what awed us can take a lifetime.

Think of a time when you were in total awe. You might notice that you also experienced some of the other basic emotions at the same time, but that unlike the others, awe is the one that could feel wonderful, terrible, invigorating, and frightening at the same time. You may want to write down on an index card one of your most awe-inspiring experiences and use it as a bookmark as you read the following chapters. Compare it with the experiences shared by the people you will read about, and read it once more after you finish this book. When you do, remember Grand's challenge while you're doing this, because the person reading your awe experience won't be the person who wrote it.

AWE LITE

Author Douglas Adams describes his choice between the harder and easier life by saying that he prefers to live in awe "of the infinite and baffling complexity of life." He reflects on his choice of the path of the more difficult and more mysterious life in the quote beginning the introduction to this book, "I'd take the awe of understanding over the awe of ignorance any day."[10] Ignorance, as Adams uses the word, doesn't refer to stupidity or a lower level of intelligence but to a choice to take life as it comes or as we've been told it means, rather than to try to understand from where it comes, why it came, where it goes, and so on.

To the extent that we could choose a more ordinary, predictable life doesn't mean that we don't feel intense and busy. That's what languishing is: mistaking a hectic personal life for a connected, meaningful one. Such a choice offers the added benefit of having a life generally free of the surprising and disrupting upheavals of a life of frequent awe. A normal, less emotionally and mentally demanding life is a perfectly logical choice, one I've often wished I could make when a life of awe seems to keep imposing itself upon me. Sometimes I long for what I call an *awe-lite* life—one that is much calmer, less confusingly intense, and less full of often very unsettling surprises that throw my entire belief system and way of thinking into total disarray.

An example of awe lite is the recent request from the president of a large corporation for whose company I was going to lecture. He said, "Inspire and awe them, but keep it light. I don't want to get my people upset by thinking they have to think about the meaning of life. They have enough on their minds. Don't share any really sad or upsetting stories." I wondered what is was that was on their minds that could be more important than the meaning of life and how they could ever experience awe if they weren't ever thinking about it.

Based on philosopher Rudolf Otto's definition quoted at the beginning of this chapter, an awe-lite life offers *facinas* (interest) without the *mysterium tremendium* (complete mental upheaval). It's certainly possible to enjoy life without being in repeated awe of it, and people who end up with awe-inspired lives sometimes say they wonder whether the easier, awe-lite version might not have been preferable. A life of awe isn't one for the faint of heart or for a hardened heart, because it is stressful, and it often breaks our heart as much as it fills it with joy. With all the other ten basic emotions, we essentially know what we are getting, but in the case of awe, the range of feelings and thoughts is complex and varied.

What the easier life lacks in exhilaration it makes up for in predictable comfort and less suffering, stress, fear, pain, and anxiety. It's the life that a lot of people seem to wish they had—until they actually have it. You will read that humans evolved to be in awe, so to deny your awe-inspirable nature can result, particularly toward the end of your life, in a sense of regret and grieving for past missed opportunities. With the current emphasis on positive thinking instead of deep thinking and the philosophy that we should do all we can to be incessantly upbeat no matter what happens and not "think too much" and just "do it," an awe-lite life can end up causing you to feel that you had a remarkable life in which your only regret was that you weren't truly there to live it.

Based on the SAI that serves as the basis for the following chapters, an awe-lite life can end up feeling somehow less of a life in which something is always missing. It can make us more prone to languishing than flourishing. However, for some of us, a less contemplative and more mentally restful life might be a good choice. It fits our more "cool" and less reactive temperament, helps us avoid anxiety (or at least maintain the level we're comfortable with), and lets us go about living without a lot of thinking that only raises our anxiety. As one spouse of a SAI participant said, "My husband is in awe all the time. He takes life way too seriously and too intensely. He makes such a big deal out of such little things, and I tend to do just the reverse. He just can't be happy with what 'is' and is always wondering 'why.'"

The awe-lite life is based on the pop psychology bromide "Don't sweat the small stuff, and it's all small stuff." Persons leading awe-inspired lives consider that platitude to be absurd because, for them, it's often the prior ignored "small stuff" that often serves as the primary catalyst for their awe response. They're awed by things as vast as a mountain vista but also as small as the head of a pin, and as extraordinary as a volcanic eruption or as ordinary as the fresh smell of a new morning.

People with lots of awe in their lives do sweat the small stuff. They tend to work themselves up into a sweat about almost everything and anything and take most things very seriously. Awe is a sweatier life than one of awe lite because awe is an emotion that derives from being intensely engaged in all that life offers; it regularly makes mountains of molehills and big deals out of what awe-liters see as no big deal. Awe-liters embrace the "don't worry, be happy" philosophy, but those who choose an awe-inspired life do not seem to be happy *unless* they worry. Happiness separate from full engagement with life's real problems is not possible for those who are open to awe.

Of course, none of us would intentionally choose to have fear, sadness, confusion, and uncertainty—all the things that awe produces—in our lives, and although we do inherit temperaments and reaction styles that can make us less or more awe-prone (or at least, more willing to think long and creatively about what awes us), we are not given the choice before we are born of what kind of lives we will have. Although we can't control our destinies, and it often feels like the choice of a hard or easy life has been made for and not by us, we can find our own meaning and management as our destinies unfold if we regularly use and try to learn from awe as our one human emotion designed to help us thrive and not just survive or languish through our lives.

LIFE IN THE IN-BETWEEN

Awe is something we feel when we venture into the in-between areas of life, so in an awe-filled life, you will often feel confused. Because awe causes our cognitive map to constantly change, we end up feeling lost much of the time. Awe sends us reeling between the comforting certainty of the rock of fundamentalist, rigid religious thinking and the hard place of modern science. It leaves us on our own to deal with mysteries that neither of these fields can ever fully explain. Awe is the one emotion that can cause us to think and feel in ways that help us bridge the gap between the illusion of science's total power to explain everything and the exaltation that comes from formal religion's veneration for not having to. When we feel awe, we don't experience a sense of closure, comfort, enlightenment, or "aha." Instead, we are flooded with a sense of mystery, arousal, confusion, and "oh no . . . now what?"

For many of the persons I interviewed for this book, awe was a religious experience and an encounter with what they called "the Sacred," "God," "the Power," or "the Absolute." Awe is the emotion we feel when we allow ourselves to be drawn into the murky and scary in-between areas of life, the dialectic twilight zone between the poles of good and bad, right and wrong, win or lose, faith and doubt, and perhaps most difficult to deal with, self and other.

Awe lite happens when we are drawn to something life offers but don't let go of one of its safe "either-or" poles. Sometimes, we have to find a pole and hold on to it for a while as if it were the whole truth about us and life, but a fully engaged and awe-inspired life is led at life's existential intersections and not on the safer corners.

Because we live at a time when quick fixes are the theme of the day and people move from one pole of life to the other—that is, trying to avoid staying too long in the confusing and challenging difficult areas of life where awe usually happens, the in-between— our awe response has begun to atrophy from neglect. According to popular psychology advice industry gurus, we can follow simple steps to go from alcoholism to being "born again," from low self-esteem to self-love, or from depression to elation without the pro-longed mental, emotional, or contemplative struggle in the middle ground, free of the disruption that awe creates in our feeling and thinking. Even the new field of positive psychology tends to focus on being happy and deals with the wonderful more than the tragic. It is concerned with what's right and not what's wrong. But awe happens and instructs from within and between all of these realms. People who have lots of awe in their lives are less con-cerned with being happy than they are with the search of the meaning of their being.

After hearing people describe what it was like to be in awe, it seemed something like the experience of being caught "in a pickle." That was the name of a game we used to play when I was a child. One of my friends would stand in front of a baseball base, and about sixty feet away another friend would stand in front of another base. I would start out safely standing on one base while they tossed a baseball back and forth, trying to tease or entice me off base and into the middle ground.

The thrill, stress, and challenge of "pickle" was to venture off the safe base while the ball was in the air, get someplace between bases, and run back and forth as the ball sailed back and forth. If I could tolerate the stress of being caught between bases, a throw would eventually be off target, and I could race toward one of the safe bases, but sometimes I got caught. Those who played the game best were those who could tolerate the in-between place the longest, relish the fear as well as the adventure, wait for their best chance, go for it, win or lose, and learn something from their time in the middle that they could use in the future. Sometimes they got caught, and more rarely they made it, but it was *not* fun playing when the one supposed to get in the pickle wouldn't leave the safe base. Throwing the ball back and forth became boring. The fun was in getting out and into the in-between place and staying there as long as possible. The purpose wasn't to win the game but to keep it going as long as possible, to enjoy the thrill of being a little scared and excited at the same time, to keep looking for new openings and opportunities, and to most of all just fully enjoy being in a pickle. As I look back at the times I was caught in the middle, it seems to be a lot like awe feels.

EXPERIENCE OR AWARENESS?

The choice of leading the easier life is a response primarily to the brain's egotistical commands and results in going through most of our daily life "experiencing" things from our brain's narrow, self-enhancing, and very personal perspective. Most of our other emotions work that way, but in a state of awe's diminished sense of self, we are freed to be more fully aware of life in its broadest context and with all of our intelligences, including (as you will read later) gut feelings derived from our heart and intestines that occur before our brain has the time to think.

The word *experience* derives from the Latin word *experiential,* meaning "to try." The word *aware* comes from the Greek word *horan* meaning "to see."[11] Sometimes, we have an experience like drinking a chocolate milkshake, and our awareness matches up with the experience. We participate in milkshake-drinking behavior, and we mindfully observe that we're doing it. We might say something like, "Wow, this shake tastes great, and I'm savoring the fact that I know I am tasting something great." More often, however, we suck our shake while we read, talk on our cell phone, or worry about something else. We become a participant in an act (have an experience) but not a full and total observer (have an awareness).

The awe response is our maximum state of full and total observation. It makes us more fully aware, meaning that we are then able to more completely experience that which we are experiencing.[12] For example, I've learned from firsthand awareness that there's a subtle but significant difference between what we mean by saying, "I'm having pain" (an experience), and saying, "I'm having the thought that I'm in pain" (an awareness). Having pain is an awful experience, but I found it awe-inspiring to discover that there's a crucial step in the pain cycle during which we have the chance to think about the fact that we're thinking about our pain and that this participating/observing distinction allows for some additional degree of manageability of how much, how long, where, and what kind of pain we will think about at any given time. At the very least, it allows us some precious moments when we have pain, but for awhile, pain doesn't have us. We become less reactive to the physiological reality of our pain and, for a few minutes, can regain some of the control that pain so easily takes from us.

Being mindfully aware of the difference between experiencing something and being fully aware of it provides us with the opportunity to forge new meanings within life's agonies and ecstasies. No matter how many good or bad things happen to us, a life full of experiences leads to languishing, but a life filled with awe—and the full awareness it awakens—results in flourishing.

If you've ever *experienced* driving your car and been shocked to *awareness* by nearly crashing into a stopped car in front of you, you've uncomfortably realized the key difference between going through life on self-involved cruise control, moving from one automatic experience after another, and the full, intense, focused awareness that you're in control of two tons of steel racing at sixty miles an hour in the broader context of hundreds of other speeding hunks of steel under the command of selfishly distracted brains. When you slam on the brakes just in time and just before you might have died, you become much more alive, and that's what awe feels like—a sudden jolt beyond experience and into awareness.

AWE'S COSTS—A FINAL ENCOURAGEMENT

Before you make your own choice between an awe-filled and awe-lite life, and between experiencing life and being fully aware of it, consider again some of the costs that come with making the choice for an awe-filled life.

Choosing the fully engaged, connected way of an awe-filled life means you will lead a life with companions with whom you share a love so awesomely deep that the fact you both will not be able to complete the journey with one another will bring you to your knees, weeping from the overpowering grief known only to those who experience the strangely splendid suffering inseparable from the awe of profound, companionate love. If you choose to try to have more awe in your life, even the death of a pet will leave you emotionally devastated, with your life (again) in need of rearranging.

An awe-inspired life requires the expenditure of huge amounts of persistent patience and tolerance, because it constantly teases us with subtle clues about life's ultimate purpose and destination, without ever allowing us to come up with a completely satisfying, rational answer. Awe is like trying to assemble a complex jigsaw puzzle with pieces missing. There's never any closure in an awe-inspired life, only constant acceptance of the mysteries of life. We're never allowed to know when this fantastic voyage might end or what happens after it does, but that's part of the life-disorienting chaos that makes this choice so thrillingly difficult and makes a life of blind faith so much easier.

As you have read, an awe-filled life is a humbling one that is constantly damaging to our self-esteem. Awe takes us down a few pegs and causes us to realize that our feelings of personal power and importance almost always end up being illusions. The nice thing about not assuming too much of a sense of self-importance in the first place is that we don't have to lose that sense when awe puts us in our place.

Awe can upset our stomachs. Ancient Hawaiians said they felt awe in their *na`au*, a word that means intestines, bowels, and also heart, mind, and feelings. As it so often is, their philosophy was prescient, as modern medicine is just now learning that our gut and our brain develop from the same clump of fetal tissue. One part ends up in the brain, and the other in the intestines to become what are called our *central* and *enteric nervous systems.* Our intestines are lined with over 100 million neurotransmitters, about the same number found in the brain, and these two nervous systems are connected by the longest nerve in your body, the vagus nerve. When one of the systems is responding, the other always does, too. That's why indigestion produces nightmares and why antidepressants that calm the brain are sometimes used to soothe the stomach. Awe is often experienced as "butterflies in the stomach" and something we "sense in our gut," and awe can leave us not only with a bothered brain but also an upset stomach. An interesting peripheral discovery in the SAI was that persons frequently in awe seem highly prone to severe migraine headaches and stomach and bowel problems.

Being in awe means that you will spend a lot of time feeling afraid and confused. If you check a thesaurus, you will see listed under *awe* words like *fear, terror, dread, fright,* and *trepidation.* Living a life of awe is living life on the edge of the sense of chaos and confusion that comes with the realization of life's perplexing majesty. As one of the respondents in the SAI defined it, "Awe is when you become so aware of just how tremendously frightening it is that you're alive that it scares you to death."

Because it's so difficult to describe in words, awe can be very aggravating and can leave us speechless just when we most want to tell someone what we've experienced. Being awed is fully yielding to life and allowing ourselves to be taken in by it, but just when we feel we have so much to share, awe leaves us unable to find words to express what we're feeling. The everyday emotional vocabulary that works pretty well with our other ten emotions falls far short of being able to be convey what awe feels like and means to us. Victor Hugo captured this awe-muting effect when he defined a moving piece of music as "that of which nothing can be said and about which it is impossible to remain silent."

So now that you've read about some of the high costs and consequences of your choice, which life would you choose—the awe-lite life that's easier and calmer or an awe-filled life that is much more difficult, thrilling, and confounding? The following pages can help you make your choice of a lifetime, so perhaps you would prefer to put off your decision until you've finished this book. After all, you'll be an entirely different person then.

2

TO HEAVEN AND BACK

"The most beautiful and most profound emotion we can experience is the sensation of the mystical. He to whom this emotion is a stranger, who can no longer wonder and stand rapt in awe, is as good as dead."

— *ALBERT EINSTEIN*

A RESPONSE TO THE DIVINE

Feeling suddenly elevated to the limits of indescribable delight, yet teetering on the edge of fear, we experience our rarest, most powerful, and least understood emotion: awe. It's an overwhelming and life-altering blend of fright and fascination that leaves us in a state of puzzled apprehension and appreciative perplexed wonder. If we go beyond a kind of ignorant distant voyeurism through which we gawk at life rather than fully engage with it and put in the effort to try to understand a little more about life's meaning, awe becomes less a feeling of being high and more a feeling of deep immersion in any and all of life's processes, including health, illness, love, and even death. It may not cause us to come to believe in something, but it can cause us to believe that there is something more beyond the grasp of our limited human consciousness. It can turn our stress into motivation for growth, solidify our commitment to our families as systems that can experience collective awe together, and help us find meaning, comprehensibility, and manageability at times of our most profound losses and even our own death.[1]

Whether one gasps "Oh, my God!" at the sight of a horrific accident, or sighs "Ah . . . heaven" at the taste of a Swiss chocolate truffle, or exclaims "Holy shit!" in response to a revolutionary idea, being in awe is a feeling that we are as close as we can get to heaven without dying to get there. It's less a feeling of being lifted up to a higher place, though, than it is a sudden awareness of the wonders of life on earth, being drawn more deeply in to all that is vastly wonderful in this one.

You are about to read dozens of stories from people around the world who were awe inspired. I've been collecting these reports for almost forty years, and they constitute the Study of the Awe Inspired (SAI) I describe in the introduction to this book. Using the first letters of the words in the name of the study and combining them with the long sigh that often accompanied being in awe, many of those who shared their stories began to refer to themselves as the "SIGHers."

The SAI includes narratives from patients who came to my clinic in the Department of Psychiatry at Sinai Hospital; from my medical students, residents, and psychology students; from spouses and family members of those who reported awe experiences; and from persons who would volunteer their own stories when they heard that I was conducting a study of the awe response. Many of the stories are direct quotes from the *awe diaries* that I encouraged some of my patients and students to keep, in which they were asked to record accurately and completely everything they felt and thought when they were in awe.

Many of the SAI participants said that, while they felt a sense of relief in finally being able to share their experiences, they were also embarrassed that their words seemed "too mystical," "too far out," "too new age," "flakey," or to be indicative of "living in la-la land." One respondent said, "Please don't use my name, or my boss will fire me or have me committed. This kind of stuff is just too paranormal for a lot of people and could awe me right out of a job." Because of these concerns, I've left out or changed the names of the authors of the stories, and, where a report would have identified its source, altered some of the details about location and other specifics. Otherwise, however, what you will read is completely unedited, exactly as told to and recorded by me.

From hundreds of reports, I've selected dozens of awe-response stories that seemed to represent awe's most common characteristics best. I selected samples that reflected the experiences of a range of persons in terms of gender, age, and socioeconomic background, as well as the ones that seemed to best provide the most detailed descriptions of the awe response. In order to learn more about our eleventh emotion, I've combined these with descriptions of awe found in classic literature, in religious writings, and in the very limited scientific work related to the awe response.

Some scientists are dubious about the value of sincerely told personal narratives, see them as being "merely anecdotal," and refer to their use to make a point as the "person who" fallacy, as in, "I knew a person who . . ." The more sincerity and conviction with which these stories are told, the more some scientists dismiss their value. They say that science must be "evidence based," and use only "real data" verifiable through statistical analysis, and that stories aren't "real data." This view reflects Western science's tendency to view what it considers evidence as the only "hard" data worth considering and the indigenous ancient sciences' value of stories and personal reports as at best "alternative" and not valid.

Indigenous sciences such as that of the Hawaiian culture have long used stories as data to produce remarkable insights into the human condition. Even many Western researchers believe that, as psychologist Daniel Gilbert writes, "Of all the flawed measures of subjective experience that we can take, the honest, real-time report of the attentive individual is the least flawed."[2] It is my view as a scientist that if we look back far enough, we will learn that some of our most remarkable scientific discoveries began with good stories that were repeated through generations. The SAI stories seem to meet this criterion and serve as a good starting point for learning about a response to which science has, to date, not paid very much attention.

In a kind of backward nonscience, I am aware that anecdotal accounts can and have been used selectively to prove an already decided point, so I've identified consistent threads that ran through all of the accounts of the awe response for you, because I believe that when hundreds of sincerely told stories contain enough of the same elements, it is no coincidence. When many different people in different places report common experiences, this suggests that there is something within these reports that is worth science's (and our) attention. I admit, however, that my own awe for the awe response, which developed over my years of studying it, has rendered me insufficiently subjective. I can say with certainty only that the people who told me about their awe usually described it in the way it is described in this book. Whether this is some form of mass delusion or evidence that science may have missed something by focusing only on what it sees as the ten basic human emotions, I'll leave to you to decide.

When it comes to awe, whether or not science will ever be able to fully explain what's happening and why is questionable. Including how aspirin and acupuncture work, there's a lot that Western science hasn't been able to explain and probably never will, but good science is motivated by the thrill of the continuing search. Like awe itself, the best research doesn't usually provide definitive answers. It more often raises more fascinating questions. My SAI sources constitute what I believe to be sufficient evidence to encourage research into awe, not as some rare paranormal psychic event, but rather as a regular, normal, basic human emotion that is the natural result of experiencing life's most profound truths.

My research on the awe response identified at least eight common characteristics that almost every report of the experience contained:

1. Whether awe was experienced in reaction to a natural phenomenon, an original idea, or a person, there is an experience of a sense of vastness that far exceeds our prior imagination and general explanatory system.

2. Awe involves an experience of a diminished sense of self as the naturally created and defined boundaries of "self" and "other" become blurred.

3. Awe is characterized by a feeling of anticipatory fear far beyond surprise that is sometimes elevated to the level of dread.

4. As if the discovery of the "something more" we've been looking for is more than we can handle, there's a feeling of an altered state of consciousness more focused on what exists "between" than what's "inside."

5. Awe is accompanied by distinguishing physiological changes, including goose bumps, chills, shuttering, gasping (with the feeling of having the breath "taken away"), gaping mouth, raising of upper eyelids and eyebrows, deeply wrinkled brow, increase in heartbeat and/or a

feeling of skipped beats, and a sense of warmth and openness spreading out from the center of the chest.

6. Awe results in a sense of a severe challenge to our "mental set," resulting in the need to decide between "accommodating" the awe experience through creating new ways of thinking, feeling, believing, and behaving; or "assimilating" what happened by briefly enjoying it and returning back to one's prior way of thinking and being.

7. Awe is often accompanied by a sense of, or intensified search for, contact with or becoming closer to God, the gods, unimaginable enormity, "something more," or a "Higher Power." It more often results in more searching and deeper understanding rather than a sense of closure.

8. Awe comes with an intensification of the need to connect not only with what inspired awe but to make a commitment to more loving, caring, protective relationships with others and the world in general.

The following section gives you one example of these eight characteristics of the awe response from an entry in the awe diary of a fifty-two-year-old business meeting planner.

FEELING GOD'S TEARS, HEARING GOD'S BREATH

She was a highly respected, no-nonsense businesswoman who had just finished organizing and supervising a large conference at a resort in Europe and decided to take a "long leisurely walk alone" in the forest behind the lodge. I had lectured for many of her meetings, and she had often told me how she wanted to "always have awe-inspiring speakers," so I asked how she defined such an experience. She answered by joking, "It's like the judge said about pornography: I know it when I see it." I told her years ago that I was thinking of beginning a psychological study on the awe response and asked her then to keep a journal of the times she felt she was in awe and send it to me to be included in my research. As it turned out, hers was one of the first word-for-word awe-inspired stories I received. She titled her entry "Found in the Woods," and here, verbatim, is what she wrote.

I was afraid I would get lost in the woods today, but instead I found myself there, or maybe God found me. It took my breath away. I was in awe not just of the beauty of where I was, but the sense of what it meant and what it would mean to me later. It was as if my heart had eyes and, like an excited child tugging on her parent's coat, it was urging me to stop and look.

Then I began to feel afraid. The woods seemed so huge and magical and full of strange sounds and even stranger stillness, but it was the good kind of fear that you feel when you're excited about something big that's going to happen or about someone great or famous that you're going to meet face to face. When it began to sprinkle, the raindrops felt like God's tears on my face, the joyful kind like when you've finally reunited with someone you love. At exactly that same time, a gentle breeze rustled the trees all around me, and it felt like God had been looking for me, had found me, and I could hear him breathing all around me. I was scared to death but suddenly so grateful to be alive. I felt so small and inadequate in the midst of it all that tears came to my eyes, the kind you shed when you're finally relieved of a terrible burden and feel safe again. Even on that steamy, hot summer day, I felt chilled and got goose bumps. It was like—for that timeless moment— I actually became the forest and there was no more me. Later, I began to think that I had gone to heaven and back. I don't know yet if I will tell many people about it because it sounds pretty strange even to me, but I'm still awed when I think about it.

As this woman's story reveals, awe is the soul's experience of a brief freedom from the constraints of its physical body, a quick celestial trip that lasts just long enough to allow something like a brief glimpse of heaven or at least to cause us to think about more sacred things. Awe draws us out of our increasingly dominant secular consciousness, and awakens our latent sense of the sacred. It challenges the limits of our complacent, cynical, and increasingly distracted daily consciousness, and, if we elect to think and feel differently because we have had the honor of being taken to heaven and back, awe can transform us unlike any of our more frequent and more self-oriented emotions.

By learning more about awe as the emotion that can result in a conversion of consciousness—away from our local self-involvement to a sense of what so many SAI respondents called a "cosmic connection" or "higher consciousness"—we become more likely to be willing and able to sample its wonders and experience and learn from its amazing benefits in our daily lives. We may become less afraid of its power, less shy about sharing it, and cease to see it as just a temporary, private distraction from the busy blur of what has become the languishing state of modern life. We might even become more accepting of the invitation awe offers us to change our way of thinking about ourselves and the world.

NEONATAL AWE

As any parent will tell you, we're born to be awed. Parents see it in a new child's widened eyes, quivering whole-body glee, and shy but

excited fear when she or he encounters something totally new
(vastly beyond his or her very limited experience) that's just a
little scary because it is all so overwhelming and that makes the
child feel powerless in its presence. I suspect that newborns tend
to be more easily awe inspired than adults precisely because they
spend their waking hours encountering newness, aren't limited by
a well-defined separate self, are so naturally gut-feeling-oriented,
and have little choice but to try to accommodate the constant
challenges to their still-coalescing consciousness. As every great
teacher knows, awe's thrilled trepidation can provide our most
exciting motivation for learning. As most great scientists report, it
is usually these same two contradicting components of awe—trepidation and yearning for knowledge—that generate the energy
behind some of our greatest discoveries.

A young mother in my awe study told me, "It's amazing. If you want
to see awe taking place right before your eyes, just watch your baby.
You can learn a lot about how to live from that little creature. Even
a sudden noise can awe him, a shadow on the wall, or the discovery
of his thumb. It's more than—and different from—surprise or just
curiosity. You can see the awe on his face and in how he flails, kicks,
reaches out, and gasps with eyes wide open as if they are trying to
drink it all in, even though it bothers him. You can almost see his
little brain trying to figure out what's going on. I wish I could be that
easily and intensely fascinated with things in my life."

When I asked this young mother about her own personal experiences of awe in her life, her husband offered his view of his wife's
awe: "I saw awe on my wife's face the first time they handed her
our child—and she said she saw awe in mine. All the pain and
worry was washed away, and she began to tremble, cry, and laugh
all at the same time. A new child gets rid of the old you really
quick. I know she was confused and overwhelmed by it all and, like

me, a little afraid of what we had in store for us. The beauty of our child seemed so fragile, and the fact that he was created by our love was so totally awesome. I don't think either of us has ever been quite the same after that first moment with our new son."

The young mother's description of neonatal awe and her husband's description of the awe he shared with her point out two of the key challenges in learning to tap into the power of awe's natural power. Like that of a newborn, our awe comes easier when we are not consumed by, and don't cling to, our image of a powerful separate self and aren't consumed by constantly trying to esteem ourselves. In a culture that stresses independence and personal power, this is a difficult task.

A second challenge associated with the awe response is that it gains its transformative power through our willingness to suspend our usual way of thinking in order to learn to see, listen, smell, feel, and think in new ways, not just about what we are seeing and experiencing, but also about ourselves in relationship to something more. As you will read, awe's signals don't come just from our brain but from our sentient, feeling, remembering heart and from what we may describe as our gut. For a brain-biased, busy world, this is also a difficult adjustment. When we can be innocent, open-minded, and open-hearted enough to suspend our cynicism to believe in things and happenings that defy belief and do so long enough to learn what they may mean in the broadest contexts, awe not only boggles our mind, it can change it forever.

THE "SANTA-ISTS"

For awe's natural power to have its impact, it has to be *un-adulterated*—meaning that we have to remember what it was like before being an adult deprived us of being easily awe inspired. Our threshold for being in awe is raised by our narrow version of what it means to be a grown-up, a state of being that has increasingly come to mean growing "in" to a sense of a separate, self-confident inner self that may *want* someone but doesn't really *need* anyone. Being an adult is equated with being a competent, independent person not easily impressed or swayed and totally free of our naïve inner child. It's working toward an even higher self-esteem buttressed by a cynically defensive consciousness that ignores or rejects anything that distracts it from getting wherever it is it thinks it needs to go. An adult is always supposed to be going somewhere with his or her life, but awe represents a spiritual stopover from that incessant striving by causing us to savor simply being there. Adulthood is also dominated by an impatient business that has little time for contemplation on how and why we are living as we are.

To see and compare adulterated and unadulterated awe in action, sit and observe the lines of children at the mall waiting to see Santa Claus. Some children are already cynical, little nonbelievers (or at least think they're supposed to appear that way or maintain their "coolness" by not letting awe take hold of them). In a society with too little time for awe, driven by trying to feel (or at least appear) happy, regardless of real external circumstances, trying to "look cool" seems to be setting in at a younger and younger age. Computer games may be described as "awesome," but being in awe of Santa Claus isn't "adult," and our children are in an increasing hurry to be—or look—grown-up.

Some children in the Santa line appear to be bartering a pretend awe. They are going along by feigning excitement to please their parents, either in order to increase their chances of getting a gift they want or to help Mom and Dad vicariously recoup some of their own missed awe-filled moments. Whatever awe response these mini-adults had has been muted or prematurely adult-erated. They're not shaking in anticipation, gleefully giggling, and fearfully crying at the same time, or struggling with awe's approach-avoidance feeling of being afraid of Santa but at the same time eager to go to him.

But there are those children in line who are acting just that way because they are in awe. The awed kids are easy to spot because, sadly, they're the odd ones the other kids are staring at. They're the ones with their minds, hearts, hopes, eyes, and mouths wide open, and they are scared and delighted by the confusing vastness and magic of what they are encountering. They seem legitimately moved by the lights and sounds and are so taken away by it all that they are oblivious to the cigarette smell lingering on Santa's elves. In the typical awe approach-avoidance pattern, they still cling anx-iously to their parent's hands, yet at the same time are tentatively eager to climb on Santa's lap. They've managed to keep their awe, perhaps with the help of parents who themselves have not lost their unadulterated awe and who have protected and welcomed awe as an emotion into their family.

THE A-SANTA-ISTS

Another test to compare adulterated and unadulterated awe is to listen in on the arguments in the after-Santa area. It is there that the young cynics challenge and mock the idea of a Santa Claus and point out the beard hanging away from the gaunt, bored face of a man who was distracted by the tight-fitting leotards of one of the female elves. They snidely expose this mall Santa as just another employed fraud. As if they have to protect themselves against the possibility of regressing back to being the children they still are and being in that state of innocent fascination, some of these child cynics' awe envy causes them to work hard to take others' awe away from them. They try to impose their nonbeliever "a-Santa-ist" views by pointing out the impossibility of anybody going down a chimney or being able to transverse the globe in a flying sleigh. But the awe-inspired have answers.

Like all of those who learn from their awe and engage in new, creative thinking, the little Santa-ists have concocted all sorts of creative ways of thinking about Santa's magical talents. They're not always very rational in their rejoinders, but neither are they necessarily irrational. They're nonrational, an essential aspect of learning from what inspires awe within us that is shown through metaphor, allegory, symbolism, what-if questions, and mystical and mythological ways of thinking that are highly creative. Listen to the Santa-ists' defenses of Santa Claus, and you will find wisdom about life worth contemplating.

"He's not on our time system," said one little girl almost brought to tears by the relentless challenge to her beliefs by a staunch a-Santa-ist. Empowered by her recent Santa awe and fresh from her ascension to his throne, the little Santa-ist was up to the interrogation. "This is only a Santa's helper here, but Santa is inside him. The big one is too busy to come now, and he only has his magic if you believe in him anyway. When you don't believe, you can't see a lot of things, so I think you should be more worried if Santa believes in you, or he won't come to your house. My mom says that it's your beliefs that make the reindeers fly and help Santa fit down the chimney. Santa is magic, but magic doesn't work if you don't know how to believe and pretend. He can do what he does because he's such a jolly old soul that God allows him to do special things we can never understand. My mom says that's true for anybody who is nice and not naughty."

Listen to the awe inspired, like this little girl, and you will hear subtle lessons about life and its meaning that transcend rational cynicism and are more than just blind faith and delusion. They're nonrational ways to learn about life from deep, symbolic ways that elude those with more closed minds and hearts—those who are willing to trust in the invisible forces of gravity but are numb to the subtle hints of something more within the magic of tall trees, sprawling vistas, and great mythical tales.

Perhaps our educational system would be more effective in producing smarter, more widely knowledgeable, reflective, and creative adults if it did all it could to encourage and enhance awe's drive for more understanding. If we dismiss awe as only a brief, exhilarating, emotional high; a temporary state of appreciation; or an intense sense of confirmation of a prior belief, we end up with an awe of ignorance rather than the awe of deeper understanding.

NATURAL AWE

Unlike all of the other emotions that dominate our daily lives, awe is our one human capacity that is natural, unnatural, and supernatural all at the same time.[3] Awe is a natural response because it has been documented as occurring throughout history, in all humans, in all cultures, and maybe even in animals. Although it is impossible to tell for sure that other animals experience human-like emotions such as awe, it is pure arrogance to assume that only we humans have received this extraordinary gift. Animals seem to experience at least some of our other ten basic "human" emotions, so why not awe? If it's nature itself that is so often the source of our awe, couldn't it be possible that all of its constituents might be able to experience some form of that which they elicit?

Author Jeffrey Moussaieff Masson, in his book *When Elephants Weep,* provides examples of some of our primate cousins experiencing a form of an awe response. He describes two chimpanzees that climbed high above the rain forest canopy to gaze together at the sunset in what seemed like awe. He writes about elephants' tears that seem to flow because of deep awe-like feelings related to the loss of a family member, returning to the place of their birth, or to where a poacher had slaughtered their mother.[4] Maybe it's not just that some of nature's creations might be able to experience what we consider to be *our* emotions, but that we are capable of experiencing feelings like awe that are *theirs.*

Masson also identifies in dogs what I described earlier as the key features and commonalities of the awe response. In his book *Dogs Never Lie about Love,* Masson describes how dogs seem to engage in behaviors that indicate that they are in awe of their owners.[5] I've often wondered if my Golden Retriever Li`a might not see me as "duman," a strange dog-human creature with whom she is totally in awe. While we don't speak dog fluently or understand a hundred of their barks, dogs have been shown to respond to more than 100 of our human words.

I think my dogs have been in awe of me, and I know I've been awed by some things my dogs have done and by the possibility of a very unique canine consciousness that allows them to be totally present in the given moment and no other. Research shows that they demonstrate at least four of what psychologists consider to be the seven types of human intelligence.[6] They seem to show emotional intelligence conveyed by such behaviors as their, "Hi, I love you" belly-up roll-over and exposure of their most vulnerable parts.

Dogs seem to show at least what seems to be awe-inspired love for what they consider to be their human family pack. Their combination of deferent fear, glee at the presence of the beings who inspire that fear, and unbounded physical demonstrations (such as obvious doggy depression when their humans leave) seem to indicate at least deep canine caring.

Maybe we love our dogs so much because, as author Fritz von Unruh points out, "The dog is the only being that loves you more than you love yourself," and judging from how much we think of ourselves, that's a lot of love.[7] The modern emphasis on "loving ourselves first" makes it difficult to find anyone or anything that is capable of exceeding the love we have for ourselves, but dogs seem able to do it. Moreover, being in awe seems to help us get over ourselves and past that constant effort toward elevation of our self-esteem. If being in awe teaches us anything, it intensely informs those who think long enough about it just how relatively insignificant we are and how invalid our illusion of a separate self really is. Dogs certainly seem to love us more than they love themselves. If we want to be more awe inspired, we may want to consider copying a little of our dog's canine selfless consciousness and infinite fascination with the most simple, ordinary, redundant things, like taking a walk or chasing a ball.

Scientists now speculate that what they have identified as our basic ten natural emotions (usually seen as some version of love, fear, sadness, embarrassment, curiosity, pride, enjoyment, despair, guilt, and anger) are naturally grounded in evolution and are essential to what we have and can become. This book suggests that the forgotten eleventh emotion of awe is as natural as any of the other ten and may not only play a very significant evolutionary role, but perhaps the most significant role of all. Just because most of us don't feel it all that often doesn't mean that awe isn't just as crucial to our life, well-being, and survival as our other feelings and emotions.

There seems to be no doubt that it's only natural to be in awe. However, we still need to determine what this ubiquitous human response is.

Here are a few of the questions about the nature of awe that are addressed in this book:

- How and where in the brain does awe happen, and does it even primarily happen there?

- Through our gut feelings, are we capable of being in awe before our brain knows it? Because almost 80 percent of our immune system cells are located in the lining of our gut and we feel awe in our gut, what is the impact on our general health of being in awe or lacking awe?

- Do we tend to grasp at our chests when we're in awe because it's the heart, and not the brain, that first senses something that inspires awe?

- What happens to us physically and mentally during and after the time we've been in awe?

- Why did evolution give us this unique response, and what purpose does it serve for our survival?

- Can our natural propensity to be awed lead us to blindly follow false prophets and to be easily manipulated by salespersons, various life experts, and corrupt leaders?

- In addition to awe being inspired by a sense of vastness reflected in great size, power, and perfection, can it result from deep awareness of the very small, the ordinary, the uniquely flawed, and the extremely vulnerable?

- Is awe inspired by senses beyond the physical senses and in response to a unique, still immeasurable subtle energy?

• Do we have to pay more attention in order to be in awe, or perhaps less—or do we have to pay a different kind of attention?

• Is awe necessarily connected with religious experience or faith in a Supreme Being?

• Is there such a thing as group awe or shared awe, and if so, how can it relate to love and enhance our most intimate relationships while, at the same time, lead to violence, war, and the world's worst atrocities? Or is awe exclusively a very personal, subjective emotion?

• Are there persons who are almost totally awe deprived, and if so, how do they end up feeling and behaving?

• Can awe be addictive? Can we end up so easily awed by the world around us that we lose track of our daily obligations and responsibilities to others?

• What role does awe proneness play in our intimate relationships? Are relationships with two persons of the same awe proneness more stable and fulfilling?

AWE AS AN UNNATURAL EMOTION

Because it goes against the common psychological assumption of the momentum toward an ever-developing, differentiated self and ever-stronger sense of an independent and powerful self, awe is not only a natural, but also a seemingly unnatural, emotion. While the ten basic emotions that we typically cycle through almost every day are primarily self-enhancing or protective, awe's total loss of a sense of self is so rare that it can feel unnatural and strange, and therein lies much of its unique power. Awe shakes us from our mental, spiritual, and physical self-absorbed languishing and can make our other emotions pale in comparison to its transformative life impact. One of the SAI participants defined her awe as "a kind of spiritual scolding about how selfishly I tend to lead my life and a warning that I'm not as in charge or as important as I like to think I am."

My study of awe indicates that its defining characteristic is what psychologists call *ego death,* meaning dissolution of the sense of self, replaced by a feeling of total immersion in, and connection with, something much more vast and meaningful. This loss of an independent self doesn't lead, as popular psychology suggests, to emotional and physical problems. Instead, awe's potential to briefly kill our ego or block our brain's implicit egotism is para- doxically one of our most powerful means for enhancing our mental, physical, spiritual, and world well-being.

Here are a few questions about awe's unnaturalness that are explored in the following chapters:

- Does the current emphasis on high self-esteem limit our awe response, which requires less of it?

- Can the selflessness associated with being in awe help us learn to overcome life's greatest fear—the end of the self?

- If awe is so powerful, why is it such a rare and unnatural feeling?

- Do we run the risk of diminishing awe's mystical unnatural power by studying and learning more about it?

- Because being in awe goes against the personal-growth grain of the self-help movement, can such an unnatural, selfless emotion stand a chance of getting the attention in the modern psychology of "me"?

- Can awe be addictive? Can it interfere with our working and loving and cause us to do little more than go in search of being awe inspired?

• Can being in awe seem so unnatural to those who aren't awe inspired that it causes them to mock or pull away from awe-inspired people?

SUPERNATURAL AWE

Throughout history and through various meditative techniques, mystics have reported experiencing awe. Reports of ordinary people being awestruck and moved by some force or sudden spiritual insight also have a long history in every society. Indigenous persons tell of awe for gods and gods in awe of other gods. In most historical descriptions of awe, there seems to be something about the experiences that is mystical, supernatural, paranormal, or at the very least, a little eerie or weird.

As you will read, almost every story of awe I collected contains an element of something uncanny, bizarre, magical, or even ghostly. Those who have experienced awe know that, although it may be a natural emotion with what often feels like the unnatural consequence of experiencing a loss of the sense of a separate self, it also feels like something beyond what we thought was possible and therefore in the realm of the supernatural.

When we're awed and take the time to reflect on our experiences, what we understood to be "the way things usually are or should be" changes, and how we perceive the world is altered. Our ordinary logic fails us; we feel like we have been at least briefly let in on a sacred divine secret about life. Some people even report that they've had a psychic, transformative experience.

The overwhelming suddenness of awe literally takes our breath away. What we see, sense, and feel seems not only to far transcend our day-to-day level of consciousness, but causes us to become more aware of the range and power of our senses. We may be capable of a supernatural extrasensory interaction with the world, which allows us to think we feel God's tears and hear him breathing.

Here are some questions addressed in this book that relate to awe's supernatural component:

• Is the awe response related to an intensification of one or more of our five basic senses of taste, touch, smell, hearing, and sight, or is it a manifestation of a "sixth" paranormal sense? While it is often stated that there is no research to document the existence of a "sixth" sense, there are hundreds of carefully done research projects and articles that illustrate a slight, subtle, but real "psychic" sense that could be involved in the awe response.

• Does being in awe involve activation of parts of the brain that are involved in what researchers refer to as our "spiritual sense areas" or "God spots"?

• Does being in an awe-inspired state relate to sensing what researchers refer to as "subtle energy," to which we are usually numbed by our busy, distracted approach to life?

• Are energetic signals being sensed by the heart and then sent to the brain?

• Is there some universal message that more easily comes through when we're under the influence of awe?

• How does what we experience during awe compare with the teachings of dogmatic religions and the contrasting views of god and God?

- Does awe make us deluded or profoundly insightful?

- When we're in awe, are our souls granted a brief respite from their entrapment in our physical bodies?

- Can our bodies be in awe before our brains know it?

DARWIN'S DELIGHT

Like other scientists who value objectivity and often think they are somehow immune from the mystical forces that send the less skeptical into a state of blatant naive awe, Charles Darwin, the scientist who spent his career studying nature and trying to objectively record the range of human emotions, how they are expressed cross-culturally, and their role in our evolution, himself fell under the influence of awe's power. Upon first gazing upon a rain forest, Darwin said he was awe inspired. Like most of us, and because awe is a natural human emotion that has unnatural and supernatural feelings associated with it, there wasn't anything he could do to resist it, and his awareness of nature was—as always happens with awe—expanded. Even if you are reluctant to try being more willing to stand regularly in rapt awe, it will still get you sooner or later, and it will be up to you what you will do because of it.

Describing his first encounter with a Brazilian rain forest, Darwin wrote in his journal, "It is not possible to give an adequate idea of the higher feelings of wonder, admiration, and devotion which fill and elevate the mind. I well remember my conviction that there is more in man than the breath of his body."[8] Darwin's words express what I discovered in my own study of awe. Its two primary characteristics are a perception of something that is beyond our current capacity to grasp mentally and express, and, no matter how spiritually skeptical we are, an inner sense of the divine, or at least our need for it.

THE HEART'S EYE

You will read in the following chapters that our heart, what Hindus refer to as the *fourth chakra,* is extensively involved in the awe response. Research from the fields of neurocardiology, cardio-endocrinology, and energy cardiology indicates that the heart receives signals from the world around us and sends those signals to the brain and other parts of the body. It's not just a pump responding to the needs of the brain, but an emotional organ often aggravated by our more brain-centered, negative emotions and capable of feeling its own positive ones.

Hindus see the heart as the fourth chakra because they feel it transcends the first three, which deal with the basic extrinsic necessities of everyday life. They teach that the heart is at the core of our most intense emotions. As authors Danah Zohar and Ian Marshall write, "The heart chakra is where thought and feeling meet, where we experience openness to others and to new things, an expanding sense of beauty and a deep idealism."[9] This is a perfect description of what the people I interviewed said it was like to be in awe.

Mystics have long spoken of "the eye of the heart." Mystic Bahya ibn Paquda wrote that our heart allows us to "see without eyes, hear without ears, perceive things which sense cannot perceive, and comprehend without reasoning," and again, that's what my interviews indicate awe feels like.[10] Yehuda Halevi, another mystic describing the intuitive power of the heart as a source of our creative consciousness, wrote, "My heart saw Thee and believed Thee.

I have seen Thee with the eye of the heart."[11] Halevi was describing his awe for his encounter with the Divine. In various shapes and forms, atheists and true believers alike described their awe with this same sense of reverence. No matter what their religious orientation, or lack of it, people in awe describe their version of going to heaven and back, and it seems that our heart is the conduit for this kind of cosmic consciousness.

AWE PRONE

While all of us, regardless of our religiosity, seem to experience some degree of the awe response as we do our other human emotions, devoutly religious people seem to have a lower threshold for being awed than more secular thinkers. Or like extraordinary athletic skill or unusual psychic ability, it is possible that some of us may be naturally born awe-responders. These people may have brains that are prewired to be more easily awed.

Some researchers suggest that we have a God spot nestled in the temporal lobes of the brain that can become activated when exposed to evocatively religious words, topics, or images, just as happens when we are in awe.[12] Seizure activity is often localized in this area, prompting one of my SAI respondents, a neurologist, to write in his awe journal, "I think being in awe is a kind of spiritual seizure."

Since the temporal lobes have direct connections with other parts of the brain, including the amygdala and hypothalamus, it is possible that an intense emotion such as awe might have some relationship to the hypothesized God spot. More current research on the brain suggests that it probably doesn't have a specific spot for exclusively representing anything we experience. Instead, the brain operates through the interactions of general areas or systems of interacting neurological cells. Indeed, the neuron is the simplest of cells, far simpler even than the chips in your cell phone. It works primarily by automatic neurochemical reflex to other cells' secretions that cause it to release its own neurochemicals. There is some preliminary evidence that there is an area of the brain in the temporal lobes that is particularly reactive to signals from the neurons in the heart.

Other researchers suggest that meditative states, mystical, epiphanic, or shamanistic experiences, and what they call "religious awe," are associated with the quieting of an area of the brain called the posterior superior parietal lobe. This is also referred to as the "orientation association area" (OAA), which helps us stay oriented in physical space and sets the neurological template for what is and is not "self" and where that self physically begins and ends.[13] Because being in awe is being much less aware of where "we" end and "other" begins, a quiet OAA may also help induce the awe response.

Yet another possibility is that some people have brains that are just more naturally God or "Higher Power" receptive and awe prone, because they are quieter and less selfish than other brains. When it comes to being in awe, the rule seems to be "the less me, the more awe." Some people may have been born with a heart more sensitive to, and a brain less dominated by, a separate sense of self. As a result, they may be more reactive to the signs of what is sacred about life. Whether some of us are born easily awed or not, being born and raised in a family that values and encourages being in, thinking about, and talking about awe probably enhances any awe proneness we may have.

Of course, just because the brain seems to have a spot or spots for him (or her) doesn't mean that God exists. However, the presence of brain centers associated with awe-inspiring experiences such as religious events does seem to indicate that, whatever our religious beliefs may be, we have a built-in eleventh natural emotion that will not allow the sacred to go away. If there is a God, inspiring our awe—whether by the most wonderful or even the most terrible experiences—may be his or her way of getting our attention.

No matter the extent of our faith, being in awe nudges all of us up at least a little on the spiritual scale toward whatever is heavenly about our existence. While some of us, for neurological (or as yet unknown) reasons, may more easily embrace and speak about the idea of being in submissive awe of God's power or its many manifestations, all of us can fall under the influence of our eleventh emotion.[14] While it may come a little more naturally to some of us, all of us are made by some awesome power to be naturally awe-full people.

AWE WITHOUT FAITH

Many persons of faith begin from a state of awe not unlike that of the little believers waiting to see Santa Claus, and they constantly seek to defend and confirm it. Many secular thinkers resembling the "a-Santa-ists" are either envious or demeaning of what they see as blind faith and have to have awe suddenly happen to them. This may explain why awe is almost totally neglected by psychologists and researchers but fills the pages of religious writings. The commonly shared experience of being in awe regardless of religious belief may serve as a bridge between the extremes of the faith scale.

New England's transcendentalist movement represented an attempt to deal with the undeniable power that came from the awe inspired by the sanctity of life without reliance on blind faith. It was based on the idea that the stunning majesty of life was a manifestation of a Higher Power. That Higher Power was not to be found in the existence of a humanlike personality that governs everything, but within each person and in nature. In this view, God isn't "up there" but "in here" and everywhere. As one professor of religion told me, "For the transcendentalist, the challenge isn't to go looking for God but to realize that he's here, and we need to be much more intensely here in order for him to find us."

The founder of the transcendental movement is usually considered to be Ralph Waldo Emerson. He described his sense of awe derived from going to the woods alone as his way of knowing and worshiping God. He wrote that when he was in such an environment, he felt that he became nothing, yet could see everything, and became "part and parcel of God."[15] It's as if he was becoming aware of God through the heart's eye.

You can be awed by the existence of a massive forest, the magnificence of a single huge tree, the crashing thunder of a massive wave, the fragrance of a single flower, or a single tear on your child's cheek when someone finally convinces her that there is no Santa Claus. Awe can be inspired by contemplating the tiniest space between the petals of a deep red rose or the vast nonexistence of something like the Bootes supervoid that is 250 million light years across and considered by astronomers to be the largest area of nothingness in the universe. Whether our starting point is faith-based awe in a Higher Power or a willingness to be open to evidence of that power as reflected in a scientist's awe of a rain forest or a child's innocent trust in the possibility of Santa Claus and the loving giving this demigod symbol represents, being in awe can be your most transformative state.

WHAT'S YOUR FAITH?

Because awe is so often associated with religion or spiritual issues, when I began my study of awe, the question I was most often asked was, "What's your faith?" I was never asked about my religious beliefs when I studied or spoke about the other ten emotions, but there is something about awe that brings out the divine—or at least the search for it—in those willing to think more deeply about this mysterious human gift. I used to answer "very deep," but that seldom satisfied the questioner.

Today, after years of studying awe, my answer is, "I'm a pantheist in the tradition of Spinoza," which usually puts a quick end to the discussion.[16] My answer refers to my own personal belief that a Higher Power is manifested in some way beyond our full under-standing in everything and everyone. I have faith in the fact that we were given the capacity to be in awe, because that gift indicates that there is so much more we could understand that we don't. I also believe that being in awe challenges us to keep trying to under-stand whether or not we ever will. I find that I am most often awed when I've lost temporary track of "me" or some preconceived idea or belief and allow myself to fall under the influence of a force that seems to emanate from the vast mysteriousness of the universe, and then proceed to try to accommodate its message into my daily life in the context of my family.

As I have reflected on awe and my own spiritual beliefs, I have come to understand why the genius Albert Einstein chose Spinoza's phi-losophy as his own divinity reference point and system for dealing with the mysteries his easily awe-inspired mind regularly encoun-tered. Einstein's quote at the beginning of this chapter indicates the degree of awe that motivated his studies of the confounding para-doxical workings of the universe. Spinoza, the man referred to as the

"God-intoxicated philosopher of Amsterdam" because he found God everywhere, was a perfect fit for Einstein's version of awe and the sense of the divine it inspired both in him and in his science.[17]

Spinoza was excommunicated for his beliefs, and Giordano Bruno, who preceded Spinoza in espousing the idea that God and the universe were one and the same, was burned at the stake. There's an undeniable comfort in the "one God over everything" view because it provides a sense that someone is in charge who knows the meaning of life that none of us can yet decipher. Looking up, rather than in or around, is a more comfortable point of view—and works for many people who experience awe as a confirmation rather than an epiphany, confirming a belief rather than expanding and making us struggle with it. Spinoza believed that the awesomeness of the universe we struggle to comprehend—indeed our human capacity to engage in that struggle itself—represents the grandeur of God. The more times I'm in awe and the more stories I collect describing it, the more inspired I am to reflect more deeply and more often about the issue of God or a Higher Power. So I doubt I'll ever be certain, but I'm in awe of the gift of being able to reflect on it.

The debate persists between pantheists who look for God in everything, theists who believe in a God over everything, and atheists who believe in no God or gods. It still rages between the deists who believe God set the world in motion, provided its laws, and leaves it to us to use our rational thinking to deal with it, and theists who believe in communication with God and behavioral and prayerful earning of his intervention. Believing in God, a god, or a Higher Power continues to be a source of bitter disagreement and even wars. What no one can disagree with, however, is that we humans are made to be capable of being awed by the world in which we find ourselves, and that the world itself is awe inspiring.

3

AWE FULL MOMENTS

*"Things never before seen have I seen, and ecstatic is my joy;
yet fear-and-trembling perturb my mind."*

—ARJUNA IN THE HINDU EPIC MAHABHARATA

BEYOND HAPPINESS

Happiness is an abnormal, brief respite between the stresses and strains of a fully engaged meaningful life. Life is, by its nature, a real pain, and bad is more frequent and always stronger than good. When Buddha offered his first noble truth (*dukkha*) that life by its very nature is suffering, he wasn't being pessimistic, just realistic. He was referring to the fact that what is most magnificent about life is also what makes it so difficult; nothing is permanent. As it is in nature, so it is in our lives. Nothing we attain, be it a thing, a feeling, our physical health, or a relationship, lasts as long as we wished it would. The endless birthing pains of nature's constant reinvention of itself that result in our awe response can be as anguishing as they are uplifting.

Which would you react to most intensely: a stunningly gorgeous sunset or a beautiful tiger running toward you? We seldom feel as intensely good as we do bad because evolution saw to it that we physically and emotionally react much faster and more intensely to what we perceive as bad for us or threatening to our lives. Quick action when we're under threat is essential to our survival, but happiness isn't. Despite our endless pursuit of it, happiness is just a nice, temporary bonus, and awe may or may not result in more of it. I felt heartbreaking awe as I looked at the face of my dying mother and sensed that mysteriously and frighteningly irreversible moment when the life force left her body. As I cried, my awe was given its power by the memories of how she had given me life and loved me throughout it. It was made even more intense by the wonder it caused within me about where, at that lethal split-second, her life energy had gone—and where mine would go when I die.

My mother had given me my life energy, hers had vanished, and the whole process thrust me into awe's unique state of overwhelming wonder. Author Brian Swimme refers to this kind of wonder as "being stunned by the magnificence of where we find ourselves," and I've found no better definition of our eleventh emotion. Even at times of loss or whenever we are in a place in our life where we don't want to be, we can still be astounded by being there, and as a result and in time, our awe can somehow reignite life, even though it will never be the same. As Swimme points out, there is nothing more astounding than to be able to participate in the process called life; death is an inescapable necessary part of that process, and it can be as astounding as it is devastating.[1] We seem to have a bias for bliss, but life offers no such guarantee. It's up to us to find awe wherever and however it is offered to us and no matter how harsh and difficult it and its lessons may be.

Awe can be delightful, but its intensity is always dangerous; it doesn't necessarily always feel good, and isn't always good for us physically in the short run. It stresses every part of the body and mind, right down to the gut, where most of our immune systems' cells are located. My mother held me so many times, sharing her life energy with me when I was afraid or hurt, and then hers had gone somewhere forever, leaving only the unrelenting sense of finality that's unique only to death. At this saddest of moments, my mom's mortality left me physically drained, yet I was not only in deep grief but also in profound awe of what was happening and what it meant.

The experience of being in awe can quickly shock us out of any inauthentic happiness we've tried to achieve for ourselves. Our eleventh emotion may have evolved as a human response because it offers new ways to perceive the world at the best and worst of times by warning us of our vulnerability to suffering and pain, and challenging and guiding us to learn about new sources of pleasure and reasons to survive. Mountains force us to consider our relative smallness, powerlessness, and comparative impermanence. An unending plain forces our binocular vision to converge far beyond its normal length, drawing us to consider the nearness of our mundane life versus the farness of yet unimagined possibilities.

We evolved to be successful, not happy. Feeling happy about our life is a bonus, but being vigilant to the threats to it is essential. Our ancestors who pursued personal happiness at the expense of being alert to threats would have had little evolutionary advantage. Awe seems to exist within us not only because it can make us very happy; it also offers lessons and warnings about paying more attention to, and fully experiencing, all that life offers us, be it terrible or tremendous. Because it often stirs the unsullied primitive pureness of more simple, less hectically distracted times that still resonate somewhere deep inside us, awe not only energizes us about the future but also causes us to rediscover the beauty of the past. It is how we most profoundly experience, and are spurred to contemplate, both the bad and the good.

THE ILLUSION OF HAPPINESS

Ask most people how they're doing, and except for the perpetual grumblers who almost always seem to have a complaint, most will answer not only "okay" but also "great," "wonderful," "fantastic," or "tremendous." Doing fine doesn't seem to be enough anymore. The illusion that life should be almost always delightful or the feeling that we have to be sure others at least think ours is has resulted in a cultural happiness facade that gets in the way of being in true awe of our life as it is and not as it should be.

Although there is no evidence that supports the relationship (and a lot that shows just the opposite), happiness and a high level of success are seen as equivalent, so any admission of misery represents a failure and leads to a competitive disadvantage. We assume that anyone who is disadvantaged and who isn't very, very happy must not be trying hard enough and therefore doesn't deserve to be. If we can impress others that our level of happiness is beyond their grasp, we seem to get a *schadenfreudian* buzz from the comparative unhappiness we induce in their consciousness.

We've come to believe that life is supposed to almost always be happy, with only a few distracting negative hitches along the way.[2] We're supposed to go through the appropriate stages of grief and get over it so we can move on, but awe can cause us to pause a much longer time to learn the lessons of terrible loss. As if we should deal with and treat our unhappiness separate from what's making us unhappy, and if something prevents us from being happy for too long, we are supposed to "get help" or "take something" to "feel better." Dr. Peter Kramer praised Prozac in his bestselling book *Listening to Prozac* and coined the phrase "cosmetic psychopharmacology" to refer to the prescription of drugs for the removal of unhappiness, as if it could and should be cut out of our life as so much excess ugly fat.[3]

Despite our immersion in the culture of perpetual happiness, there's something increasingly unpleasant about all the pleasantness being forced upon us, which gets in the way of true awe. As if hung everywhere by a "be-well-ian" big-brother pleasure police, there's something annoying about those ubiquitous yellow smiley face dots staring at us and nagging us to cheer up and smile.[4] Despite the cliché, a smile isn't really a "frown turned upside down." Oftentimes, it's what researchers call the "Pan American smile," so named after the robot-like, forced greeting grin required of that now-defunct airline's flight attendants. A good scowl is much more sincere and involves totally different muscles and emotions that are important to a full life; being told not to worry, be happy, and smile only leads to artificial happiness detached from real life, and that is more act than affect. Awe doesn't result from trying to be happy and can actually be prevented by the incessant effort to be in that state. It derives from intense, unedited, open-minded engagement with anything and everything the world offers.

True awe, the awe that leads to deeper understanding and not a brief temporary interesting distraction, involves the power of negative thinking. After all, it is pessimists who are more likely to have more frequent pleasant surprises and it is the depressed people who are often more in touch with the real threats and negatives of daily life than the perpetual optimists who work hard not see negatives anywhere. Confronting, accepting, and learning from our negative feelings—even the worst and saddest ones—can turn the anxiety that comes with being alive into a facilitating, enhancing, even fascinating emotion worth learning more about. Based on what the SAI participants told me, they never felt more alive than when they felt the terrible pain of an awe-inspiring negative life transition. Because the awe of understanding leaves lingering doubts and more questions than answers, many of them were pensive, worrying people, not smiling optimists—another argument on the side of choosing the easier, less-awe-filled life.

People who defy the pop psychology axiom of "don't worry, be happy" seem more capable of awe than those who constantly try to be happier than they are. This is because people who strive for happiness believe they must close themselves off to the negative by always thinking positively and, in doing so, end up censoring the darker half of life that often inspires the most understanding kind of awe. So not to expect life to be happy, not to see happiness as normal, and to consider unhappiness as bad can lower our threshold for being in awe and thus being more fully alive. The SAI participants were not an upbeat, smiling, perpetually positive-thinking group, but they were the most alive and engaged people I've ever met.

I was never unhappier in my life than the day my son Scott was born. As I described in the introduction, I could see right away that something was terribly wrong and that he, my wife, and I were in for a difficult life of struggle and pain. I never imagined that we would lead such a constantly, intensely challenging life. At the same time, I have never felt such profound awe as I did when I received the gift of my son, for life itself, and for the way in which his loving spirit seemed to shine through the horror of what he was experiencing with his spasmodic body. It was, as has been written, the worst and best of times, the kind of times that can inspire the awe of deepest understanding and the need to understand more.

PUBLICIZED PLEASURE

It seems that it's no longer enough to be a little happy once in a while; we have to be sure everyone knows when we are. Bumper stickers publicizing that strangers want other strangers to know that they "heart" their dog, a city, or a football team causes some of us to ask "Who in the hell cares what you 'heart'?" For others, it might lead them to wonder why their own daily lives don't cause them to go around wanting to announce to the world something that they're "hearting." There's an increasing tyranny of happiness that gets in the way of a full, sincere, meaningful awe for being alive, and it's based on the myth that happiness is normal.

As the real, terrible pain in the world seems to be becoming more evident, widespread, and awe-inspiring enough to cause us to think long and hard about its meaning, there seems to be a contrasting mendaciousness to the frantic "Have a nice day" that morphed to the command to "Have a wonderful day" and more recently to the more pressuring "Have a great day." As the American modernist poet Wallace Stevens pointed out, this apparent abundance of happiness or demand to be happy seems to radiate an "unwholesomeness because it emanates from an unnatural source, not from real life."[5]

What's most "real" about living is that painful and bad outweighs good most of the time, and the good news that does come through doesn't ultimately matter as much as we thought it would or last as long as we hoped it would. We're made to thrive through the worst that life offers, and much of our joy derives from relief from those times and renewed confidence that we can make it through some of our worst fears. While no amount of feigned positive attitude will change the "bad trumps good" rule, being more available to being in awe of all that real, ordinary life offers can lead to our fullest and most engaged life. It may not be *the* good life we're all supposed to pursue to be happy, but it can be *a* good one, lived with full, reflective engagement.

THE LIABILITIES OF PLEASURE
AND BENEFITS OF PAIN

Popular psychology preaches that happiness is the natural, normal state; that we can be and should always try to be happier than we are; and that we "owe it to ourselves" to keep trying to be "all we can be" by being happier and happier. Until very recently, psychotherapy has generally been less concerned about helping people actually do better than teaching them how to "feel better" no matter how or what they're doing. The stories from those who most regularly experience the awe response indicate, however, that they're also the ones who have had the most pain and unhappiness in their lives and are doing better, not in spite of—but often because of—that pain.

Particularly when we are in awe of a traumatic event, research shows that the most common outcome is resilience, not an enduring devastating emotional reaction or mere survival.[6] My son Scott's life is evidence of the validity of that principle. Despite his cerebral palsy, he has become one of the most trusted financial advisors in Hawaii, designed and built one of the most unique homes in the islands, overcome his speech and movement problems to become a skilled pilot, and studied medical literature to become my protector when I was dying of cancer. At one of my most down times during my treatment when I said I was worried about whether or not I would survive, Scott laughed and said, "Dad, if you're going to have to get through all this, you should be thinking about more than just survival. I've learned with my CP that just being a survivor wastes a lot of energy with very little pay off. You should be thinking about thriving, not just surviving." To this day, and because of Scott's own hard-earned lessons about resilience, I cringe when someone refers to me as a "cancer survivor" or my son as a "survivor" of a birth injury. We're both in far too much awe of life to settle for that.

Because of the discrimination he regularly encountered, Scott is seldom very happy, but he is more alive than most persons who are free of the burdens he carries, who burden him with their ignorant gawking at his struggle to walk, and who fail to be in awe of a person who has transcended the worst that life could give him—to struggle to not only survive but thrive in a world that keeps rejecting him. I sometimes worry about how much energy and personal strength it must take on Scott's part to keep thriving in the face of repeated social rejection and isolation from those who don't thrive, because they have yet to learn to be in awe of a loving wise spirit that transcends the shaking awkward body that takes their interest.

As I watch Scott bounce back and beyond his challenges, my awe and the awe of those who know Scott's essence grows every day. The mail lady stopped her truck when I was leaving Scott's house and as she put letters in Scott's mailbox yelled out to me, "Aloha, Dr. Pearsall! I just wanted you to know how in awe I am of your son and how much he inspires me. Just seeing how he lives gives me chills and makes me so uplifted."

While more than half of us will experience such terrible trauma as physical assault; rape; a sudden, tragic, untimely loss; or the devastation of natural disaster, most of us still manage to do very well or even better after our challenge has been met and often because of, not just in spite of, our experiences.[7] Our eleventh emotion, our capacity to be in awe of what challenges us and the lessons and new ways of thinking that come from awe, may be an essential component of what psychologists call SIG, "stress-induced growth."

My SAI interviews indicate that those persons who are most regularly in awe of their lives tend to be those who've had what most people would consider the worst ones. Looking through the stories of the frequently awe inspired, I noticed a pleasure paradox. Those who had had the most severe pain and least continued happiness seemed to often be those who were most generally content with their lives and suffering the least, while those who had experienced comparatively much less pain in their lives tended to gripe and grumble and seemed to be suffering the most. The awe study findings extend the popular exercise maxim of "no pain, no gain" to our psychological life.

In my book *The Beethoven Factor,* I discussed Beethoven's transcending his deafness to be able to write some of the world's most awe-inspiring symphonies. I point out in that book that some of our greatest strengths are often forged in the crucible of adversity.[8] Psychologists Carol Ryff and Burton Singer write that when we become fully aware of and learn from the blend of the positive and negative features of the human condition, we discover—I would say are awed by—what they call the "irony of well-being," which is "the paradox that human strengths are frequently born in encounters with life difficulties."[9]

Ancient psychologies and modern research reinforce the fact that the cliché "pain is fact; suffering is optional" has some validity. I've learned this not only from my son Scott's life of awe, but also from the stories of the SAI participants. Awe elevated these people above the limits of their pain to be able to embrace more fully what their awe was teaching them about how to connect with things, people, and events that mattered much more than their pain. I also know this personally because there were days when I had cancer that my pain was at its worst yet my suffering was minimized by my awe for my wife, my family, and the gift of the moments I could still share with them.

Even the physiological aspects of the awe response, including the warm, open feeling in my chest when my wife entered the room and the goose bumps I felt when she told me she loved me as she brushed the sweat from my brow seemed to diminish or at least distract me from my physical pain. I still had it, but it seemed to have me less. It didn't make my happy, but it made me a little more content, and that seems to be awe's greatest gift: it doesn't always make us very happy, but it renders us more fully alive.

During my cancer, I was experiencing firsthand the dreadfully vast power of nature to destroy, but I also felt poet Wallace Stevens's encouraging words, "The imagination is man's power over nature."[10] Awe's magic derives from its capacity to broaden and deepen our imagination, and it's this capacity that gives us power over our pain and perspective for our pleasure.

DIGGING IN THE BLACK SAND

A lesson that emerged from the hundreds of examples of the experience of awe is that life not only isn't really about trying to be happy, but that even if we could be happy all the time, we would still end up leading half-lives. Without the ever-looming reality of inevitable loss, how could we be in awe of those limited, special moments shared with someone we love? If we never knew the pain of endings or our extraordinary capacity to let go and move on, how we would know the thrill of nature's many new beginnings and be in awe of the hope and promises they offer?[11] The awe stories reveal that there's as much awe to be experienced from giving up and moving on as in persistent striving.

Charlie is a neighbor of ours. He's a Hawaiian man who works as a commercial pilot, and when I told him of my research on awe and we discussed the idea that losses are necessary, that they can inspire the thrill of new beginnings, and that our eleventh emotion relates as much to pain as pleasure, he began to rub his arms.

"Wow," he said. "I'm getting chicken skin [the Hawaiian version of goose bumps] getting ready to tell you my awe story. I was standing there not far from where the lava was still flowing, and I saw where Pele's [the Hawaiian goddess of the volcano] tears had turned to black sand. For some reason I'll never know, I fell to my knees crying and started digging in the sand with my hands."

Charlie stopped talking for awhile, but he kept moving his hands much like a dog digs with its paws. As he illustrated his digging by moving his hands in space, he continued to share his tale of awe.

"I really don't know what I was digging for, and maybe it was the old white sand beach that used to be there. No matter how fast I dug, the black sand kept falling back into the hole I was digging. I could feel Pele's *mana* [energy], and my whole body felt like it was buzzing with it. I dug and dug until I couldn't dig anymore, and then I just sat back on my knees crying. I thought about my dad who had just passed and how much pain I felt, so maybe in some strange way I was looking for him. It was not a very happy time for me down there at the new black sand beach, but it was one of the most intense times in my life, and I'll never forget it. To me, that was awe. It was awe for the feeling of the sand in my hands that seemed to symbolize how things end and keep being created and affirm that even though we hurt, some force keeps creating and filling up the holes in our lives."

Sometimes it is best not to keep digging for life's treasures and to take more time to treasure all that is good and bad about the life we have. It's probably a complete waste of time to try to be happier than we are, because research shows that we are already as happy as we'll ever be.[12] However happy you are as you read these words is probably as happy as you're ever going to feel. Most (from 50 to 80 percent, depending on which study you look at) of how happy we tend to be is genetic, but how fully alive and connected with the world we will be is largely a matter of how often we choose to be in awe of the life we're leading, as opposed to striving for a happier life later. Based on the lives of the participants in my SAI study and the work of other psychologists, temperament almost always trumps circumstances.[13]

A good life is about meeting the challenge of carrying pain without amplifying it into suffering and savoring pleasure without becoming a slave to pursuing more of it. It's our eleventh emotion, and it is its capacity to expand our imaginations and open our minds to all that is available to us in the present moment—be it good or bad—that offers creative ways to meet that challenge. The capacity to meet challenges in creative ways refers to a *creative consciousness* that facilitates a fuller engagement to try to understand, rather than the easier awe of ignorant acceptance and a sense of confirmation.

A RICH IMAGINATION

Every morning of our lives, we're given the chance to see the world anew. The first time we open our eyes, our previous day's thin top layer of vision receptor cells is literally scorched away by the entering light, and new cells are exposed that have never before seen the light of day. The first sound we hear vibrates away the prior day's layer of auditory cells, giving us the opportunity to hear fresh new sounds. The first time we smell a new morning's coffee, the old odor-receiving cells are whisked away to expose new ones that give us the chance to breathe in odors as if for the first time. How we choose to use this daily physiological fresh start sets our course for "just another day" or for one full of awe. Whether we languish or flourish is up to us and how easily awed we choose to be.

Whether we will allow ourselves to be awestruck by the ordinary magic of life or, as in the movie *Groundhog Day,* essentially relive the same day over and over again, not only determines the quality of our lives and the lives of those around us, but also influences how long, how well, and how meaningfully we and the people we love will live. The challenge is not to wait for something to inspire awe but to look as if we have never seen, listen as if we have never heard, and be alert to aromas as if we had never breathed them in before. In other words, we can't "will" awe to happen to us, but can help create the consciousness environment where it is most likely to occur. People could choose to be in awe of my son Scott and to learn from how he deals with his disability, but many just stare at him without really seeing him. They look and move on, missing the opportunity to experience awe for, and learn from, a soul that resists succumbing to challenges that would overwhelm many others.

You have read that awe is first and foremost *the* emotion of self-transcendence. It's encountering something, someone, or even an idea, a disease, or a terrible crisis that is not only a violation of our expectations, but a revelation of what is beyond our wildest imagination. Awe results in what author Edmund Burke described as a "dilation of the imagination" that can lead to entirely new ways of thinking about how we interact as one with the world.[14] Burke asserted that our deepest awareness of what is beautiful and sublime about our existence is related to what he described as a kind of childlike, innocent, ignorant openness of the imagination, and the people I interviewed who described their awe response all reported this childlike state. Awe doesn't seem to happen much to persons who lead their lives in arrogant certainty or constant pursuit of an unattainable happiness.

OVERCOMING OUR AWE-A-PHOBIA

If awe can help reduce our pain and free us from the relentless, endless search for more happiness so we can more fully engage with a full and real life, why don't we know more about our healthiest and most transformative emotion? It may be that we are a little too awed by awe and are allowing its intensity, the fear it induces, the overwhelming sense of the majesty of life that it inspires, the mental work it takes to make sense of it, and the degree to which it diminishes our sense of self to cause us to avoid it.

Some of us who have known the full impact of the awe response might be concerned that we could become addicted to it. It's as if we think that if we indulge in it too much we might become awe dependent, seen by others as an "awey." Maybe we think that, by being in awe more often, we might somehow spoil it or wear out its effect. This might explain why some who shared their stories about awe said that they didn't want to go through it too often but only experience it as, as one put it, "an occasional jolt of spiritual awareness when I need it; a kind of blissful break for a moment of fascination with the world, and then it's back to the grind of just trying to survive in it—a motivator, but not a way of life. Only mystics and gurus have time to be in awe all the time."

My research shows that we can greatly and safely increase the

amount of awe in our lives without allowing our eleventh emotion
to become our only one. Because of the "bad trumps good" evolutionary principle, we can be confident that we'll always have more
than enough of the bad emotions. Those who regularly experience
and are transformed by their awe and by engaging in the crucial
step of reflecting about it reported that their loving, working, and
living not only were not interfered with but were greatly enhanced
by their eleventh emotion.

DYING TO BE IN AWE

I could find only three scientific articles ever written about the
awe response, yet when I was dying of cancer, many of my fellow
patients and I experienced it almost every day.[15] As I lay near
death from Stage IV lymphoma, I often wondered what it was
about my looming death that could sometimes make me feel more
in awe of being alive than I had before I became sick—in addition
to being in what felt like a strange awe of death that has not left
me to this day. I still know of nothing more awe-inspiring, as I have
defined that response, than death, and it still leaves me in a state
of utter confusion at the power of love, life, and death that can
result in such agonizing grief at life's irreversible end. I discovered
that the answer to why closeness to death is associated with feeling more alive was related to my daily experience of the cancer—
it imposed a diminished sense of my self that seemed to nudge me
a little closer to the sense of selflessness that is a prerequisite for
the awe response. The mystery of it all also imposed the dilation
of imagination necessary to be awed. Feeling fear, experiencing
confusion, being literally drilled down to the marrow of my bones,
being helpless in the face of the vast mysteriousness of my cancer,

and living in the cancer unit itself, where so many miracles and tragedies happened every day, all seemed to create the perfect mental state and environmental setting for awe to happen.

Like birth and death, cancer comes with all the prerequisites for being in awe. It's shocking, overwhelming, frightening, and so vastly mysterious that those who have had cancer still can't fully grasp what happened and those who have never had it can't imagine what it's like to have to deal with it. When it comes to "bad," cancer is right at the front of the pack, but its mind-boggling blend of wonder, confusion, dread, pain, unhappiness, hope, and enhanced valuing of life makes it one of life's most awe-inspiring phenomena.

You have read that awe is most often found in situations where fear, mystery, and a challenge to the self suddenly resonate together, and it was in the bone marrow transplant unit where I first decided that, if I would live, I would try to learn as much about awe as I could. I saw awe's helpless, childlike ignorance in my fellow cancer patients, and I felt it myself. I became profoundly aware of the intensified connections within families and saw patients looking at spouses, children, and grandchildren in ways that reflected the strange mixture of dread and delight that comes with being in awe of every moment one has left.

Even though chemotherapy and radiation had numbed our physical senses, many of us dying of cancer seemed to become more life energy–sensitive and more easily in awe of what we could have been all along. Of course, the children with cancer—with their youthful, broadened imaginations and not-yet fully differentiated selves—were awe experts. As one little girl who had gone through two bone marrow transplants said, "This is so terrible, it's kind of like awesome. Just look at all the little red holes where they drilled out the inside of my bones. Aren't they fascinating? They're marks where the inside of me was sucked out. I keep looking at them all day, and they keep changing, so something's going on that I think it is really awesome."

LESSONS FROM THE OFTEN AWED

To make my points about the awe response, I've included mostly dramatic examples of the awe response in this book, but like all of our other basic emotions, awe exists in degrees. Sometimes, we might be briefly awed by stealing a quick glimpse of a child's smile and, other times, we are awed by the sight, feeling, and even smell that come with our first look at the cascading waters of a towering, powerful waterfall. Just as long as we feel the diminished awareness of self, have a sense of life's vast mysteriousness and ordinary magic, and stop for awhile to accommodate what we experience into our life, we are in awe.

There was a small but fascinating subgroup within the SAI that seemed more frequently in awe than the others. This frequently awe-inspired group (the "serial sighers," as the less-often awed SAI participants referred to them) constituted about 10 percent of the more than 500 people who shared their stories of awe. This more easily awed group said that their awe response had been a life-altering event that somehow lowered their threshold for being awed again and again. The rule seemed to be, once deeply awed, twice as ready to be awed again. They seemed to experience a kind of consciousness conversion not unlike descriptions of sudden intense religious conversion. It may be that being in awe a lot alters our physiology, enhances our senses, leads to a new kind of attention, and/or increases our cardio-sensitivity, to make it more likely that we will be awestruck in the future.

By contrast, most of the SAI participants said being in awe was "wonderful" when it happened and seemed like more passive recipients of it who hoped it might happen to them again sometime. As if awe is like lightning that strikes randomly, this majority group of respondents assumed that awe somehow flashed into their lives in the form of a random cosmic gift by which they were struck as innocent life bystanders. They remembered being shocked by what happened to them, wanted it to happen again, but were not significantly or lastingly changed in terms of how they approached their daily lives (or perhaps didn't know they were changed).

When I was dying, I learned that I didn't have to wait for something awe-inspiring to just happen to me and that, if I thought long and deeply enough about it, awe could have a life-altering impact far beyond a nice surprise. Awe became less something that just happened to me and more a way I chose to think about what was happening to me. I learned that, if I was going to experience more of my eleventh emotion and less of the mostly negative other ten, I would first have to get much more into life and much more out of my self. I discovered that I could help bring awe on by being mindful of the ordinary magic in life that I used to take for granted.

If I put my mind and heart to it, I could experience all the features of the awe response by paying more attention to the loving care of my nurses and the warm touch of one of their hands to comfort me in the middle of the night. I had never in my life seen an icicle formed from beginning to end, but the hours of doing nothing, which cancer provided, allowed me to look outside my window in awe of slowly dripping water that turned into a long, sharp, invincible-looking icicle that slowly melted away right before my eyes in the morning sun and mysteriously returned again in the late evening. I saw colors in that icicle that I had either never seen before or had failed to realize I had seen.

I was in awe of the courageous struggles for life going on all around me and the brave audacity of patients and families dealing with and growing through the dying process. For the first time in my life, I was in awe of time and how the clocks around me seemed to be measuring some other dimension of life, which was certainly not mine. I was in awe of my own body and how it looked and felt when whole body radiation burned away its hair, making me look like an adolescent even as cancer accelerated the aging of my body.

Big or small, awe always makes us more awake, alive, and consciously engaged, despite whether what awes us is a positive occurrence or a horrific one. I would sometimes cry for hours after being in awe of the love I felt for my family, intensified by the real possibility that I would soon be losing all of them. Other times, I would share a good laugh with another cancer patient who shared my awe for the workings of a body that seemed at the same time so sacred and so stinky. We were awed by the idea that, no matter how abused our bodies were by our disease, it fought back not only to try to heal but by doing something as embarrassingly silly, relieving, and attention-getting as issuing a gaseous protest with a far-reaching toxic intensity only those who have had their abdomen cut open can appreciate.

A FAIRY DANCING IN THE ROOM

Based on my research, a working definition of awe might be that it is "the humbling experience of our own lack of imagination in the face of a prodigious stimulus." It's important to recognize, however, that just how extraordinary the event is that we face is determined by our own selfless, ignorant, open-hearted, open-minded, and ready-to-be-dilated imagination. While usually used to describe something huge, the word *prodigious* does not just refer to gigantic, enormous, massive, or beautiful. Among its other definitions are words like *abnormal, extraordinary, unusual, exceptional, remarkable,* and *impressive.* An antonym for prodigious is not only *small* but also *average* or *ordinary.* An awed sense of encountering something that we discern as prodigious could be inspired by something unusually small, exceptionally vulnerable, and sometimes even phenomenally gross or remarkably ugly. As the true stories of awe you read in this book reveal, we can be awed by great tragedy as much as by impressive triumph, and each kind of awe holds its own lessons for the personal transformation that awe can inspire.

It's when we are underwhelmed with our selves that we're more likely to become overwhelmed with the wonders of the world around us. We may have briefly noticed and heard the constant cooperative signaling within a flock of geese navigating together to the south for winter, been too "into" our selves to be awed by this remarkably choreographed air parade, and finally took time to allow ourselves to be in total awe of it. Other times, awe's prodigious stimulus is as simple and ordinary as a light shimmering through the window to reflect off of a glass sitting on the kitchen table, but if we're consumed with ourselves, we'll never see the light.

Being in awe, or at least being awe prone, results from a mental set or choice of how we will engage with our world, not just suddenly and involuntarily being overwhelmed for a few moments by an external event. The dilation of our imaginations is crucial to being awed, and children I interviewed about awe often showed the natural innocent ignorance imposed by their immaturity that made them easily awe inspired.

One six-year-old girl I interviewed about what she thought awe meant spoke about how she felt when she first saw her new baby brother. She said the experience was, "So . . . like . . . *totally* awesome." But she stopped talking suddenly, gasped, and placed her hand over her heart. I tried to look where she was looking and saw that she had noticed the crystal on my watch casting a rainbow-like image that danced all around the room. I wondered why she had become suddenly mesmerized. "What's wrong?" I asked her. After several seconds of silent, amazed, wide-eyed gazing at the light, she moved her hand from her chest to her open mouth, as if to prevent her breath from being totally taken away. In frightened whisper, she said, "Oh my. Oh my. Oh my. Be very quiet. There's a magic, tiny fairy flying around in here. Don't scare her away. Do you see her?" I never noticed my watch casting that light before, but I sometimes look for it now, and I'll never see it the same way.

A frequent comment from adult participants in the SAI was that their mind "was blown" by their awe. One SAI participant said, "It blew my mind, man. They call it the Grand Canyon, but the word grand doesn't at all describe what I felt. There is no word for it. It just blew my mind." From a light reflected off the crystal of a watch to one of the wonders of the world, that's what awe does to us. It "blows" or expands our minds, activates our imaginations, and our explanatory system into total disarray.

ADDIE'S GIFT

The accommodation inspired by awe is making a major change of mind and heart. True awe requires being on the alert for examples of exceptions to our mind's status quo and its cynically selfish rules of life. It's being on the alert for that which diverges from our current consciousness, not just for what confirms it. For example, it involves abandoning the commonly held belief that almost everyone is looking out "for number one" and protecting their own personal welfare over all else.

Humankind's vast capacity for altruism can be extraordinarily uplifting, and when we are in awe of it, it can open our hearts and completely change our minds. When we accommodate a remarkable act of altruism, how we think and feel about humankind is changed forever, and that's awe inspiring.

A woman in the SAI described her awe when she saw the actions of a young child. "This kid was in second grade. She had won a new bike as a reward for a school contest, and they showed the whole thing on television. The kid was in total awe of that bike. Her eyes became as big as apples. She cried, she shuddered, and she was overwhelmed by the whole thing. She stroked it and said it was exactly what she had always wanted, and you could see that she had never received anything as wonderful as that bike. She seemed shy and afraid not only of the new bike and trying to learn to ride it, but of the kindness she was receiving. But then *I* was in awe. That wonderful little girl gave the bike one last hug and kissed it, and then set it aside. She began to call out to one of her classmates, a girl suffering from leukemia.

"'Addie!' she screamed, and her classmates began to join her call. 'Addie, Addie, come here!' they began to sing together, and little Addie came running in childish glee. You could see that she was sick. She was pale, she was out of breath from her short run, and her hair was just growing back after her latest course of chemotherapy. The winner of the bike took Addie's hand and led her to the new bike. She said, 'Here, this is for you, Addie.' The rest of the class gathered around and hugged Addie and the little girl who gave Addie the bike. It was all so wonderful that it was scary, and I just lost it. A warmth began to spread out from my chest through me whole body, and my heart began to race. I got chicken skin, I began to cry, and I was in total awe of those two little girls. It really changed my mind forever about human nature."

Addie herself seemed in awe, not only of the gift she has just been given, but of the loving generosity of the little girl who had given it to her. Addie had long been giving the gift of the example of her courage and resilient joy in the face of her painful suffering. Her teachers and the students seemed well aware of the sacredness of that gift. Everyone seemed in awe of the giving nature of this group of loving people, a gift Hawaiians call "aloha," literally translated from *alo* meaning "to share" and *ha* meaning the "breath of life." Maybe awe so often takes our own breath away because there's something about it that involves a sudden and profound sense that we are all ultimately breathing the same breath.

HOW AWE KILLED KING KONG

I've learned a lot about awe by watching the movie *King Kong*. Unlike other movies with grotesque monsters that destroy everything in their paths, induce terror, and arouse violent reactions, Kong seemed to inspire awe as much as fear and love as much as dread. The human characters seemed to be in frightened awe of the gorilla's massive size and power and didn't know what to do with the overwhelming realization of their own smallness and powerlessness in his presence. Their ignorant awe caused them to see only great size and not a unique natural spirit. They couldn't dilate their imaginations enough to be able to accommodate what could have been a great natural gift, and, as you will read later about the downside or dangers of being in awe, fear-driven violence resulted.

Kong inspired awe because he was too much for human consciousness to handle. He could have helped the people expand their consciousness, but that would have required a completely new way of thinking about Kong's life, as well as their own. Maybe that's what awe is for: to act as a consciousness stimulant that makes us more aware of just how unaware we usually are and the need for a more creative, forgiving, loving consciousness. Maybe it's our emotion that serves as nature's alarm clock designed to awaken us to its wonders before we sleep right through our lives.

Despite their fear, the humans were irresistibly attracted to and emotionally moved by Kong's presence. For the same reason, we tend to gawk at disturbing scenes like auto accidents; there seems to be something within us that needs to be scared to death in order to become more fully alive. Like the powerful back-surge of water just before the tidal wave hits, awe presents the opportunity to experience the vastness of nature. What we do with the opportunity is up to us.

Kong was eventually killed because his captors lacked a king-sized imagination. They failed to acknowledge their ignorance and be inspired to learn. In the absence of true accommodation of the existence of the beast, they allowed the fear that comes with awe to become the dominant emotion. The message may be that we feel threatened by extraordinary beauty, particularly when its grandeur exposes our illusion of personal control or the ability to ever fully grasp the nature of the universe. Instead of being transformed by our awe, we often do what they did to Kong. We're stunned, entertained, attracted by what awes us and then run away from it, or try to capture and control what inspires our awe in the first place. Failing that, and either by our neglect or destructive selfish actions that turn inspiration into zealotry, we end up destroying it.

THE WONDERS OF THE BOGGLED MIND

Based on what's been written about it in the fields of religion, art, nature, and even politics and what I've now learned from my interviews in the SAI, awe always inspires people to try to deal with something big and baffling. *Big* refers less to pure size than to something, even an idea or image, beyond our imaginations and current ways of thinking. *Baffling* refers to the struggle between assimilating what creates the awe and making the major mental shift. Those few psychologists who have written about the awe response refer to these two of its characteristics as "vastness" and "accommodation."[16]

Accommodation is making significant changes in what we thought and in our ways of thinking because we are baffled by what is happening to us. Accommodation is not only making a new experience a part of our consciousness; it is creating a whole new consciousness that makes room for the new meanings awe awakened within us. If we go beyond the ignorant awe of brief interest translated quickly into confirmation of our preexisting thoughts and beliefs, the awe of understanding allows us to draw a completely new mental map of our world so we can see even old experiences in entirely new ways.

Unless we return to it by thinking again and again about it, awe—

like happiness—comes and goes very quickly. It's up to us if we want to make the moment not only last, but also become a part of our consciousness by continuing to accommodate its lessons.[17]

Awe's vastness refers to anything that we experience as being much larger than ourselves or our ordinary day-to-day levels of experience or frames of reference. Vastness can be experienced as something as simple as huge size ("My God, just look at those mountains!") or remarkable smallness ("Oh, look at the size of the baby's tiny fingers!"). It can also derive from a cosmically vast question ("What is heaven and where is it?") or a locally important but simple one ("Why does he or she love me?"). It can also be experienced as "social size" in the form of fame, authority, obscurity, or prestige ("Look! There's Barbra Streisand!").

Sometimes even the trappings and symbols of vastness lead to awe, as in the president of the United States' Oval Office or *Air Force One*. Awe's vastness might be sensed in the form of tiny, distant images finally coming to a huge stage, surrounded by massive speakers and hundreds of lights, as thousands of fans roar in anticipation of actually finally seeing a Rolling Stone. Celebrity is a creation of the manipulation of some of the aspects of the awe response, and creating a sense of vastness, distance, and rarity that inspires a little fear and humility is how fame—however fleeting or bizarre—is manufactured. As the ubiquitous images of the likes of Paris Hilton, Jessica Simpson, and Britney Spears and the various American Idols reveal, the manipulation of elements that inspire awe can result in the ignorant awe lite that can catapult almost anyone into instant fame. Regardless of talent, those who know how to act in ways that create a sense of special uniqueness, difference, distance, and even frightening reckless behavior and know how to use the trappings of wealth, status, or even outrageous behavior to appear to stand far out and beyond the experiences of the rest of us can become famous simply because they first became celebrities who manipulated some of the characteristics of the awe response. It may just be awe lite that draws so many to know more about the likes of Jessica Simpson and Britney Spears, but the distance, strangeness, and bizarreness of the awe response can still be seen.

Awe can also be elicited by something that strikes us as extraordinarily wise and funny at the same time. When I briefly met the Dalai Lama years ago, I was in awe not only of his wisdom and how his words challenged me, but also of his sense of humor. I remember his giggling when someone in the audience asked whether dogs were reincarnated. With gentle humor and a wit used to teach deeper lessons, he laughed as he said that it was possible that really nice dogs might transcend upward in their reincarnation.

Awe also happens at moments of deep sadness. I remember feeling all the effects of awe as I looked at my parents at their funerals. I was in awe of their passing and couldn't grasp the scope of their absence, where they or their energy was now, or how we could relate with each other now that they were gone. I was awed by their lives, our life together, and the vastness of that existence. Its meaning overwhelmed me with a welcomed, deep sadness that felt more real than any sadness I had felt before. I needed that sadness to help me grieve deeply and meaningfully. I felt awed by how I felt and also by my built-in capacity to let go, grieve, and move on. My awe of understanding caused me to realize that anyone worth loving deeply is worth grieving intensely and lastingly.

A young woman recently described the intensity of the most powerful version of awe, the awe of understanding the full catastrophe that is life itself, when she told me, "I was in awe when my grandmother had weakened to the point that the hospital moved her to a nursing home. The place smelled and was depressing, and I just looked at her and thought, *Is this is why we work so hard?* This is why we try so hard and create families and stress out and push ourselves and our children? So that we ultimately die in a place that smells like piss?! That's what life is about? I was in utter awe of my feeling of disgust as well as of what I was in disgust over—the utter letdown of life."

My severe unhappiness at my own parents' deaths seemed to (in ways I still don't understand) honor and give meaning to their lives and the life we had shared together as a family. I was the furthest from happiness that a human can be, but I felt more alive than I ever remember feeling and motivated to be more alive with those I love, despite my intensified awareness of how short and cruel life can be. Just as every beginning gives us joy but can frighten us with new responsibilities, every loss renders us a little less happy and overwhelmed in our search for meaning, and these starting and ending moments are the ones that fill our life with awe. As the old song says—and awe makes us so intensely feel—"That's life."

Sometimes the vastness of awe is sensed in the form of a loud sound as from a booming symphony, in a unique sense of movement as in the rumblings of an earthquake, or in the bone-rattling experience of not only seeing but feeling a spacecraft roar away from the Earth. Awe can even be inspired by itself, as when another person's awe response causes our own experience of sympathetic awe, or our own memory of being in awe inspires it all over again.

RELIGIOUS AWE

While science has largely ignored the awe response, religious writers have embraced it as central to conversion and spiritual insight. For instance, Paul's conversion on the road to Damascus is an example of awe-altering consciousness of faith.[18] In this well-known story, Paul (as Saul) is on his way to continue his persecution of Christians (thought to be heretical Jews). He is suddenly blinded for three days by an overwhelming heavenly light. He is disoriented and hears, but cannot see Jesus asking why Paul persecutes him. When Paul regains his sight, he becomes the most devoted and prolific disciple of Jesus. Again, the themes of vastness, woven in with required suffering, pain, and unhappiness, illustrate the need to accommodate to be truly awe inspired. In the religious or spiritual context, this change of consciousness is often referred to as "conversion" or the sense of being "born again," and if we think deeply enough about what awes us, that is how our eleventh emotion can make us feel—reborn. We may not always feel as happy as we think we deserve to be, but we will surely be much more alive than we have ever been.

Perhaps what might make us the most truly content is to be in awe of the fact that happiness doesn't come naturally and that life would not be nearly as awesome if it did. As Buddha taught with the first of his four basic truths mentioned at the beginning of this chapter, once we accept the first truth, "life is suffering," we are able to flourish in a more mindful and heartfelt selfless engagement with all the good and bad that life offers. Once we are no longer held hostage by the pursuit of personal happiness and we free ourselves from the ignorant kind of awe inspired only by beauty, intensity, vastness, and size, we are free to have many more connective awe-full moments that help us keep trying to understand more about life because we are stunned by it.

THE CASE FOR AN ELEVENTH EMOTION

"Were any man to keep minutes of his feelings from youth to old age, what a table of vanities they would present—how numerous, how diverse, how strange."

— AUGUST W. HARE

EMOTIONALLY MOVED

Think about the last time you were deeply moved. What did it feel like? How was your body acting? What were you thinking and what did you think later? How did your experience make you feel about other people? Science shows that we are in fact literally moved by our emotions, and my research on our eleventh emotion indicates that it can move us like no other.

As derived from its Latin roots, the word *emotion* literally means "energy in motion." A feeling is the brain's awareness of a sensation, and if you pay attention, you're "feeling" right now. The chair you're sitting in is pushing on your buttocks, and this book is pushing against your fingertips, but an emotion is a very strong feeling, something to which we attach meaning through our conscious processing of something happening to us. It's this conscious registering that is the key to all of our emotions, particularly our eleventh.

All of our emotions generate measurable energy that leads to mental and physiological changes, which, in turn, generate their own energy. So when we feel emotionally moved, we are actually experiencing energy moving throughout our body. Unless we consciously interpret them, however, feelings quickly pass, and our emotions just "are." Emotions are energy neutral, meaning that until our consciousness gives them meaning, they're pure energy manifested and registered primarily through our autonomic (or automatically reactive) nervous system.

For example, feeling angry and actually being angry are two different states. No one "makes us angry." We consciously make ourselves that way depending on how we interpret what our body's signals are telling us. Our body might automatically react in an agitated state when someone threatens our safety by cutting us off in traffic (feeling angry), but it's up to us as to what we do with the emotional state our body is in. We can ruminate about a revengeful driving maneuver and get ourselves angrier (being angry) or we can decide to choose peace over being right, ease up on the accelerator, and clear our consciousness by focusing on "this" moment rather than on the one to which we just surrendered our consciousness and that we allowed to agitate our entire body.

This same "feeling-emotion-consciousness" cycle also pertains to our eleventh emotion. Ignorant awe happens when we just experience intense fascination or attention that "turns us on," but the true awe—the one of understanding—becomes life altering when we are turned in and become consciously reflective on what is happening.

HEARTFELT HUNCHES

Awe is a sacred hunch, an overwhelming emotion that indicates that something within us is sensing something about the world that our brain has yet to discover. It's a gut feeling, a sensation in the form of an unconscious bias about the world that influences our decisions and guides behavior before the brain gets fully involved.

A groundbreaking study on emotions by psychologist Antoine Bechara illustrates how it may be possible that we are in awe before we know it.[1] Bechara and his colleagues asked subjects to pick cards over and over again from any of four decks, two of which yielded better cards. They were only told that some of the decks yielded higher scores over time and that they could see if they had lost or won points whenever they turned over a new card. As the subjects made their selections, the researchers monitored their emotional responses by measuring how much they were sweating. This skin conductance test, which is sensitive to the amount of salt in sweat, has long been used to assess degree of emotional response. This time it yielded stunning results that provide insight into how it may be possible we're in emotional awe before we know it.

Even though the decks were rigged to make it far too complicated for the subjects to figure out which the best ones were, almost all of the participants were eventually picking from the winner packs. They clearly had all developed emotional hunches about where to select their cards because their skin conductance shot higher whenever they began to pick from one of the losing decks. While they were still randomly selecting cards willy-nilly, the indicator of an emotional reaction—the amount of sweat on the fingertips—shot up whenever (and before) they picked from a bad deck that

their brain didn't know yet was a loser. It was only *after* their emotional reaction that their card selections began to show what their
gut feeling had finally registered, and they began to act on their
finally realized hunch.

We often think after we feel, and awe seems to function as a sixth
sense for the sacred or "something more" that we "just feel" before
we think. Like being drawn to the good deck of cards before we
know it's good, awe seems to cause us to be attracted to something
magnificent about life and the world. You will read later that our
heart and even our intestines may be playing a role in these newly
discovered gut feelings and may be the sources of the emotions.
We may admire the brain's rational brilliance, but our emotions
are taking place faster than the brain can think. That's why truly
transformative awe requires lengthy reflection *after* the event.
Only then can we put what inspired us into the context of our lives
and decide how it will be stored in our consciousness.

GETTING EMOTIONAL

"I'm going to admit something to you now, but don't get emotional." After months spent in marital therapy accusing his wife of
not showing him enough love, appreciation, sex, and trust, these
words were the preamble to a husband's confession to his wife that
he had been having two affairs, one with her best friend and
another with her sister. His warning failed. As she applied wads of
tissue over her eyes and sobbed bitterly, her cheeks flushed bright
red, her pupils dilated, and sweat began to dot her forehead. Her
husband's next statement was the last straw. As he defensively
protested, "I knew it. I knew you'd get all emotional, but you have

no right to be so upset. It's not my fault. You drove me to it," she picked up the tissue holder and threw it at him.

The stunned wife certainly looked like she was having emotions, and you'd think psychologists would now clearly and definitively know what they were, how they work, and why we have them, but they don't. Until recently, emotions have received comparatively little scientific attention. To fully understand awe as our most powerful emotion, we have to be clear on what science says any emotion is.[2]

"Good morning, my beheaded. . . . Oh, I mean my beloved." These words might have slipped out of the mouth of King Henry VIII as he greeted one of his wives. Humans are the most emotional of all nature's creations, and we aren't very good at trying to hide them. Sigmund Freud wrote, "He that has eyes to see and ears to hear may convince himself that no mortal can keep a secret," and all of us have had the experience of detecting feelings others wish we didn't and displaying those we wished we hadn't. St. Jerome wrote, "The face is the mirror of the mind, and eyes without speaking confess the secrets of the heart." Try as we might, the degree to which emotions influence our thoughts and behaviors is undeniable, yet new fields like affective neuroscience are just now beginning to reveal how they operate.

One thing is already clear. That we "get" or "become" emotional or "begin to have feelings" is fallacious. More than our perceptions and mental inferences, it's our feelings that we experience most intensely; but until the last two decades there's been more scientific attention to and agreement regarding how we perceive and think than how and why we feel. As leading emotion researcher Robert Plutnick writes, "Despite the obvious importance of emotions in our daily life, the topic of emotions has not received the attention it deserves in academic writings. Most colleges and universities still do not have a course devoted entirely to the subject of emotion."[3]

Although sometimes we are more intensely and demonstrably emotional than others, we don't "become" emotional; we are naturally emotional all the time. You're emotional as you read these words, but whether you become conscious of them or not is up to you. Just try thinking about how you're feeling, and you will sense your current emotional status. It may not be intense, but you might feel a little sad, happy, worried, anxious, or even depressed, even though you may have been too busy or distracted to know it.

EMOTIONALLY TOUCHED

How do you feel right now? Are you happy, sad, surprised, or still a little angry at the philandering husband you just read about? Most of us know only too well how emotional we are, and we believe that we know what an emotion is, or at least know one when we have one or see one in someone else. But you've already learned that our emotions have touched us before we can get in touch with them.

How, why, and where do our emotions happen? As if emotions are like steam that needs occasional releasing, we are told by psychologists that it's important to our "emotional health" to "get in touch" with and express emotions so they don't build up inside us. Are our emotions really some kind of expansive emotional gas that we have to vent? Why do we have them in the first place? Why can't we just eat, go to work, have sex, and die without all the emotional upheaval that comes with these life processes?

Until the last several years, most scientists have tended to consider the idea of emotion to be too subjective to measure. As if it were really possible for any scientist to be free of emotional investment in what they are studying or any doctor to be devoid of any emotion regarding the well-being of her or his patient, professionals who become "too emotionally involved in their work" are seen as losing their objectivity and becoming unscientific and therefore ineffective, even though we know the opposite is true. Emotions drive the interest and concern that motivate intense caring and carefulness about and in whatever it is we do. Moreover, as the card-drawing study illustrates, they have profound influence on how we make our decisions, even before we make them. Without them, life is like a warm cup of coffee without the coffee or a glass of wine without the wine.

Awe, particularly the awe of understanding, starts with something a little like what author Malcolm Gladwell calls consciousness "thin slicing," by which he means discovering interesting and fascinating patterns and meanings in situations based on very narrow slices of experience.[4] Awe is a heartfelt hunch about more than the eyes can see, the ears can hear, the nose can smell, or the skin can feel. Sometimes, one glance at my sons' faces causes me to feel awe not only for them but for life's endless energy represented by their still-growing bodies and evolving energy.

In the 1920s there was strong interest in trying to learn more about emotions. While there were many articles written about them, the emergence of behaviorism and its emphasis on our conduct being regulated by strict rules put a stop to this initiative. Behaviorism's view of the relative unimportance of what we think and feel as compared to what we measurably do and what happens after we do it restricted research on what behaviorists considered to be such a hopelessly vague and romanticized concept: emotion.

Fortunately for the world, science does not proceed in a linear fashion or with the objectivity it brags about. It moves forward in accordance with the general psychological and political ecology, the emotional climate of the times, changing philosophies, and the mortality of the scientists. So the story of emotions didn't end with the "if it exists, it's measurable—if it's not measurable, it doesn't exist" scientific ethic.

As psychological theories always do, behaviorism eventually fell out of favor to be replaced by cognitive psychology and its willingness to study how we think and feel. Psychology began to embrace author Christopher Cranch's view that, "Thought is deeper than all speech; feeling is deeper than all thought." As a result the 1960s saw a rebirth in studying things—like emotions—that aren't always easily measurable.

As modern psychology was becoming more emotional, Charles Darwin's last book (written in 1872), titled *The Expression of the Emotions in Man and Animals,* began to garner the attention it had long deserved. It had introduced a bio-evolutionary approach to emotions and the idea that they have been essential to our survival and development. Inspired by Darwin's work, scientists began studying emotions from this psychobiological evolutionary point of view.[5] Today, a science of emotions is continuing to develop, but it's largely the study of almost every conceivable emotional state but one—awe.

WHY THEY FORGOT AWE

The word *awe* is derived from words in Old English and Old Norse that were used to express fear and dread as experienced most often toward a divine being. Its relationship to the word *awful* is no coincidence for, as you have read, the awe response can be a very bothersome, upsetting, frightening, wonderful, terrible, mind-altering, stimulating (yet numbing), and personally challenging event that doesn't always have predictable consequences. Awe may not have yet made the lists of other emotions produced by scientists because it's so difficult to pin down.

As the English language developed, the word *awe* came more and more to include ideas like profound new respect and admiration. Now the *Oxford English Dictionary* defines awe as "an attitude of a mind subdued to profound reverence," and this poetic definition fits well with what I've learned about awe in my own research and from others' descriptions of the awe response.[6]

I have suggested that awe is our eleventh and most transformative emotion, but does it really qualify as an emotion by current scientific criterion? Through the Study of the Awe Inspired (SAI), I've discovered that it has its own distinguishing characteristics that qualify it as a basic emotion beyond surprise, amazement, an occasional passing feeling related to some other emotion, or a religious act of contrition. It's perhaps our most unique, complex, multidimensional human emotional response in that it challenges us to expand our thinking not only about how all of our emotions work, but even, as you will read later, where they reside in our bodies and what causes them.

Because it's not easy for scientists to be there with their measuring equipment when a person encounters a gorgeous sunset or for them to put a rainbow in a test tube and then record our reactions to it, the scientific study of the awe response is a difficult challenge. Unlike the other generally accepted basic ten emotions (and although there are a few indications that might qualify), it doesn't seem to have a consistent, single, distinguishing facial expression that everyone in awe shows.

When it comes to most of our emotions, Freud may have been correct in pointing out that we just can't keep a secret and that we wear our emotions on our faces and all over our bodies, down to our twitching and often emotion-exposing sweaty fingers. Angry people look mad, embarrassed people look ashamed, and sad people look like Eeyore, but some people in awe look terrified, others stunned or thrilled, and still others have their eyes glaze over in a state of apparent psychological absenteeism that is almost impossible to interpret.

Another difficulty in studying awe is that those who experience it are unlikely to record and measure it with the necessary scientific rigor that has been applied to separating out what are now considered to be the other ten basic human emotions. In fact, to try to do so might stop awe in its tracks. Descriptions of awe by those who feel they are struck by it are highly subjective, and this is another characteristic that is something most researchers would prefer to avoid. Reports of awe like those I've collected for the SAI often sound too poetic and mystical for the comfort of the skeptical scientific mind or for the editors of most technical journals.

The ancient Hindu classic prayer-dance uses the body and face to express the accepted ten basic human emotions, but awe isn't included. Darwin made lists of human emotions but never mentioned awe. As the "basic lists" indicate, researchers of emotion seem to have a "bias for bad" or at least realize that survival of our species depends on vigilant, quick, and intense reaction to "bad," so it's not surprising that at least six of the basic emotions that do make most lists—fear, sadness, embarrassment, despair, guilt, and anger—are negative.

H. L. Mencken pointed out, "For every complex problem, there is an easy answer, and it is wrong." It's not easy to understand awe, and I still don't. Awe is so fascinatingly powerful and important precisely because it's not easy to study or understand. However, it has apparently also been too easy to just dismiss it as an occasional, nice reflex. Studying awe is looking directly into what is most human about us, and that's as fascinating as it is frighteningly complex.

WHAT'S AN EMOTION?

Even though we talk so much about them, it's not easy to define an emotion. I found over thirty different definitions of *emotion* offered in various psychology texts and research articles and almost as many theories of what emotions are and how they operate.[7] Not one list contains *awe* or even refers to it as a secondary emotion. My review of twenty of the most recent lists of "basic" emotions did not yield a single mention of awe.[8] While no one seems to agree on a definitive basic list and researchers often have their preferences for different ones, everyone seems to agree that there are basic emotions from which all our others flow and that it is important to study and understand them. I suggest that leaving awe off the list relates to a pervasive but erroneous assumption in the field of psychology that all of our emotions exist within us. Awe is experienced as something that happens between us.

After my review of the literature, I still find William James's definition of emotion to be a good starting point. James was one of the most influential figures in the history of psychology. His ideas about emotion, published in 1884, are still found in psychology textbooks and impact the thinking of clinicians around the world. James described his view of emotion by writing, "My theory is that the bodily changes follow directly the perception of an exciting fact, and that our feeling of the same changes as they occur is the emotion."[9] In James's view, our emotions don't just exist simmering somewhere inside us as mysterious hot or cold humors.[10] They are perceptual, physical, and mental events that occur in our interactions with the world, which was how the SAI participants described their own awe response.

Except for the usual cautions, setting up experiments to test our memory, our ability to learn the range of our perceptual abilities can be done without much worry about damaging the subjects being tested. However, there are unique ethical concerns about trying to manipulate emotions in the laboratory. Because of this, instead of trying to create emotions and observe them, scientists usually have to try to study them as I've studied awe, *after* they've already happened, and often anecdotally. We have to look for them as they already exist in the field, but this reduces the chances of making any direct causal connections between a stimulus and a feeling or taking "on the spot" physiological measurements. Although it's a fact that we have an emotional reaction to a deck of cards just before selecting a card and before consciously suspecting if the deck's a good one or a bad one, getting a handle on an emotion is one of science's most difficult challenges. It's enough to get a scientist emotional! Even Benjamin Franklin couldn't catch lightning in a bottle—only its results.

There were SAI respondents who were, in fact, in awe of lightning, but had already been stricken by their awe for it, and all I could do was assess their reports of the results. One of them said, "When that lightning flash sparked across that dark Kansas sky, my life changed. I was thrilled and scared to death at the same time, and my heart went a mile a minute. I was in total awe of how the whole world seemed to light up and become energized. I not only saw it, I felt it. I heard it. I tasted it. It was like the door to heaven opened up a crack and its light flashed out."

As I have in exploring the awe response in my SAI study, researchers in the field of emotions have tended to rely primarily on verbal reports of experienced inner states. But because our brains often do not even know we're having an emotion, this also can only be a rough approximation of whatever an emotion really is, what causes it, and what it does to—or how it might be caused by—our body. If our brain isn't aware of the impact our emotions are having on it, it can't always be accurate in helping us describe our emotions. As psychologist Neal Miller pointed out, our verbal responses are fascinating samples of our behavior, but they are not necessarily a clear window through which to view our emotions.

My study of awe suffers from all of the above limitations, and what indirect physiological data I was able to collect only offers clues for further research on awe. I couldn't cause people to be awed. I could only ask them about it after they were. Nevertheless, what they had to say is helpful in identifying awe as one of our basic emotions, deserving of more study for its relevance to every aspect of our daily lives.

IS AWE REALLY AN EMOTION?

My review of the accepted definitions of *emotion* indicates that researchers in the field of emotion usually require five characteristics that they believe are necessary to label a response a basic emotion.

1. There has to be an identifiable eliciting or exciting stimulus.

2. There should a physiological response to that stimulus.

3. The response should be innate.

4. There should be evidence of thinking and feeling about the body's response.

5. There should be some kind of action taken as a result of the emotion.

Here's how awe fits these criteria.

1. **An identifiable eliciting or exciting stimulus:** The emotion of anger is usually elicited by something or someone in our environment that obstructs our progress toward a goal. The emotion of sadness is typically elicited by something in our world being taken away from us. Awe's electing stimulus that excites our body into its awed state is usually something vast that makes us feel small, powerless, or at least much less concerned about the self and more focused on the outside world. It's not something blocking us or being taken from us that leads to the awe response; it's something drawing us in so profoundly that whatever frustrates us, makes us sad, angers us, and so on, our self has little relevance to our consciousness at that awe-filled moment. It's the sudden absence of a drive toward a specific goal, and what's lost is a dominant sense of the self. As one of the SAI respondents said, "Awe stops you in your tracks. It sort of turns you inside out, and there does not seem to be a boundary between who you are and where you are. It's like your body recognizes it's not just yours but connected to, and part of, something much more than you."

2. **A physiological response:** Have you ever been afraid *after* your body was frightened? Maybe before you knew it you slammed

on the brakes just in time as a child ran in front of your car. Moments later, you found yourself sitting with a white-knuckled grip on the steering wheel, feeling your heart racing as you begin to realize that your body was scared and agitated *before* you were. It's as if your body was saying, "You should have seen what I just felt."

In the case of awe, we gasp because our breath has literally been taken away by what is happening. We grab at our chest because our heart is racing or sometimes feels that it is skipping beats (actually having extra or premature beats). We feel fear as shown by the goose bumps we have before we know it and as they begin to spread over the skin.

3. **An innate response:** We don't have to be taught to be afraid. Fear evolved within us as a natural human response. It's an emotion because it's built into us as an evolutionary survival reaction and dictated by the "bad trumps good" principle. It helped keep our ancestors away from predators and other bad ancestors.

   Awe is also a natural, inborn, unlearned response. As mentioned earlier, it may be that being capable of being in awe made it more likely that our ancestors would be drawn to gazing out over vaster vistas in order to be drawn to a wider range of sources of food, shelter, approaching threats, or good ancestors. The wide-eyed gasping and thrill experienced by a very young child to her first encounter with a puppy illustrates the inborn nature of the awe response. There is no need to take an awe training class before visiting the Grand Canyon.

4. **Thinking about the body's reaction:** "I wondered what it was about him that really pissed me off," said the young police officer. "I didn't even know he got to me like that until I got back

in the squad car and started writing his ticket. My heart was racing, I was biting my lip so hard it was bleeding, and I felt my blood pressure going through the sky. I was angry with this guy's attitude and demeanor even before I knew it." A reaction is defined as an emotion when we are influenced by how our body is reacting. In the case of awe, the blend of dread and delight and avoidance and approach first excites our body and then we match up the reaction with what caused it and begin to think about it and what it means to us. We don't just behave as we feel. We also feel as we behave.

5. **Taking action:** Scientists define a response as an emotion if they can detect some kind of action that results because we become aware of our body's excitement. When we're in awe, that action might be to sit down and reflect on what has just happened, to have a good cry, to just stop and be totally still, frantically grabbing for the camera, calling out to a family member to come quick to share in the wonder of what has taken place, or eventually to make a major life change.

THE THREE AWES

Psychologists still argue about how emotions happen to us. Some say we feel an emotion after our body experiences physiological changes. Others say we experience the emotion at the same time as the body does. More recently, however, others say that all of our physiological responses to the world are pretty much the same, and we don't "feel" an emotion *until* we have thought about it. My study of the awe response suggests that either awe is so intense that it somehow involves some yet-unknown reaction, or it is a strange combination of all of these theories of emotions. Thus there may be three ways awe happens or is experienced in our bodies—delayed, immediate, and reflective.

Delayed awe: William James was fascinated with how our emotions work. He wrote, "We feel sorry because we cry, angry because we strike, afraid because we tremble."[11] That's why we say we are "in the grips" of our feelings and talk about "getting emotional." James and a Danish physiologist named Carl Lange asserted that we don't run away from a bear because we are afraid. We feel afraid because we are running. Our ancestors survived because their actions clicked in before they had time to think about them and related emotions followed later. This is the so-called James-Lange theory of emotion and describes at least the most frequent way in which people in the SAI described their awe response. One of them said, "I had chills, trembled, and gasped before I knew it. Something was happening to me before I knew what was happening, so I think my body was in awe before I was. When I caught up with how my body was feeling, it was a fantastic emotion."

Immediate awe: Based on other reports from the SAI, however, it may be that there just aren't varying degrees of awe but other kinds of awe response. This one's related to the Cannon-Bard theory of emotions that says that we experience our emotions and their physiological manifestations exactly at the same time. Physiologist Walter Cannon is the researcher who gave us important research on stress and our innate fight-or-flight response. He thought the James-Lange view of emotions made little sense because our body's responses were not separate and distinct enough to lead to a specific emotion. He argued that our racing hearts could have the multiple meanings that we want to run away from someone, hit them, or make love to them. Could it mean that the body is telling us that we're feeling fear, anger, or passion?

Cannon also thought that physiological responses were too slow to set off immediate emotional responses. Cannon joined with another physiologist named Philip Bard to theorize that the body's response and the interpretation that leads to the associated emotion happen simultaneously. You don't feel afraid because you're running; you feel afraid and run simultaneously. In the Cannon-Bard view, your heart races, you have chills, and you gasp in awe as your body experiences awe and not after or because of it. Some of the people in SAI described their awe response that way. One said, "I not only felt in awe, I said it immediately when I saw my new grandchild. My whole body quivered just as soon as I felt the fragile warmth of the child. My heart pounded, and tears started to run down my cheeks, but I didn't even know I was crying until I saw my tears on my grandchild's cheek. It all happened at the same time and was so intense I was afraid I would drop him."

It seems clear from the James-Lange theory of emotion that the physiological aspects of awe are crucial to experiencing it. From the Cannon-Bard point of view, it also seems that there can be more to being in awe than a post-reading of the physiological response associated with it. In my discussion with one of the SAI participants about this issue, she said, "I don't know if I was in awe because the hair was standing up all over my body, or if I was awed and my hair stood up, or if everything happened at once. I can only tell you it was like nothing I felt before, and it scared the hell out of me and thrilled me all at the same time."

Reflective awe: There may even be a third kind of awe response, a more delayed, mentally reflective kind. Psychologist Stanley Schachter's more recent theory of emotion asserts that all of our emotions are essentially similar, and they aren't really anything at all until we cognitively label them. As baseball umpires are fond of saying, a pitch isn't anything until they call it. This cognitive umpire approach relates to what is called Schachter's "two-factor theory" of emotion.

Schachter agreed with the James-Lange view that our emotions stem from our immediate physiological responses to our world, but he also saw value in the Cannon-Bard position that many of our physiological reactions are very similar and that our conscious interpretation of what is happening to the body plays a key role in what emotion we finally experience. He emphasized the role of how we think about and label our life experiences and our bodies' responses to them.

Stories from the SAI also suggest that awe is an emotion that can happen to us suddenly and under the stimulation of our body without our giving it a thought until after it happens to us.[12] It may even be possible that some of us experience a kind of "subliminal awe" and don't know we've been awed at all or until someone else describes their awe experience, which triggers a "memory trace" kind of awe to spark within us. Maybe this kind of awe shows itself in a dream or subconsciously leads us back to the place or person that, unknown to us, had inspired awe.

Other times, our body and our consciousness seem to go into awe at exactly the same time. In yet other circumstances, we may have to think awhile about what happened before we are fully tuned into our body's signals that it had been awed by what happened to us. It may be that this third kind of awe response is most likely to lead to the true transformation and accommodation I call the "awe of understanding."

We have a luxury our primitive ancestors didn't. Whether we are taking it or not, we have more time to just think than our primitive cousins did. We no longer spend much time worrying about being consumed by a predator or running out of food. If we take advantage of it, we have the privilege of being able to consciously evaluate and become responsible for the onset and impact of any emotion. Learning more about the hows and whys of our emotions, particularly the complexities of our forgotten eleventh one, could have profound effects on our daily lives and probably reduce much of the stressful languishing that characterizes modern life.

In the case of awe, we can all be scientists. We can keep an awe diary and carefully record our experiences of being in awe. We can look for patterns, common events that elicit awe, common reactions, and life impacts. We can be more attentive to what it is that inspires awe, what kind we are having and why, lessons it offers us about not only accepting but even finding peace and comfort in the realization of our powerlessness. Perhaps then we can live our lives a little higher up on the disgust-divinity scale.

For the atheists or agnostics among us, awe offers the opportunity to experience an emotion that deals with divinity without the requirement of blind faith in God or a religious system. Whether or not we believe in a Higher Power, awe has the power to awaken us to a deeper appreciation of a sense of what's divine (with a small "d") in the daily life that resonates all around us. We don't have to look "up" or even believe in something or someone "up there" to experience the profound, intense, and thoughtful moments that awe can inspire. No matter how bitter or brief life may be, awe enables us to gratefully relish and savor the gift.

Life doesn't owe us anything more than itself, and awe is how we come to fully appreciate that fact. Even atheists might be encouraged to seek more awe in their lives by considering the words of poet Emily Dickinson, "That it will never come again is what makes life so sweet." Whether or not there is a Higher Power or a better life later, those who are in awe regularly realize that being fully alive *now* is powerful enough.[13]

AN EMOTIONAL PLACE

The construction of a list of basic emotions stems from the idea that we all have a pallet of a few primary emotions and that all the others that we feel are secondary blends or derivative mixtures of them.[14] Understanding our emotional core can help us learn more about who we and others are. If awe is indeed one of our core or basic emotions and all of us feel it, we've been neglecting one of the most powerful of our transformative feelings that could help us all be more appreciative of what we have and less combative about what we don't. It can help us learn more about all of our other emotions.

By adding awe to our basic emotional pallet, we could be painting a much richer life tapestry. If awe were accepted as a basic or primary emotion, it might help us see that we're all probably in awe of the same things, and that could be the fulcrum point that brings more balance back to a world that seems so chaotic.

For decades we have been urged to get in touch with our "inner self" and the emotions of which that self is supposed to be made. As author Stewart Justman points out, pop psychology has told us for decades that living is a matter of technique and that we should learn these techniques from experts who offer their various well-marketed sets of steps to emotional health.[15] These techniques are almost always based on the idea that our emotions exist somewhere within us and are slowly but surely building up. We're warned that we have to get in touch with them by being more self-aware and then outing our emotions by confessing and talking about them as much as possible.

Social critic Wendy Kaminer writes that, "What might have once been called "whining" is now exalted as a process of exerting self-hood."[16] She adds that "self-absorption is regarded as a form of self-expression," but as you have read, awe happens when we lose all sense of self.[17] The SAI respondents seldom (if ever) talked much about themselves and much more about the stimulus and the experience itself. Being in awe is less about our own feelings pouring out than feelings pouring in.

We're even told that not being aware of our feelings and failing to express them may be a major health risk. Diagnosing disease in emotional terms is now in vogue, and all sorts of theories abound about what feelings are related to what disease and what feelings kept inside did what damage. In his mega-selling book *Emotional Intelligence,* science writer Daniel Goleman touts the value of personal emotional awareness and publicizing our emotions as possibly being more important than traditional intelligence quotients. In the case of cancer and other serious diseases, he suggests that tuning into our emotions and sharing them can be as powerful as some medications in extending the lives of cancer patients.[18] While there is little science that supports these conclusions and some that shows the exact opposite, people who are reluctant to get in touch with their emotions are often seen as not yet fully evolved, defensive, or emotionally obtuse.

Based on the reports of the awe response I've collected, we are transformed and seek new understanding because we become aware of the emotion elicited from the awe experience. While it is related to being open to and more fully aware of signals coming from our body and heart, searching inside for an emotion to express only distracts us from these signals. Awe's signals are plenty strong enough to get our attention without chronic introspection, and we can't be in awe when we are self-focused.

Awe happens when we are focused on the "between" more than the "within.'" Awe's absence from the basic list of emotions might be due not only to the difficulties inherent in studying it but also to some extent to the current "milieu of the emotional me" that author Christina Hoff Sommers and Yale University psychiatrist Sally Satel describe as dominated by an "emotional correctness." This is the view of the healing power of public emoting that is based on the unproven assumption that turning inward to identify our feelings and then outward to vent them is the ultimate form of personal authenticity and mental health.[19]

Awe may not have made the list of our basic emotions because scientists wouldn't find it where they're looking for it. Both the science and most of the therapies of psychology and psychiatry don't deal with it because it doesn't fit well with where they think our emotions exist and their view of what constitutes the healthy way of dealing with them.

THE "PLUS" IN ONE PLUS ONE

Our emotions don't exist within us, but between us, and it's when we're in awe that we most profoundly experience that reality. Even when what we're experiencing is troubling, being in awe is feeling more deeply and profoundly connected with life and the world. Persons in awe feel they have been going through the motions of daily living in a numbed state of languishing, the increasingly common psychological state discussed in the Introduction, which happens to us when we experience awe deficiency in our lives.

Maybe there's a psychological equivalent to the looming environmental crisis of global warming. Maybe the pace at which we think, feel, react, and live is so intensely fast that it's overheating our consciousness and making it numb to what nurtures it and makes it grow and connect with other consciousnesses to celebrate and protect what is precious about life.

If we include awe as a basic human emotion equally deserving of the attention given to all the others, we may discover that our capacity to be awe inspired is central to our character, new insights into our consciousness, and deeper caring about life and others. Perhaps, in the long run, the awe response will be revealed as essential to not only our survival, but the survival of the planet. Maybe awe doesn't just deserve to be added to the list of our basic emotions. Maybe it's *the* basic one.

5

THE REAL SECRET

"When we quit thinking primarily about ourselves and our own self-preservation, we undergo a truly heroic transformation of consciousness."

— JOSEPH CAMPBELL

OUR WAY OR *THE* WAY?

Unless awe shakes us out of them, we're spending most of our life under the influence of two absurd delusions. One is that we're independent, separate, powerful beings who, if we will only think positively enough, can have the life we desire. A current book titled *The Secret,* which guarantees this miracle path to the life of our dreams, has become the fastest-selling self-help book in history.[1] Using a conglomeration of the ever-popular positive thinking approach with a little distorted science, ancient philosophy, and mysticism; the usual new-age platitudes; and misapplied principles of quantum physics, television producer Rhonda Byrne has joined the psycho-guru authors of the likes of Wayne Dyer, Tony Robbins, Dr. Phil McGraw, and Deepak Chopra to offer her version of the myth that we can and should be happier than we are and that we are the final arbiters of what happens to us.

Byrne says that secret of life is "the power of attraction," the idea that not only do our good or bad thoughts attract whatever it is that they're about, but that our thoughts actually change objective physical reality—if we think it, we can have it. Like most self-help gurus, Byrne's secret prescription for the good life is just what the doctor ordered for a culture convinced that we can and should be happier than we are and that our thinking can make it so. However, my years of studying the awe response indicates that exactly the opposite is the case and that the real secret to a life well lived may be to not try to create what we think we should have but instead to try our best to be fully engaged in life and share our awe of the life we have been given. In other words, if we have it, we should try to fully experience and learn from it, no matter what it is. It's life, and although we don't, and maybe weren't, made to understand why the cards are dealt, some aren't very good no matter how positively we try to influence the deal or the dealer. We can play the cards we're dealt and do our best to find awe in the full grandeur and even catastrophes that come with our one chance to be alive in an over-whelming world. We aren't all-powerful individual beings, attracting what happens to us with our thoughts. Instead, we're reactive parts of an incomprehensible system that from time to time grants us glimpses of the extraordinary perplexing nature of life. It's at those times when we can be in awe that we sense we're not in control, and that no matter how hard and positively we think, none of us gets our way. We just get "the way."

That a book promising more self-control over our own individual happiness became so instantly popular may be evidence of the severity of the worsening of the epidemic of our languishing and what happens when we operate under the illusion of personal power. As the editor of *Publishers Weekly* pointed out regarding the ceaseless popularity of happiness-helper books, "Nobody ever went broke overestimating the desperate unhappiness of the American public."[2] It's our failure to flourish by being in awe of whatever life gives us that leads to the lingering, nagging, pervasive, searching unhappiness that characterizes the languishing that sends millions in search of the secret.

OTHER WORLDS

The second delusion under which we lead our daily lives is that the everyday world as we perceive, experience, and think about it is the only real world. Modern science and particularly quantum physics and its concepts such as "quantum entanglement" suggest that there are not only worlds that we can't imagine, but that we may never be able to imagine. Its findings show that there are worlds much smaller, larger, and faster than the one our brain spends its time in. Awe happens when, for just a brief moment, something about those other worlds slips through into our version of reality.

What's most inspiring about awe is that it seems to be the emotion we feel when we sense that there are things about life we don't, and might never, know but that we're supposed to keep trying to understand anyway. It seems that life will never leave us alone. It constantly and—often when we least expect it—suddenly draws our deepest and most intense attention to just how infinitely, complexly, aggravatingly, often terribly perplexing life is. It's as if life is saying, "Hey, look at me. You're having an exceptional life, and it's too bad you're not here for it. I'm really something, aren't I? You're part of me, but you only know and experience so little of what I am, and there's so much more you don't and may never know, so here's a little taste to let you know how much more there is. You might limit yourself, but in the final analysis, there are no limits, so get over yourself and get with me. There's so much you're missing, so I offer you awe to invite you to come back to life, stop languishing, and happy or not, start flourishing anyway."

A CONSOLING AWE

Sometimes, one of the other many worlds we're not evolved to know much about or experience exerts a force on us we can't deny or understand. For example, there's the quantum world that still baffles our greatest minds while leaving them in such awe they can't resist grappling with its seductive surprises and paradoxes. As the famous physicist Niels Bohr is said to have remarked, "Anyone who is not shocked by quantum theory has not understood it." Just as we have come to think of it as normal or business as usual that we're living on a revolving, rotating globe to which we're stuck by an invisible force, the impossible things that go on regularly in the quantum world are "normal" in that world of parallel universes, where waves and particles are the same thing and become what they seem to be depending on who's looking, how, and for what. What this mind-bending science and other discoveries about other worlds and their rules of operation keep revealing and hinting at about life may not offer the comfort of a firmly held unquestioned belief or the idea that the secret to life is that we can make it whatever we want it to be, but awe and the new thinking it can inspire lead to an expanded consciousness. The fact that we have such a consciousness and that there's something about life that keeps tugging at it, much like an excited child pulling at a distracted parent's coat to point out the wonder of a butterfly, can be consoling no matter how good or bad life seems.

When things get so bad in the world that we feel we can barely stand them, awe offers a way to answer two proverbial questions. The first is, "Why me?" which is more often asked during the bad times than good times. We seem to be born with a sense of entitlement to "good" and a psycho-allergic indignation reaction to "bad," but of course that's another illusion. The answer life offers us when we're in awe is, "Of course you. You received the rare gift of life, and you're an inseparable part of all the best and worst of it. You don't get to pick and choose. You've already been given the greatest gift. You're alive. Live and be in awe of all of it." Being in awe of all of life, both good and bad and happy and unhappy, is flourishing; it's the opposite of languishing, which sends us off in search of the latest secret to how to have a better life.

Awe also offers a way to answer a second proverbial question, one asked by so many who suffer from languishing. That question is "Is this all there is?" and the answer awe offers is a resounding, exhilarating, and often frightening "No!" The awe of understanding can cause great love to become the worst fear and terrible grief to awaken a sense of love and value of life beyond what we ever experienced or imagined we could experience. To ask, "Is this all there is?" is to throw the gift of our being back in the face of the Giver.

Awe's way of consoling us may not make us feel good, but it does make us feel more deeply than we ever felt and think in ways we never thought. One difference between the tragedy of committing suicide and trying to struggle on may involve, on at least some level, the capacity to retain enough of our eleventh emotion to balance against the emotion of despair, so that the person has enough awe for life left—or the world and others have left that person with enough opportunity to keep engaging and learning in the world—that she or he can still choose being depressed over being dead. The awe of understanding can be as dangerous as it is delightful, and depressed people are often more in touch with "reality" than those who use denial and illusion. So being in awe of life is risky emotional business.

Awe can really mess up our thinking, disrupt our certainty, and expose the false beliefs many of us use to get us through the chaotic, random, unfair evil that permeates so much of life. False beliefs are the consciousness's narcotic, but as biologist Richard Dawkins writes, "False beliefs can be every bit as consoling as true ones, right up until the moment of disillusionment."[3] Awe can console us because it offers *enlightened illusionment*—a time to dream, fantasize, and stretch our consciousness beyond the bonds of our middle-world brain. The awe of understanding shakes up our thinking and makes it difficult to cling to beliefs engrained in us as children or based only on blind faith, and the upsetting, startling result can be the disturbingly astonishing, and wonderfully troubling feeling that there is so much more not only than we ever knew there was, but also that we may never be able to know. Perhaps most exciting and consoling of all is how awe can offer the promise that the limits to the narrow view of what constitutes life do not exist, despite what our brains tell us, and that there is so much more to know, even if we never manage to finally know it.

WALKING THROUGH WALLS

Because of his unrelenting advocacy of Darwin's theory of evolution, Richard Dawkins is often described as Darwin's fierce Rottweiler. He argues that evolution provided us only with the kind of brain we need to assist us in the surroundings in which we evolved.[4] It didn't give us quantum consciousness, because we

don't spend our daily lives on that level, or at least not in awareness of it or trying to comply with its rules. The neurons, brain,
and body that evolution has given us so far just can't perceive, be
sensitive to, or understand quantum signals from the other worlds
all around us, but awe may happen when for just a fleeting
moment, we can or are challenged to.

Our consciousness is designed to help us walk around walls, not
through them, and it constructs ideas like "solid" and "impenetra-
ble" and "rock solid" even though science knows for sure that
walls and rocks are mostly space with a few atoms scattered here
and there. Even though our brain didn't evolve to help us live day-
to-day by the rules of this atomic world, that world is nonetheless
there. The body we evolved with can't walk through a wall not
because the space isn't there to do so, but because of the energy
field holding the atomic particles of the wall in one place at least
for the moment. We didn't evolve to deal with that "other" world
even though we aren't the stuff we are made of, and at any given
time, we're really only a temporary gathering of matter and mostly
space ourselves.[5] Until awe makes it do it, our brain isn't made to
reflect about or even care about what it considers the nonsense of
the workings of the other worlds in which we also exist.

If we had evolved on the level of the neutrino, with a body and
brain designed for a world of that size and speed, the brain that
came with that evolution would understand full well the possibility that we might be able to take a stroll through a wall. However,
as Dawkins says, we're "middle-worlders," made for walking
around trees, rocks, and walls and not through them. We evolved
in the middle world between the infinitely huge and the
inconceivably tiny, and it is our evolution in this middle world that
helps us know not to bang into the coffee table. It turns out that
most of "what is" is beyond our brains' capacity, interest, and

evolutionary purpose, but that same evolution gave us our oft-neglected awe response that might be a rare time when we experience or sense what the middle-world brain usually doesn't, and as a result we are left gasping and grasping to know and understand more.

Dawkins points out that what we call "reality" is a model used by our brain to help get us through the day. It's a reality our brain needs to deal with so it can help us stay alive. If we had evolved to live in one of the other worlds that our best and smartest scientific brains are struggling to understand, we would never be awed by the sometimes overwhelmingly moving signs of Einstein's principle that we are an inseparable "part of a whole, called by us *the Universe.*" We wouldn't be killing one another while operating under the illusion that we are "something separate from the rest" and wouldn't suffer so from the consequences of what Einstein called the optical delusion of a self-consciousness that says we are individuals separated by boundaries.[6] Our brain would consider such an idea "reality" and not just a noble altruistic dream, but maybe that's what awe is for—to deeply sense not what is but what could be.

A DILATION OF CONSCIOUSNESS

You have read that awe dilates the imagination by offering you the chance to expand your consciousness and that a tendency toward self-focused, materialistic thinking results in languishing rather than flourishing. Because it takes us out of our usual model of life, awe in a sense takes us out of this world for a little while. Psychologist William James wrote, "Most people live, whether physically, intellectually, or morally, in a very restricted circle of their potential being. They make very small use of their possible consciousness and of their soul's resources in general, much like a man who, out of his whole bodily organism, should get into a habit of using and moving only his little finger."[7] Whenever something awakens our eleventh emotion, we become aware of worlds we usually don't think about and then tap into the extraordinary power of our connective consciousness.

Researchers Doc Childre and Howard Martin of the HeartMath Institute in California write, "The collective energy generated from the feelings, thoughts, and attitudes of the almost six billion people on this planet creates an atmosphere or 'consciousness climate.' Surrounding us like the air we breathe, this consciousness climate affects us most strongly on energetic and emotional levels."[8] These two researchers are not just referring to some abstract, metaphorical energy but to the real, measurable, powerful energy generated by our emotions resonating in our hearts and minds as we experience them. Being in awe is experiencing a severe change in emotional climate.

One of the SAI participants, the wife of a former governor, described her experience of awe on September 11, 2001, and how it related to her awareness of the danger of the delusion of a separate consciousness. Her description illustrates how awe can be inspired not only by the remarkably wonderful but the dreadfully horrible. She wrote, "I was in awe when those towers just tumbled down upon themselves. It was as if their shoulders just sagged under the horror of it all, and they collapsed in horrendous grief. I thought about how it could be possible that we humans can do such cruel things to one another. I thought how terribly, terribly stupid of us to think that we don't all ultimately share the same spirit, the same consciousness. How did we become so dreadfully deluded? We all create the consciousness and the spiritual climate we live in. If only we could all be more aware of how we are ultimately all of one mind—of one consciousness. What a world that would be to live in. That would be such a wonderful global warming."

EXPLAINING CONSCIOUSNESS

Perhaps because we have to so radically expand whatever our consciousness is in order to try to define it, consciousness is a concept that often ends up in the same category of ideas like mysticism, an idea middle-world science prefers to avoid whenever possible. The idea of consciousness is itself awe inspiring because it seems beyond our capacity to understand yet fascinates us at the same time. It's such a vast, stupefying concept that the mind—perhaps because it's part of what's ultimately being looked for—has real trouble wrapping itself around the idea of whatever it is, how it works, and why we have it.

Whatever consciousness is, it's certainly much more than neurons releasing and reacting to each others' chemicals. Two neurons neurochemically soaking each other's dendrites and axons aren't conscious of what they're doing or thinking that they're sharing a nice bio-bath, but something strange emerges when billions of them bathe together, and that something strange is our consciousness.

Scientists refer to a phenomenon that arises from a combination of huge numbers of really small parts, like the brain's 100 billion cells and trillions of subatomic particles, as an *emergent property,* meaning that the resultant whole does things that the individual sub-parts can't because the whole isn't only much more; it's way different.[9] Combinations of large numbers aren't just like small numbers, only bigger. They're also capable of doing things the small numbers within them can't because something unique emerges due to the fact of sheer numbers and their interaction, and that "something" is consciousness.

The wild and weird world of quantum physics provides clues to how emergent properties might influence how consciousness works as related to being in awe. It teaches us that trillions of inconceivably small things going unimaginably fast can lead to some surprises. Although our self-focused here-and-now brain resists the idea, the fact is, subatomic particles can exist in two places at once. Where they are depends on who's looking, when, and how, and the same seems to be true with the awakened consciousness we experience when we are in awe. When our consciousness is expanded by something we encounter, our looking deeper may in some way result in a temporary quantum breakthrough. It provides a mind-boggling glimpse of the fact that there are many levels of reality beyond the one in which we spend most of our time. When we're in awe, we're reacting on some level to the emergence of things and phenomena that our busy brain doesn't often have the time or tolerance to deal with.

If we lived our daily lives solely in terms of the quantum world's rules, we'd never have to worry about whom to marry, where to live, or what career to pursue. We could be married to several people, live several places, and work at all kinds of jobs all at once, but we can't. But if experiment after experiment proves the fact of the "two places at once" emergent property of large tiny numbers working together, why can't we make our already hectic pace more efficient by being two places at once ourselves? After all, we're made up of billions of particles, and they can do it.

We can't literally be two places at once because of another feature of very large numbers called *fixedness*, meaning that even if it would seem in some quantum theoretical sense that we could be home making love and at work making money at the same time, fixedness dictates most of our daily consciousness. We end up feeling—except perhaps when we're in awe—that we are where we are.

AN ASTONISHING HYPOTHESIS

If the preceding discussion of consciousness sounds like complete hogwash to you, you may be right. But I think you'll agree that you are conscious—whatever that is—of the fact that you disagree. I certainly don't know for sure what consciousness is or whether all the quantum speculation and ideas about emergent properties ultimately have anything at all to do with it. Whatever force created it must be laughing at our efforts to figure it out, but I do know that my study of the awe response indicates that it's something our eleventh emotion seems to intensify and expand. I do know that we "feel" we have it, so a working definition that at least seems to describe how we experience it might be as follows: Consciousness is a mysterious blend of how and what we say when we talk to ourselves, what's doing the listening, how it feels about what it hears, and what seems to be doing the speaking.

My awe-tinted, imprecise, and admittedly mystical description has been far too subjective for most of my scientific colleagues. Most of them are still digging through the proverbial cortical haystack of the pile of billions of neurons in our heads, hoping to find the needle that will provide the answer to how we know that we know. The problem is that it's difficult to find a needle that distinguishes itself from the other needles in a stack full of hay.

"You, your joys and your sorrows, your memories and your ambitions, your sense of personal identity and free will, are in fact no more than the behavior of a vast assembly of nerve cells and their associated molecules."[10] These are the words of the Nobel laureate Francis Crick, who claimed in 1953 to have discovered "the secret of life" when he and co-founder James Watson unraveled the mystery of the famous DNA double helix that unzips to make copies of itself. In addition, he was proposing that we look for consciousness in much the same way that he, Watson, and other neurobiologists searched for the keys to heredity.

Crick was convinced that consciousness, like the elusive genetic code, could one day be totally explained by science—in this case, neuroscience. Crick himself labeled his ideas about consciousness's origins as his "astonishing hypothesis," and indeed it was. He was convinced that our sense of who we are, our ability to "think about how we think"—or in my words, what it is that does the talking and listening when we dialogue with ourselves—were really the workings of a soggy sack of about 100 different kinds of about 100 billion neural cells. It's an amazing theory because it suggests that we have no soul and no spiritual self that transcends the cells of our brains and bodies. In other words, no cells, no consciousness, and ultimately no "us" beyond the workings of our brains.

At least, unlike some other scientists who can't understand why human consciousness has been elevated to science's Holy Grail, Crick acknowledged and was fascinated by the importance of something called "consciousness" that keeps confounding attempts to scientifically explain how we think and feel. Having discovered the secret of life, he was now in search of how it is we are aware that we're alive. He was convinced that science would eventually understand this nagging mystery by shrinking consciousness down to cell size. He thought the complexities of how the vast network of neurons in our brain constituted consciousness would be discovered to ultimately be no different than any other physiological function. If scientists would only put their minds to it, stop thinking about consciousness as some unique mystical transcendent miracle, and study it with the same steely objective dedication as they do any other natural phenomenon, they would eventually find the neurological equivalent of DNA.

THREE SMART POUNDS OF GLORIOUS MEAT

Like hearing, smell, taste, touch, and particularly sight (which Crick discussed in detail as a possible model for beginning to understand the neurology of knowing that are all physiologically explained), Crick thought our consciousness could eventually be understood in totally neurological terms. Crick challenged the view of consciousness that embraced the "fallacy of the *homunculus*" (Latin for "little man"). He said that although it might feel as if we have a little person somewhere in the brain talking to, about, or for us, the cortical chatter is really the buzzing of neurons. In his view the awe response that is so entwined with our sense of consciousness would be just an intense neurological event, not a transformative emotional and mental experience that somehow transcends the way our senses function.

Crick was right in his emphasis on the importance of the scientific method that led to the remarkable discovery of the double helix molecule. It in turn led to the human genome project and how diseases are located and genetically copied. But can our capacity to have our consciousness altered by being awe inspired merely be a pop-psychology version of electrical-chemical events taking place only in our brain, an organ that philosopher Patricia Churchland refers to as "three pounds of glorious meat, wonder tissue"?

I'm aware of the danger of challenging the idea that rational science will eventually fully and finally describe the materialistic basis of what we experience as consciousness and the awe that seems to awaken and change it. I'm also aware of the irrational end of the explanatory spectrum. It takes the form of hundreds of books, seminars, and gurus telling us how to find our "true inner conscious being," how to increase our consciousness, and urging us on to a higher and higher "level" of consciousness so we can rise to a higher astral plane, talk directly to God, and for a price, get a picture of the energy fields that are supposed to radiate from our consciousness. In the middle of this spectrum is our nonrational thought emanating from our sentient heart and experienced in the form of intuition, a "sixth sense," or awareness of "something more." Astonishing ideas of all sorts form when we're in awe of something that might transcend the physical realm like the idea of human consciousness and an eleventh emotion capable of altering and expanding it.

TWELVE CHARACTERISTICS OF THE AWE RESPONSE

Reports by the respondents in the SAI, along with the work of the few scientists (for example, Abraham Maslow and William McDougall) who have dared to study such a complex concept as awe and the issues about consciousness that it raises, provide a general profile of the awe response. We might find within these characteristics hints regarding the nature of the consciousness that is so impacted and expanded by awe, or at least we may find some new places for which to look for the process that bears that name.

Based primarily on my interviews, I present in the following section a list of the twelve most frequently described characteristics of what the awe response feels and looks like, as reported by the SAI participants and as written in their awe diaries. The list raises questions worth pursuing about the nature of being awe inspired, why we were made to have this response, and about the nature of our consciousness that seems so profoundly altered by the power of our eleventh emotion.

A Look of Awe

Because it can show itself in so many ways, it's difficult to tell whether someone is in awe by just looking at him or her, but those who see people experiencing their eleventh emotion, particularly their loved ones, say they can see it. Even with eyes wide open and jaw dropped with nostrils flaring open, as if to take in as much as possible, people in awe can appear to others to be really happy, terribly sad, or totally gone. Two very early attempts to identify how we look when we are "in awe" offer very different descriptions.

In the Hawaiian language, there's a word *ihihia* (pronounced ee he he ah), which means "to be stricken with awe." It refers to the idea that we can enter a state that is completely free of time, space, and self and experience a connection with—or at least a sense of suspicion of—the collective consciousness we sense when we are in awe. An ancient Hawaiian proverb states, *"Hakanu i no luina Rusini"* (pronounced ha ka new e no lew e na Rew sea knee), and it translates as, "speechless with awe." It is said that when the first Russian ships approached the Hawaiian shores, the natives observed them in *ihihia* or "awed reverent silence." Hawaiian elders teach that *ihihia* was expressed by the ancient Hawaiians by a stone-faced deferential silence, and some of the SAI respondents' spouses and family members said that was the way they showed awe. One SAI participant wrote, "My wife took a picture when I was looking out at the ocean, and I look totally stoic and almost dead. She asked me why I wasn't happy. I guess I wasn't. I was just really moved and taken away."

A different appearance of something that seems similar to the awe response was described in 1872 by Charles Darwin. Although the response he observed seems to lack the expression of a sense of full vastness and a mind-changing characteristic of awe, it does seem to be at least a close relative of it. In his *Expression of the Emotions in Man and Animals,* Darwin presented his observations of classification of what he called the expression of "admiration."[11] He defined this response as a mixture of a look of surprise, pleasure, approval, and astonishment. This might be equivalent to the word "awesome" so frequently used by people today but lacks reference to the fear I've found essential for a full awe response.

Darwin's description of admiration was based on his observations of manic patients whose hair would stand on end prior to the onset of a manic episode. He also described what he called the admiring expressions on the faces of Australian aborigines as they first set eyes on Europeans. He noted that the aborigines' reaction was characterized by "raised eyebrows, bright eyes, gaping mouth."

There was one facial feature associated with the awe response that I've noticed in persons in awe or even when they try to describe it. There is often a thin set of "wonder wrinkles" or deep folds of the skin in the forehead shaped like upside down smiles and the exact opposite of frown lines. I don't have enough data to prove that awe comes with these "wonder wrinkles." It may be they're just a muscular reflex, and those who don't show them have used Botox, but I've noticed them particularly in babies and children.

Heart First?

Awe usually happens to the entire body before the brain has the chance to "think" about it. That's because the basic five senses may be receiving signals from the environment faster than the higher levels of our brain can recognize and interpret. It is also because neurohormonal and electromagnetic signals come from the heart that convey what the heart can literally sense and convey to the brain before it "knows it" itself.

At least in the most common form of the three or more kinds of awe described in Chapter 4, most people seem to notice that the body is "feeling" awe after it has actually already started. In a way, it can seem that we're awed by the fact that we're in awe.

One of the SAI respondents described this "body first" awe reaction by saying, "I was just standing there waiting with the others for the water to spurt up out of the blow hole near Sandy Beach [on the Hawaiian island of O`ahu]. When it exploded up into the sky, my wife told me she saw chicken skin break out all over my arms and legs. It was a really hot day, but I was getting chills from just staring at the water shooting up, but I guess you could say I must have been in awe of what I was seeing and didn't know it until after I was."

As well as other subtle sensations received by the body at a subconscious level from the basic five senses, people also experience awe due to the afferent (sending) neurological connections that run from the heart to the brain and via the electromagnetic energy that resonates from the heart to the brain. Research also shows that energetic information from the heart ends up in the brain's amygdala, and changes in the electrical activity of the heart are reflected in the cells of the amygdala.[12] This is one of the ways changes taking place in the heart can be experienced in the brain.

A recent study showed that over half of the patients diagnosed with symptoms of panic disorder showed prior undiagnosed, irregular heartbeats that were the cause of their severe anxiety. Once the arrhythmias were treated, their panic disorder went away.[13] The idea that any emotional or physical problem or wonderful emotion like awe is "only in your head" is a physiological impossibility.

The heart doesn't just react to the brain; it communicates to and with it. One of the SAI participants said, "I think that awe comes from your center somewhere, not your top. It floods over you before you know you're awash in it. It's a heart thing first before it's a head thing."

If you doubt that the heart can impact the brain, just ask any golfer about the "yips." They're the sudden involuntary movements of the hands and wrists that cause golfers' putts to become true adventures. Basketball players shooting foul shots sometimes get the yips, and so do my surgeon friends, although they are understandably reluctant to talk about it.

The yips are often attributed to a condition called *focal dystonia*, in which a muscle or group of muscles goes into spasm, but no one really knows for sure what causes them. It has been hypothesized that overuse of one certain group of muscles can cause us to have a case of the yips or that perhaps the brain's anxiety about the situation causes it to make our muscles misfire, but there's evidence that the heart's involved.[14] It seems to be able to sense what's going on, get emotional about it, and then send a report of the emotional state to the brain. Ask a professional golfer who just lost a tournament on a single missed putt, and she or he will tell you that, if the yips were involved, they "had them before they knew it." Some golfers report success in curing the yips by trying to slow and steady their heartbeats.

A Gut Feeling

Awe seems to be an entire body experience, but it is most often reported as a gut feeling that begins in the area of the heart and stomach and spreads out in a feeling of warmth from that center. People in awe tend to grab their chests or stomachs, not their heads. This may be related in part to the most important nerve in our body, what scientists call Cranial Nerve 10.

The vagus nerve is the tenth of our twelve paired cranial nerves. It starts in the brainstem, weaves its way down through the neck, and then meanders down to the abdomen. The *vagus* (literally "wandering" and "vague") nerve is also called the *pneumogastric* nerve since it innervates both our lungs and our stomach, resulting in the awe sensation that we "sense something in our gut," or "feel butterflies in our stomach," or that something is "gut-wrenching."

In a way, we all have at least three "brains," all of which are involved in our eleventh emotion. One is the assertive one in the head that seems to think it's the only one and that it alone defines "you." The other is the more humble heart that is capable of beating on its own, reacting to the environment, and sending signals to the brain. To distinguish it from our central nervous system (CNS), the third brain is known as the enteric nervous system (ENS). It's located in the linings of our esophagus, stomach, small intestine, and colon and is full of neurons, neurotransmitters, and neuropeptides, so named because of their peptic or digestive tract location.

Like Siamese triplets, these three "brains" make up one mind, so whatever is "on" your mind is also in your heart and intestines. These brains are intimately connected, and when one is agitated, all three are. When we say we "trust our gut," we're being smart because almost one-half of all of the nerve cells in our bodies are located there, and they're constantly secreting neurohormones that influence a sense of well-being. A healthy ENS contributes to healthy psychological, physiological, and immune systems.

A tourist visiting Kilauea volcano on the Big Island described her awe "gut feeling." She said, "I could feel the slight rumbling of that volcano in my gut. It was like it was some leftover primal sense of the energy still stored in the miles and miles of lava resonating inside my center. I was in total awe. I felt butterflies in my stomach just like before I have to give a big speech at work on the mainland. I even thought that the god the Hawaiians call Pele was punching me right in the stomach."

That Loving Feeling

The hormone oxytocin, the same one that is secreted during sexual orgasm and when women nurse, plays a major role in the awe response. This hormone also works with the vagus nerve to produce feelings of loving calmness, connection, and bonding.[15] One role of oxytocin is to cause lactation in mothers who are breast-feeding, which in turn increases feelings of attachment between mothers and their babies. If you've ever watched a mother nursing, you may have seen the awe she feels for her child, for the process, and for the awe that her baby seems to show for her.

In a fascinating study conducted by Jen Silvers, one of psychologist Jonathan Haidt's undergraduate students at the University of Virginia, lactating women came with their babies to a laboratory and were asked to insert nursing pads in their bras while being videotaped watching a videotape. Half of the group watched an *Oprah Winfrey Show* video clip that showed a musician expressing his sincere appreciation to his music teacher not only for inspiring him, but also saving him from a life of gang violence. After that moving scene, the musician himself was surprised when Oprah then brought out the young man's own students to express their gratitude to him for doing the same thing for them. The other half of the group watched video clips of comedians. The results of this experiment yielded what Haidt describes as one of the "biggest effects" he has seen in any study.

When Silvers weighed the nursing pads to assess the amount of milk that had been released during the videos, the pads worn by more than half of the mothers who had watched the awe-inspiring (what Haidt called "elevating") video showed evidence that the mothers had leaked milk. The tapes of them watching the video also showed that many of these mothers began to spontaneously nurse their babies while watching the *Oprah* clip. Only a few of the mothers in the comedian-watching group leaked milk or nursed. The videotapes of the participants also showed that the mothers watching the *Oprah* tape engaged in more touching and cuddling of their babies.[16]

Love and awe are closely related. The respondents in the SAI often used words like feeling "enraptured" or "in ecstasy" in describing their experiences. Some said that they felt like hugging somebody right away. They said they felt "totally lost" and, as one of the study participants described with some embarrassment about her sexual candor, "I felt like I melted away into that sublime blissful state after you have just come."

While I've not been able to conduct scans of the brains of people in awe, their verbal reports upon which I have to rely in this first study of awe at least suggest that the same parts of the brain involved in sexual orgasm are in some way involved with our awe response. What SAI participants report seems to indicate that the sensual dance between our sympathetic (arousal) and parasympathetic (calming) autonomic nervous systems that is essential to the sexual climax also takes place when we're in awe. As one embarrassed SAI respondent said, "I know I'm really blushing now, but I must say that the kind of awe I experience is pretty sexual, so maybe you could say that sexual orgasm happens when you are in awe of the person you're making love with."

A Feeling of Being Uplifted

Awe often involves a feeling of being "elevated" or somehow removed and "taken up" and away from daily hassles and worries about personal issues to a new insight into the higher or better side of humankind and the world. It's a sudden feeling of joyful relief at "finally being above it all" and freed from the emotional burden that results from our cynical and often negative view of the world and the people in it.

As pointed out earlier, the sense of being elevated was first identified and studied by psychologist Jonathon Haidt. He described it as an open, warm, glowing feeling sometimes accompanied by chills, "choking up," and a feeling of warmth in the chest area.[17] Again, I can only speculate as to the physiological causes of this sensation, but increased circulation to the chest area, a surge of adrenaline, stimulation from the vagus nerve, or perhaps the pounding of the heart might be related to what Haidt described.

A SAI participant described the elevated feeling she experienced when she was awed by Addie's gift, described in Chapter 3. The gift of one little girl to another little girl battling cancer is one of my favorite awe stories. The woman who observed it said, "It's like you suddenly become above all the negativity about people and have your faith renewed in mankind. Seeing something like that made me feel as if I could rise above all the stupid consuming distractions.

That generous little girl gave me a great gift, too. For at least a little while (until I watched the next TV newscast), I became way more optimistic about people and life in general."

A Delightful Dread

Some level of excited fear is always associated with being in awe. It seems to be a unique kind of excited, curiosity-based fear more like a fear you might experience if someone told you that the ghost of your deceased grandmother was in the next room than that of being told that a poisonous snake was in the next room. It's an anticipatory-based more than an escape-based fear.

This delightfully disturbing state combined with a sense of a sur-rendering of an independent, separate, powerful self that comes with being in awe may explain why the awe response can be used to manipulate, intimidate, and win wars. In this state, we feel excited and can become highly agitated and ready to act. Crowds at soccer games and audiences at concerts can be so awed by what they are experiencing that they behave in ways they never would in other situations.

In 500 B.C.E. Chinese military writer Sun Tzu wrote about "awing enemies into submission." Although actually born in Russia, North Korea's Kim Jong-il portrays himself as a god born high in the mountains under several rainbows, energized by lightning, and having published thousands of books. He regularly conducts mas-sive military displays and more recently missile launches designed to awe his own people so that they remain under his control and ready to act. The United States proudly used its own version of "shock and awe" as an opening salvo to initiate its invasion of Iraq.

Aroused Awe

Depending on how we elect to mentally process what's happening to us when we are in awe, the initial intense response in the SAM system (sympathetic adrenal medullary system), which arouses the body, can be followed by or even cause the rebound of the calming influence of our relaxing PAC (parasympathetic-adrenal-cortical) neuro-hormonal system. This system is characterized by hormones secreted from the cortex or the outside layer of our adrenal glands that help produce an emotional calming down from the crescendo of the intensity of SAM-excited awe response.

Another SAI respondent, this time an embarrassed man, described his awe response as being similar to what he called his "sexual cycle." He said, "First I get excited, followed by—at least if we do it right—a profound sense of being totally gone, and then of deep relief and total relaxation. That's also what it feels like when I'm in awe. It's kind of a rhythmic thing, you know, getting into the rhythm of life, and good sex has good rhythm, if you know what I mean. At least that's what our most awesome sex is like."

Some authors go so far as to define sexual orgasm as "the sweet death," meaning a total loss of the sense of self like that experienced in the state of awe. Whether we experience *post-coital remorse* or a fond longing for a repeat performance depends on how we think about what happened. In the case of the awe response, the more we make significant changes in our thought processes to think about our connection with what we are experiencing, the SAM and PAC systems can operate in balance together. If we stay with the awe-inspiring experience despite its intensity and our initial fear of its vastness and feelings of powerless smallness, we eventually can become relaxed, at peace, and safely grounded.

One of my physician friends in Hawaii described the SAM and PAC rhythm of the awe response by saying, "When I finally met my guru in India, I felt this sudden need to run home and hide, but then I suddenly realized that, my God, I *am* home. Calm down and enjoy this, and learn from this." If we interpret what inspires our awe response in new ways that make us feel calmer and connected, there is an ultimate counter-balancing decrease in stress hormones, particularly the one called cortisol. When cortisol is decreased, immunity is strengthened by an increase in T-cells and immunoglobulin that help fight off disease.

A Quieted Excitement

Sometimes, we can be so awestruck that we go into a trancelike state that one of my SAI respondents identified when she described her awe as "suddenly forced meditation." Our SAM or arousal system can become so intensely and suddenly excited that it spills over to cause our PAC or quieting system to kick in to quiet it down. Another SAI participant said, "Awe is kind of like being shocked into silence." Neurologist Andrew Newberg and his colleagues describe this "shocked silence" as "hyperarousal with quiescent breakthrough." Further, they said "it can result in "a trance-like state experienced as an ecstatic rush of orgasmic like energy."[18]

One of the SAI respondents was an accomplished violinist and music teacher. She described this state Newberg describes as being so high that we end up feeling low by saying, "I was so in awe that night the symphony performed Beethoven's *9th*. After my cancer and everything, it was suddenly all just way too overwhelming for me. My husband said I seemed to go into a coma or something and was just gone, but I've never felt more energized and safe at the same time. For me, that was total awe."

An Excited Calm

In another and more atypical version of the awe response, the nervous system goes into what Newberg calls "hyperquiescence with arousal breakthrough," or so much PAC that the SAM system kicks in. We can become so profoundly calmed by something that inspires awe that the usual balance between the sympathetic (activating) and parasympathetic (relaxing) parts of our autonomic nervous system is disturbed. Our quieting system spills over to our agitating system, and we suddenly experience a profound alteration of consciousness and feelings of great exhilaration.

A nun who was one of the SAI participants described this "so up, we end up down" feeling by saying, "There was a loud and violent thunderstorm outside, and I was sitting alone in the chapel in very deep prayer. Suddenly I felt, and I mean I felt and didn't see, the lights go out. I opened my eyes, and all I saw was one candle and the wind blowing in from the storm that blew the flame to one side and into the shape of a cross. I had been so totally relaxed that I barely heard the storm, but now I was totally energized. It felt like I was becoming a part of the flame."

Leaving Us Breathless

When we're in awe, there's a feeling of initial breathlessness caused by a quick gasping inhalation and holding of our breath. This is due in part to signals from the vagus nerve that influences our lungs and also to the effects of stimulation from the SAM system.

One of the physicians in my study described his awe response by saying, "I think awe happens somewhere in that strange place between our heartbeats and breaths. It takes place during that mysterious time when we aren't really breathing and the heart is between contractions. It's kind of a sweet, little quick mini-death, and then you come back to life." Most SAI respondents said that, following what seemed like a few moments of holding their breath, they sighed and began to take deeper and fuller breaths.

The Third Tear

When we're in awe, our eyes often fill with tears, and there may be weeping or sobbing. Crying is a complicated process, and we shed many different kinds of tears. What are called "basal tears" keep our eyes lubricated constantly, and "reflex tears" are the kind that are produced when our eyes get irritated by onions or something getting in them. However, when we're in awe, we shed a third kind of tear. These tears are elicited by a strong emotion and contain certain kinds of chemical hormones and proteins, particularly the prolactin and manganese that are related to feelings of intense emotion and are the substances that are "cried out" when we grieve or feel intense sadness.

Having a good cry can be one of the healthiest and most uplifting things you can do. One of the SAI participants described this effect when she said, "I don't cry just because I'm sad. I sometimes cry so I won't be. I love to have a good cry once in awhile, and when it happens to me when I'm in awe of something, it really seems to feel like a great de-gloomer."

A professional woman going through a major career change and under immense pressure in her new job told me, "Sometimes, women just have to have a good cleansing cry. I know I do, but I sure don't do it at work. I know women like me who purposely rent sad movies just to make them cry; it's cathartic, and we sort of look forward to it. I think men have given crying a bad name."

The Need to Be "Herd"

When we're in awe, the profound sense of connection associated with that state causes us to want to join with others to share the experience. We feel we want to tell the world what we're experiencing and share it with everybody we can.

Awe may be our most basic social impulse and related to our need to organize ourselves into groups. Before the world's largest trees and highest waterfalls and standing on the edge of the deepest precipices, all of us feel equally small and vulnerable. By experiencing the awe of our shared connection to nature and ultimate common vulnerability and subservience to it, we can recognize more fully our undeniable dependent connection to each other and the consciousness climate we all share.

One of the SAI participants described awe's sudden intense "herd reaction" when she said, "Standing on the edge of the Grand Canyon for that first time, all of us there, including all the strangers around me, seemed to be in awe together. There's no 'you' when you're in awe, so we all sort of shrunk together in the presence of what we were seeing and, without saying much to each other, I think we all were having the same frightened, awe-inspiring experience, and we knew we were all moved the same way. That was a great feeling of unspoken togetherness."

The preceding features of the awe response not only serve to strongly support the argument to include it as one of our basic emotions, but also encourage us to learn as much as we can from it, to try to experience it more than we do, and to see it as one of the most powerful paths to leading us out of the languishing lives so many of us have fallen into. Maybe, if we allow ourselves to be awed more often, we might even discover that our consciousness transcends the limits of the three pounds of "glorious meat" in our heads, is far more sacred than new-age psychobabble can describe, and is more astonishing than even Francis Crick imagined.

6

THE FLOURISHING FACTOR

"Our brains are no longer conditioned for reverence and awe. We cannot imagine a Second Coming that would not be cut down to size by the televised evening news, or a Last Judgment not subject to pages of holier-than-thou second-guessing in the New York Review of Books.*"*

— JOHN UPDIKE

ADD: AWE DEFICIENCY DISORDER

Are you flourishing? Research indicates that almost eight of every ten of us aren't.[1] Instead, the majority of Americans are languishing their lives away in a kind of psychological purgatory in the form of a mental health "in-between-ness," in which they are neither totally mentally healthy nor mentally ill, and spend their days in the pursuit of a happiness that forever seems to elude them. Despite how full their schedules, to-do lists, and mission statements seem to be, languishers often describe their lives as "feeling hollow" or "empty," the exact opposite of the flourishing experienced by those who are regularly awed by their gift of life no matter the nature of that gift.[2]

Languishing is indolent and sneaks up on you over time. It's characterized not by depression, high anxiety, or the presence of negative feelings, but by the absence of the regularly intense feelings about life that flourishers experience, including the good, the bad, and the ugly things that life brings. It's important to understand that flourishing from an awe-inspired experience isn't always characterized by the happiness languishers keep seeking. Like a flourishing garden that withstands the storm, flourishers are vibrantly alive even though life may deal them the most severe challenges. They're not just positive thinkers but deep, reflective ones who intensely engage with anything that happens in their lives and try to understand more about life, whether things are going well or not.

Unlike flourishers, languishers have busy bodies but anesthetized souls, unable to fully celebrate even the most wonderful victory or deeply and legitimately grieve a terrible loss. Languishing results in constantly feeling on the go but seldom feeling moved; feeling that life is leading us, rather than the reverse.

My clinical staff and I have treated thousands of languishers, and I think I finally know the cause of their languishing. They were suffering from a new kind of ADD—a chronic version of attention deficit disorder manifested in the soul-sapping condition of *Awe Deficiency Disorder*. I've also found from the Study of the Awe Inspired that the more regularly awe-inspired people flourish because they've shown a creative and adaptive ratio between the positive thinking that suggests what can go right and how to enjoy it, and the necessary negativity to understand what might go wrong and how to learn and grow from it.

WHAT DOES "AWESOME" REALLY MEAN?

If we say something is "awesome," do we usually mean it? I doubt it, because languishers seem to use the word a lot, and the more easily awed, not nearly as much. When we so easily say "awesome," are we really experiencing a full awe response, or are we saying that we're going through something that feels vaguely "like" it, and that we could be awe inspired if we only had more time to dwell and reflect on what we're experiencing? The use of the word *awesome* has become more an announcement of a shopper's discovery than an indication of a transformative spiritual insight in progress. Our consumer consciousness converts being in awe to the same thing as having a need that only a few hours ago was a "want."

The word *awesome* has become almost as ubiquitous and meaningless as the word *love*, another word thrown around quite a bit by languishers but reserved for very special expression by the frequently awed. The quick and emotionless phrase, "Love you," often becomes a salutation used to replace "Have a nice day" or "See you later." You hear it from people ending their cell phone calls, and it serves as a superstitious check-off as something we have to say to family members "just in case" as we dash out the door grabbing our keys, pager, and laptop. (I don't recall any of the SAI participants reporting having been on their cell phones while in awe.)

The word *awesome* is used so often that it barely draws our attention. It's often used to save us the time of talking longer, more sincerely, and in more depth with other busy people. In our day-to-day discourse, when something in the conversation causes us to feel the chills, goose bumps, and emotional upheaval that comes with our eleventh emotion, we use the word *awesome* as a way to get back to the task at hand. It's often easier and maybe a little less embarrassing or self-revealing to just say "awesome" and leave it at that.

When leading a languishing awe-less life, people's emotions tend to become deadened and expressed in a kind of Stepford-wife speak. We get angry so often that even though its impact on our body can still kill us, the brain in our head thinks "been there, done that" and has gotten used to it. When we tell someone that we're "enraged," we seldom really are. When we answer "fantastic" when someone asks how we are, we usually aren't and are too busy and distracted to know whether we are, or are too busy to go into detail about how we really feel. We do so much at one time that when we say, "That was wonderful," our check-off consciousness is really saying, "That was kind of nice. Now, what's next?"

GETTING OUT OF TOUCH WITH OUR EMOTIONS

Our basic ten human emotions—love, fear, sadness, embarrassment, curiosity, pride, enjoyment, despair, guilt, and anger—are seen by most psychologists as what they call "self-interest monitors," meaning that they're designed to force our bodies and minds to care about and take action in terms of what is good for us as individuals. This is why therapy and the self-help personal power movement has been so enamored with getting "in touch" with what's "inside," but this comes at the expense of connecting and focusing on the between, where the awe response emerges.

One of true awe's most important lessons is the discovery that our greatest strengths and weaknesses and full joyful engagement in life do not exist within us; they exist and happen between us. True, unadulterated, sincere, understanding awe involves awareness of significant spiritual needs being drawn out of us, not wants finally being met for us. It leaves us bothered and thoughtful, not satisfied and full, and it's as likely to make us sad as happy. Awe is the basic human emotion that lifts us far above languishing, not because it makes us feel good, but because it makes us feel.

Self-help's bromide of "one must love oneself before it possible to love another" conveys the idea that we must work hard to become more in awe of our self by striving for higher and higher self-esteem, yet decades of this how-to-be-happier psychology hasn't made us either happier or more lovable.[3]

The esteem-thyself movement has flourished since the early 1960s, but as author Gregg Easterbrook points out, "The percentage of Americans who describe themselves as 'happy' has not budged since the 1950s."[4] While awe is found outside of ourselves in the in-between spaces of our lives, where the wonders of the sense of deep connection occur, our modern emotionalized culture has turned our attention inward. Listen to people describe real awe in their lives, however, and you will hear descriptions of feeling being pulled out of and away from their sense of self and becoming less aware of their own personal emotions than ever before in their life. Except for the emergence of the humbling fear that is a necessary side-effect of being in awe, persons who are truly awe inspired become almost emotionless in a state one SAI participant described as "spiritual suspension."

Persons in real awe are so completely absorbed in and by what awes them that, at least in terms of a highly emotional individual self, they cease to exist. They're "gone" and not "tuned in." They have little concern for trying to feel better or trying to get in touch with their inner feelings. Awe is less introspective than "inter-spective" in the sense that it involves full engagement and merging with something much vaster than the self has imagined or we can imagine when we are self-consumed or busy consuming.

AWE-INSPIRED LOVE

While my interviews of persons about their experiences with awe were mostly of individuals, and most respondents said that awe happened to them most often when they were alone, it is a mistake to assume that awe impacts only one person at a time. In fact, the awe of understanding is first and foremost a feeling of profound connection. Some SAI respondents described how awe also worked its magic in their most intimate relationships and even in teams at their workplace. An emotion as powerful as awe, which is elicited by vastness and freedom from the illusion of boundaries and separateness, by its very nature extends its influence far beyond the single person.

We may often be too emotionally numb to know it, but languishing is always lonely. Flourishing is always shared. Even though we might be physically alone when we experience it, awe awakens our sense that we are never truly alone and that our sense of separateness is exactly as Einstein described it (in Chapter 5), a mental optical illusion. Awe results in a sudden conversion from "me" to "us" and "everything," and it is in this sense that it may be our most loving emotion. We are more likely to feel love by looking out together in awe for what's best about the world than gazing passionately into one another's eyes to see whether we've found someone who thinks we're the best.

In addition to awe being a means of falling in deeper love with life, it also carries with it multiple interrelated benefits that can lead to a sense of flourishing with someone else. If we don't diminish its divinity or settle for awe lite, the awe of understanding can be the emotional antidote with the power to convert our languishing to flourishing.

DEFINING FLOURISHING

Just as the new field of positive psychology has introduced the concept of languishing as a distinct diagnosable condition, it has also become interested in its opposite, the awe-inspired state of flourishing and the one most often elicited by our eleventh emotion. The concept of flourishing was first introduced twenty-three centuries ago by Aristotle. It translated from *eudaimonia,* which literally means "fortunate in one's genius," and it was used to refer to humankind's fulfillment of its natural potential.[5]

While Aristotle emphasized rational thought, flourishing doesn't just involve one of our mental capacities. While they probably aren't aware of it, I'm certain that animals, gardens, and mountains can flourish in their "other worldly" ways, so I don't see any purpose in excluding them from the idea of flourishing we experience in our "middle world."

Author Thomas Pogge wrote, "Flourishing is the most comprehensive 'all-in-one' assessment of the quality of human lives."[6] Because awe leaves us with a deepened sense of how incomplete we are and how much more mental, emotional, and spiritual work we still have left to do, I use the word *flourishing* to describe its impact, because it implies a process, not a finished state like "being fulfilled" or "totally happy." What's awe inspiring about a flourishing garden is that, even with its weeds, it seems, and even feels and smells, vitally alive and growing. Like life and the world, it's a work in progress.

As you will read at the end of this chapter, people who are flourishing tend to tilt toward thriving more than merely surviving. I say "tilt" because these people also have the necessary negativity to help them think deeply about all of life and not just the best of life. For many SAI participants, thinking negatively helped them manage their anxiety, providing a way to more likely be pleasantly surprised than those who always expect the best.

Flourishers have more positive than negative feelings and thoughts, but not always by much. Persons who work hard to always accentuate the positive not only expend a lot of energy trying to whistle past the graveyard, but also miss out on the awe that can be experienced by fully engaging with life's traumas and challenges. The frequently awed flourish not just because they've discovered what's tremendous about being alive, but because they become totally mindful of all that constitutes life and can immerse themselves in both the best and worst that happens, and they grow from and through both.

Because awe not only thrills us by making us more aware of the complex good and bad grandeur of life, it can help us not only survive but thrive through life's tribulations by helping us fully engage with them in creatively shared ways. It is in this sense of profound awareness of life even when life seems at its worst that awe can help us heal, and we can manage to flourish even when—and sometimes because—we are suffering.

AWE AS HEALER

Perhaps no other human experience has such wide-ranging positive impact on our lives as being in awe, and one of its most powerful influences and one that has received very little attention from modern medicine is its role in health and healing, two processes essential to flourishing. Research shows that the physiological and mental state that comes with awe's uniquely intense mindfully connective state and total engagement with the world tends to speed recovery from the negative cardiovascular aftereffects of our negative emotions.[7] The toxicity of our hostile angry moments is cleansed by the untainted purity of being in full contact with what is grandest about the opportunity to take on the challenge of being alive, sometimes even when we wish on some level that we weren't.

One of my respondents described awe's emotional cleansing effect by saying, "After I've had one of my angry outbursts, the aftereffects last for days. I feel icky and even dirty and all agitated and emotionally drained. I can feel my blood pressure being high and my heart still racing and missing beats. One day, I noticed something remarkable. The day after I had really blasted one of my employees for screwing up, I was out jogging the next morning. For some reason, the early morning air was unusually fresh and moist, and just as I came up over a hill in the park, I saw the big full moon ahead of me. I stopped to look, and it took my breath away. It was probably some kind of optical illusion, but I swear the moon was as huge as a massive planet looming right there in front of me. Then I felt warmth on my shoulders, and as I looked back, I could see the sun just coming up over the trees behind me. I sat down on the ground, hugged my knees to my chest, and began to cry. I was in total awe, and somehow all the poison of the anger from the day before was completely gone. I think our bad emotions dirty our soul, and awe can somehow cleanse it."

Experiments have shown that being in awe and the mindful state it induces alters what neuroscientists call "frontal brain symmetry."[8] In a cortical sense, life itself is pushed to the front of our awareness. By causing what seems to be a sudden, almost involuntary, meditative state with all of its salubrious effects on the immune system, our resistance to disease and healing processes can be enhanced.

While my interviews of the awe inspired do not provide enough data to prove it, one of the things I noticed about people who are easily awed is that they said they seldom felt sick or had colds or flu, and when they did, they either got better quickly or seemed able to enjoy and relish the experience of being sick for awhile as an escape from the pace of modern life. Sometimes, being sick can cause us to be more aware of our body and both its fragility and strength. Sometimes we can even suffer in the paradoxical comfort of a chance to curl up, be cozy, be cared for, enjoy a little self-pitying misery, and feel our body's healing process at work. When I was dying of cancer, I remember being in awe of the vague feeling of my body fighting for my life.

Being in awe might even be a cure for, or at least increase our resistance to, the common cold. Research now shows that the brain changes that occur when we are in awe and the immune enhancement that comes with them increase our resistance to the rhinovirus, one of the most frequent causes of a cold.[9] The next time you feel a cold coming on, try taking a couple of awes.

Awe and the ability not only to survive but thrive through adversity are also related. The persons I interviewed who reported being frequently in awe said that they found these experiences not only strengthened them and made them feel healthier, hardier, and more vigorous but that they seemed to enhance their resilience or ability to bounce back from life's adversities, and research bears this out.[10] The awe of understanding seems to build up our emotional coping resources and provides new ways of finding meaning, comprehensibility, and manageability at times of trauma.

Like a very hard spiritual stretch, awe can be an exhilarating and exciting release that borders on stress followed by a reactive sense of comfort. Research shows that this unique combination of responses has a salutary effect on the stress hormone that has the most negative impact on our health. Experiments have shown that cortisol, the hormone that pressures the heart, raises blood pressure, and lowers immunity, is reduced when we are engaged with the world in the way that awe inspires us to be.[11]

Based on all the good news about the effects of being in awe, it's not surprising that the best good news of all is that people who are easily awed not only seem to enjoy their lives more but also to have longer ones than those who spend less time experiencing their eleventh emotion. Because being in the physiological state associated with awe can protect our cardiovascular system, reduce our chances of having a stroke,[12] enhance our immunity, increase our resilience when we are under stress, and help us be and feel more creatively adaptive and mindfully connected with life, it seems logical that these factors would help the frequently awe-inspired to live longer than those who are less so, and many well-done longitudinal studies have proven it.[13] In fact, the data is clear that one of the best things we can do for ourselves if we want to age well, live long, and die gently is to be in awe as often as possible.

There's another awe paradox that emerged from the SAI reports of awe. For the persons who were most often awe inspired, life was, in fact, usually longer than the lives of persons who reported less awe in their lives but often felt—as a 100-year-old frequently awed woman put it—"as if it went by so fast and was far too short." For the awe inspired, there just didn't seem to be enough time to embrace all that awe opened up in the consciousness of those who spent many of their days living in the state of their eleventh emotion. It seems that a life full of the awe of understanding will always end with more questions than answers and with a sense that there is much consciousness expanding left undone and so much more that could have inspired awe. I noticed in my interviews of those who were dying with me in the cancer unit that one unavoidable price of a life without awe was an intensification of the natural despair that life could have somehow been lived more fully.

Of course, if we're hurrying through our life, going through the motions without a lot of emotion, life can also seem to be flying by with never enough time to do what we really wish we could do. However, the often-awed weren't bothered by not having enough time to get things done. They were motivated by the need to become more fully aware of what they were doing now.

As if they had no control of their lives or the attention they could have invested in it, persons suffering from languishing complained about their lack of time while remaining in the mad dash on the hedonistic treadmill as if they had no way to get off. They sometimes self-rewarded their busy languishing by granting themselves temporary psychological leaves of absence from the rat race. As if they had no "middle gear," some languishers used their vacation to "totally crash" and sleep on the beach while others even geared up by engaging in "power vacations" that were as intense as their work, but these brief respites often ended up leaving them in a state of post-vacation fatigue.

IN AWE OF PAIN

One of the most significant findings from my own study of awe was its impact on pain, and other researchers are now confirming that the physical and emotional characteristics of awe may help reduce or at least help us manage and even learn from our pain.[14] Because some of my interviews were conducted on the oncology unit with my fellow cancer patients who, like me, were suffering excruciating daily and nightly pain, I wondered what effect awe might have on pain. What I learned caused me to be in awe of awe's pain-managing potential.

When I experienced my own pain from stage IV lymphoma and the related chemotherapy, whole-body radiation, and bone marrow transplant, it often seemed that there was nothing that reduced it. The advice from popular psychology was to "get my mind off it" and "try to visualize pleasant thoughts," but I discovered that, at least in my case, I didn't have many pleasant thoughts to visualize and trying to do so caused me more stress and made my pain worse. What I finally did was what the awe-inspired cancer patients told me they did; I tried to focus intensely on my pain and put it into a larger context.

You have read that awe is a wonderfully intense mixture of wonder and fear inspired by encountering something vast that stretches the imagination and current way of thinking. We don't just feel "in awe" of good things. Sometimes a horrible tragedy can result in us feeling in awe of what transpired, even though—and sometimes because—it was so uniquely terrible. We can't go on thinking and feeling as we did. The world calls us out to face its mysterious remarkable chaos, and we are forever at least a little less self-focused. The rational fear of real harm is at least a little diminished or crowded out by the presence of awe's nonrational fear related to much more abstract issues such as mortality and the meaning of life and death. It is in these ways that being in awe can help us not only survive, but also be transformed by trauma. This may be why those of us who have known great suffering feel that our greatest strengths have often been forged in the crucible of adversity.[15]

Of course awe doesn't alter the reality of pain, but it provides a sense of meaning and comprehensibility that provides a degree of manageability. The pain of cancer was certainly horrendous, but by focusing on it instead of bracing myself until it would go away, something surprising happened. It took on less local and more cosmic proportions, and I felt as much in awe of it as I was in dread. I still hurt and I don't want anyone reading these words to think that I'm implying that the pain she or he is feeling is not real, severe, and disruptive to daily life, but at least for me and many of my fellow cancer patients, my mind, and perhaps my soul, suddenly had a context that transcended the limits of the pain. I still had pain, but it didn't have me as much as it did before I was in awe of it. At least to some degree, I could flourish again even in the face of impending death and chronic pain.

For instance, I began to have thoughts about such issues as why pain does exist, what it is supposed to teach us, and why we have to have it. I had fewer thoughts of "why me?" and "when will it end?" I began to feel more alive and alert than I felt before I became deathly ill, and being in understanding awe of my pain seemed to soothe and comfort me as I came to feel my body's healing strength at work. I could, at least I thought I could, feel my immune system doing battle on my behalf, and I felt the same energy I felt from my young son Scott when he was fighting for his new life. I was equally in awe as Scott stood at the end of my bed in a surgical mask to protect me from infection, and that he was now saving my life as I had helped to save his. I've always found one of the greatest sources of awe is the power of loving bond between parent and child, and when that bond is intensified by the threat of death, the awe becomes even more profound.

Over time, the physical pain did seem to reduce, but not by a lot. It came back often, but I was no longer at war with it. In a way I still don't understand, I seemed to forgive my pain and came to understand that it was only doing what it had to do and the only thing it could do. My pain became less an enemy than a sign of life's struggle for itself. It was still disrupting my life, but it no longer controlled it. I had a context in which to come to grips with my pain and something to think and reflect about and not just try to reduce.

FROM LANGUISHING TO FLOURISHING

The awe response is one of the most powerful ways in which we move from languishing to flourishing, defined by psychologists as living at the optimum range of human functioning no matter what is happening to us.[16] Psychology has long taught us that "being happy" is one sign of health and well-being, but new research in the field of positive psychology goes further to suggest that intentionally focusing on, and putting ourselves in, situations that bring out intensely transformative emotions of all kinds relating to our real life produces physical and mental health.[17]

University of Michigan professor of psychology Barbara Fredrickson is a leading researcher in the field of positive psychology. She has proposed what she calls the "broaden and build" theory of human emotion. She asserts that our positive emotions evolved as psychological adaptations that increased our ancestors' odds of survival and reproduction. Unlike negative emotions that help us survive by the fight-or-flight principle, Frederickson's theory holds that it is our positive emotions that widen the array of our thoughts and actions and increase our behavioral flexibility. It is awe's capacity to help us "broaden and build" our consciousness that makes it the powerful eleventh emotion that it is.

The "broadening" that Fredrickson refers to is the new way of thinking and seeing the world that being in awe can facilitate. Broadening is forming a wider and more accurate view of the world and, as Fredrickson puts it, "This greater knowledge becomes a lasting personal resource," a process related to the mental accommodation inspired by the awe response.[18] Based on the SAI reports, I would add only that it's not just greater knowledge but coming up with better and deeper questions that are a major part of that resource.

The resourcefulness in dealing with their pain that came in part from being able to be at least as much in awe as in total fear of it was an earmark of the cancer patients I interviewed about their awe response. Despite their extreme distress, they had a blend of both positive and negative emotions that tilted toward—but not too much toward—the positive, what I call the "flourishing factor." With a blend of the energy of positive emotions and the necessary negativity to fully understand and cope with the crisis at hand, they were living in a world broadened by their capacity to be awed.

A NECESSARY NEGATIVITY

Although our negative emotions are as much a part of experiencing a meaningful, fully engaged life filled with awe, they can become toxic if our positive feelings don't outnumber them. Awe can frighten and bring us down us as much as it thrills and uplifts us because it often elicits the sadness, anger, fear, shame, and other negative feelings that come with awe's deepened awareness of life's brevity or how much we and others are squandering our gift of life or damaging the sources of that life. Without our negative emotions, we can't feel the full brunt and range of our eleventh emotion that leads to the drive for more understanding.

If we accept and confront our negative feelings, we can transform some of our anxiety into a facilitating and not just a debilitating state. Despite the current positivity zeitgeist of self-help psychology and its emphasis on thoughtless optimism often divorced from real life, awe can help us go beyond the oversimplified idea that being happy and up is always good and is something for which we must strive, and being sad or down is always bad and something we should avoid at all costs. As one of the SAI participants said, "I think people who try to be happy all the time put in an awful lot of energy fooling themselves, and they're either phony or stupid. That's just not life." While he was probably overstating the point, author Raymond Aron seemed to agree with my SAI respondent when he wrote, "What passes for optimism is most often the effect of an intellectual error."[19]

The evil in the world is dark, vague, enormous, and menacing—all characteristics of what inspires our awe response. Living our life in the pious pretense that evil either doesn't exist or that it must be denied through preservative positivity is like trying to be in awe of a massive tornado without acknowledging its deadly force. People who flourish do so with full experience of both the dark and light sides of life.

Without necessary negativity, we can become superstitiously fixed in our ways. In our effort to keep negativity out of our lives, it paradoxically subverts and controls life. We become uncreative and inflexible, and can lose our ability to adapt and grow. Some researchers call this "appropriate negativity," the kind that offers us useful, rational feedback for at least a limited time about the effects of what we do and how life operates. We can enhance our chance to flourish and to be in the awe that comes with that state by avoiding both global or gratuitous positivity or negativity.[20]

Our negative emotions aren't useless, nor should they always be avoided at all costs. Sometimes, anger is appropriate, and taking action related to it is necessary. We need to feel fear when we are really under threat, and sadness is essential when terribly unfair things happen. Anger can intimidate enemies and energize us when we need to fight. Looking sad and forlorn can draw the social attention and emotional comfort we need. Without our inborn negative emotions, we can become rigid and unresponsive, and fail to take necessary protective and creative actions when necessary.

Life isn't wonderful. It just is, and that's more than enough to inspire awe. Our negative feelings are as essential as our positive ones; however, being in awe usually leads to the best part of being alive, a sense of sincere elation with life that includes a blend of excited approach and avoidance. We need our negativity in some measure in order to experience a full-fledged awe response made up of intense "approach" feelings mixed with a dash of the avoidance system and the fear that it induces. Being in awe is a lot of things, but never boring. It's not being a positive or negative thinker, but it is "being" and thinking about being to the fullest extent humanly possible.

Of all our emotions, awe is most unique in its powerful blend of the influences of our approach-avoidance system. One of my interviewees, a forty-year-old engineer, provided an example of the role of our negative emotions in the awe response. He said, "I was immediately in awe when I saw that magnificent ship. It took my breath away, I gasped, and it felt like my heart would beat right out of my chest. I felt like a tiny dot compared to it and it loomed over me as I stood near it. What a marvel of engineering it was, the largest cruise ship ever built, and I could only imagine the planning that went into it. But then I began to feel this sudden rush of fear that intensified my awe. I was literally shaking. I thought of how many people were sailing on it and what would happen if it sank. Thousands were having so much fun on it, but they were really very vulnerable on it. It suddenly seemed too big for me to feel safe, but that was part of what made it so awesome to me. It was hissing and groaning like a mechanical monster. I've never been on a cruise ship, and I wanted to get right on this one [approach] but at the same time I recoiled from it [avoidance]. My wife said I just gazed and gazed at it and kept saying 'God damn it.' I'm still in awe of that ship when I think about it, and it made me feel in awe of what human engineering can do and the dangers it can create by doing it, but I don't know if I can ever get past my fear of how awesomely huge it is and how small and helpless I feel in comparison to it." My interviews of those who have known awe often contained the kind of fear and fascination reaction described by this elated but alarmed engineer, but there are often bonus positive emotions that can eventually come with reflection about what awes us, and that can be well worth the emotional and analytical disruption awe imposes on us.

Always trying to stay positive prevents us from learning important lessons from the negative aspects of living, and artificial happiness divorced from the real elements of life can cause us to fail to recognize and make necessary life changes. Feigning a positive attitude does little to facilitate a flourishing life, and the people I interviewed who were frequently in awe were not always upbeat and cheerful, but their tilt toward positivity always seemed appropriate, genuine, and real. The fake smile of the "always up" person, totally remote from real circumstances, is not only disingenuous, but studies of the brain show that forced smiling is actually associated with the region of the brain from which our negative emotions emanate.[21] There is even some new evidence that feigned, forced, and trivial positivity relates to activation in parts of the brain related to abnormal heart function.[22] Trying to "put on a happy face" might put pressure on our hearts.

As in most things in life, flourishing is a matter of balance, but not perfect balance. We need to lean a little more toward our positive feelings than our negative ones, while not being falsely positive. Like a sailboat at good speed, we need to tilt safely toward one side to catch the full force of the wind, and being in awe is the perfect state for working toward this special kind of "almost" balanced. Its blend of dread and delight offers the challenge of feeling positive with just the right touch of cautious negativity to make life excitingly real.

THE FLOURISHING FACTOR

Barbara Fredrickson and her colleagues have shown that the ratio of at least 2.9 positive emotions for every one negative one seems to be a key number. Why that number seems to be the key measure relates to some complex mathematical calculations that are in turn related to something called "sensitive dependence on initial conditions," a reference to the *butterfly effect* of chaos theory, through which the flapping of a butterfly's wings in one location can eventually result in a wind storm at another.[23] That's how awe seems to work. It's the initial consciousness condition at one moment in our lives, to which our entire lives at later moments is sensitive. A little of our eleventh emotion, including its positive and negative elements, can go a very long way.

Fredrickson's research has also shown that flourishing begins to disintegrate when the ratio of positive feelings to negative exceeds 11.6. This degree of positivity seems to be insincere at best or delusional and maladaptive at worst. Fredrickson's numbers derive from an experiment in which subjects logged on to a website to report the extent to which they felt each of twenty emotions in the past twenty-four hours.[24] By comparing the ratio of positive to negative emotions experienced with a measure of the degree to which the participants were flourishing in a fully engaged and meaningful life, the researchers established the ratio of almost 3 to 1 in favor of the number of positive emotions to be essential for flourishing, but not to exceed 12 to 1.

Based on Fredrickson's and other positive psychologists' work, I designed my own "Flourishing Factor Test" for use in my study of awe and, sure enough, the more a respondent said she or he understood, could describe, and experienced awe as I have defined it in this book, the closer that person was to the magic 2.9 ratio of positive to negative emotions. I invite you to take the Flourishing Factor Test to determine whether you're sailing through your life with the emotional list to be more easily awed by, and flourish through, whatever storms might lie ahead.

The Flourishing Factor Test

Use the following scale to score yourself on the following items.

0 = Not at all

1 = A little bit

2 = Moderately

3 = A lot

4 = Extremely

In the last twenty-four hours, to what extent have you experienced the following positive emotions?

1. ____Amusement *(hard laughter)*

2. ____Fascination *(amazed wonder)*

3. ____Compassion *(heartfelt sympathy)*

4. ____Contentment *(calm gratification)*

5. ____Gratitude *(profound appreciation)*

6. ____Hope *(eager anticipation)*

7. ____Serenity *(quiet calmness)*

8. ____Joy *(gleeful delight)*

9. ____Love *(selfless devotion)*

10. ____Pride *(basking in deserved praise)*

11. ____Zeal *(eager enthusiasm)*

12. ____Sexual desire *(physical attraction)*

____Total Positive Emotions

In the last twenty-four hours, to what extent have you experienced the following negative emotions?

1. ____Anger

2. ____Contempt

3. ____Frustration

4. ____Disgust

5. ____Embarrassment

6. ____Worry or fear

7. ____Guilt

8. ____Sadness

9. ____Shame

10. ____Loneliness

11. ____Panic or helplessness

12. ____Negative surprise

_____**Total Negative Emotions**

Divide the total from the positive column ____ by the number in the negative column _____ =

_____Your Flourishing Factor

If your Flourishing Factor is somewhere around 3 or so, you are more likely to benefit from the understanding kind of awe. But be warned. Most of how positive or negative (or optimistic or pessimistic) you tend to be is due to your genes and not your success or failure at being a positive thinker. By thinking about and being aware of your score, you might be able to tilt yourself a little more toward the positive or negative, but not by much.

Natural-born optimists and pessimists both can experience awe in their own unique ways, but not by trying to be what they can't be or by trying to live their lives trying to comply with some special secret about the power of positive thinking to bring them the life they desire. Awe isn't a matter of finally realizing the life you've always wanted. It's a matter of being more fully and reflectively aware of the sacred gift of having a life and being granted the privilege to experience all it offers from its highest peaks to its lowest valleys. As one SAI respondent said, "You can't be in awe of how great life is unless you're also awed by how rotten it can be. Awe is becoming so intensely alive that it can be really terrifying and make you rethink everything."

7

ELATED BY LIFE

*"Gratitude bestows reverence, allowing us to encounter every-
day epiphanies, the transcendent moments of awe, that change
forever how we experience life and the world."*

— JOHN MILTON

IN SEARCH OF THE REMARKABLE

I went for the results of my annual physical today. More than fif-
teen years after I nearly died from cancer, and even though I've
been in wonderful health ever since, I still approach each of these
appointments with great trepidation. As the doctor sat thumbing
intently through the pages of my lab results in search of a negative
finding, he finally looked up and said, "Well, I don't see anything
remarkable here." Those words were barely out of my physician's
mouth before I felt the stirrings of the awe response.

Tears welled up in my eyes, and I felt chicken skin. As if it were
jumping for joy, my heart skipped several beats, and I felt a sense
of warmth radiating from my chest. I was mystified by the miracle
that continued in my life and felt a chill go down my spine as
something I don't understand made me grab immediately at my

right hip, the original site of my cancer. The rational dread of what could have gone wrong subsided, as did the irrational terror that any slight sign could mean cancer's return. Yet I felt awe's unique nonrational fear of the magnitude of what life can hold in store for us, how being so close to death brought me so much nearer to life, and how vulnerable I have felt since having come so close to nature's seemingly random power to kill or heal.

It's still almost impossible for me to imagine that, after being so close to death and having my body ravaged by chemotherapy, my body had done more than bounce back. It was even stronger than those of many men my age who had not been through the torture I had experienced. Then, without warning, I began to feel anger.

Nothing remarkable? I thought. *How could the doctor think or say that?* I had gone through stage IV lymphoma, two courses of intense chemotherapy that my oncologist called his "scorch-the-earth" approach to treatment, full-body radiation, three major surgeries, and a bone marrow transplant, and I had nearly died three times in intensive care, yet the numbers he was looking at said I was in perfect health. Throw in two detached retinas, several attacks of excruciatingly painful kidney stones, and a prolapsed mitral valve that causes the sensation of skipped beats, and every day without pain is quite remarkable to me.

As I had when I felt the life force growing in my newborn son despite the doctor's pessimistic doubts, I felt for the mysterious force that spared my life and his and restored my health. I felt strangely protective of nature and whatever mysterious processes were at work. It felt like my doctor had committed a blasphemy against my body and the sacred energy that gave it life and helped it heal.

How can he say "Nothing remarkable"? I kept asking myself, no longer paying much attention to what the doctor was saying about lowering my cholesterol, losing a few more pounds, and eating less fat. My wife and I always go to medical exams together, and I said to her, "Isn't the whole report he's reading amazing? Why isn't he astonished by the extraordinary miracle portrayed right before his eyes? Why doesn't he feel the awe I'm feeling at the magic my body has worked?"

My wife was in awe, too, but she has always been calmer and more forgiving than I, so she just smiled and patted my hand. "I'm sure he does," she said, and the doctor nodded in what seemed like compliant toleration of someone in awe of what the doctor saw every day.

Like most physicians, attorneys, teachers, and other professionals claiming to deal with our health and well-being, my doctor really spent most of his time looking and thinking about states of being unwell. Either by his training or a temperament preselected by his medical school admissions committee, he looked only for weakness, vulnerability, pathology, and what needed remediation, and that's certainly an important focus. But he seemed too distracted by what could be wrong to be in awe of the fact that—as long as we're breathing and alert—there has to be more right with us than wrong. Insurance companies don't cover the diagnosis of "remarkable," and my doctor didn't have the time to sit and celebrate nature's capacity to make his science look so good.

LANGUISHING LEARNERS

Like most of us influenced by the "bad trumps good" principle, my doctor was constantly on the lookout for trouble. Thinking that "good" is essentially only the absence of "bad" and that being healthy is being not sick, he was in pursuit of signs of something wrong. He had found nothing bad or, as I so ironically put it, "nothing too awful," so he believed he had no work to do and no role to play, other than to continue to help me prevent illness. This preventive mode is usually only proactive negativism, based on avoiding the worst more than maximizing the best. It may be that we're experiencing less awe in (and for) our lives than we might, because our constant focus on what's wrong and what can go wrong causes us to look right past what's wonderful.

I often ask the medical students, residents, and practicing physicians who attend my lectures to define a healthy person. Most of them struggle to give an answer, and when they do, it's usually based on the absence of something wrong rather than the presence of something right. One of my residents offered her definition of a healthy person as someone on whom we had not yet conducted enough tests. Many of my students find my question distracting to their already overburdened brains, consumed with memorizing or keeping up with all sorts of negative scenarios and symptoms that they dare not miss. If they hadn't already lost it, they were having their awe drummed out of them by the constant bombardment of numbers and labels.

When I tell them my definition of a healthy person, they seem to doubt my sanity. When I say a healthy person is someone who experiences awe for the life he or she has and is flourishing with others regardless of symptoms, pain, and test scores, the reaction is one of polite acknowledgment as they wait for me to get back to "real medicine." For many students, medicine is the science of preventing death, not celebrating life and all that it gives us, both bad and good.

What seems to draw the attention of my students most are the worst and most gross diseases. When they say they have a "really interesting case," they mean they've stumbled on something very serious, bad, and complex. I, too, am awed by nature's dark side, and I don't want to discourage my students' awe for how horrendously wrong things can go. As awe nearly always does, it energizes, fascinates, and motivates them to learn. However, many of my students are already enslaved to an almost exclusive paranoia that their whole careers could end because they've missed something really bad. There are few malpractice lawsuits brought against doctors for failing to recognize how perfectly healthy someone is, but there are plenty because a physician mistreats or fails to identify something bad.

THE POWER OF BAD

Because of the dominant power of bad and the evolutional imperative of our ever-ready quick and intense reaction to it, we aren't typically in a pre-awe state, ready to be easily elated by the good life has to offer. For example, it's a wonderful feeling when you pull the handle on the slot machine and change rattles out, but studies show that the pleasure of winning money is far outweighed by the lingering bad feelings of losing it.[1] When asked what it would take to form a more positive view of a murderer's character, respondents said it would take at least twenty-five heroic, life-saving acts to even soften their view toward, or expand their understanding of, someone who took someone else's life.[2] Thinking we've been feeling great is quickly overwhelmed when a problem-focused physician finally finds "something remarkable" at an annual physical and warns us about a bad number or test result.

As Ben Franklin pointed out, "We are not so sensible of the greatest Health as of the least Sickness."[3] A bunch of good numbers
reported by your doctor are quickly and easily outweighed by one
"bad" one, and people tend to talk in much more detail about their
various aches and pains than they do about the specifics of "feeling fine."

The "bad trumps good" principle is one of the major obstacles to a
more awe-inspired life, not because of the negative feelings that
can come with it, but because it can make us more chronically
defensive against trouble than open to the tremendous. However,
by being aware of the evolutional dominant power of "bad," we can
put in the extra effort to look a little harder for what is good and
even remarkable. As a result, we might become more often in awe
of the miracle of those rare days when things are "just okay."
Those who learn to be in awe of the ordinary magic behind a day
that is "just okay" have far fewer regrets than those who waste
their time looking for trouble and hoping for more happiness. We
don't have to wait to be awed only by life's big deals. There's plenty
within the grace of everyday living that is awe inspiring, and those
who find that kind of awe for the ordinary in their lives are less
likely to have their lives totally dictated by the "bad trumps good"
principle.

POLLYANNA

Whenever I lecture about the awe response, use the flowery language necessary for describing it or encourage my audiences to be
in awe even of the "bad trumps good" principle, recognize how it
helps us survive and thrive, and be more vigilant for what is best

about life, someone accuses me of being a psychological Pollyanna.
They say I'm "out of touch" with reality and offering false and
unrealistic encouragement to people living in a harsh and dangerous world, and that I'm only setting them up for disappointment.
Actually I tend to be a pessimist by nature and have to work constantly to overcome my own propensity to comply with my natural bent toward the bad. My score on the Flourishing Factor Test
in Chapter 6 is below the key 2.9 ratio, and I'm a natural-born
negative thinker. Trained as a pre–positive psychology clinical psychologist to diagnose disease, nearly dying of cancer, and being the
father of two sons with severe impairments, I know only too well
the prevalence of what is bad in the world and the importance of
being clearly aware of and responding realistically and construc-
tively to it. I've also learned, however, that tilting at least a little
more toward the good emotions as described in Chapter 6 is also
essential to avoiding languishing and to being able to flourish, no
matter what life offers.

Pollyanna was the name of the little girl who was the main character in the 1913 novel of the same name by Eleanor Porter, but
unlike the current popular image of someone we call a
"Pollyanna," she was not at all a starry-eyed, ignorant optimist
who was out of touch with the real facts of life and its terrible
downsides. She was wise far beyond her years and saw the bad in
the world perhaps even more clearly than many others. Had she
taken the Flourishing Factor Test from Chapter 6, I suspect her
score might have been the 2.9 ratio and not much higher. She was
able to find enough good in most situations to learn but also
remain just negative enough to be realistic—and even forgiving
of—the wrongs she encountered.

Instead of being dominated by the "bad trumps good" principle,
Pollyanna was able to find some gladness in her life no matter what

she encountered. She could still be in awe of life even when—and sometimes because—things went badly. She was much more a deep thinker than just a positive one. Likewise we often have to go deeply, think not only with our heads but with our hearts, and feel with our entire bodies in order to prevent our evolutionary "bad" preset from dominating our life and lowering the Flourishing Factor score far below the 2.9 ratio.

THE TWELVE ELATIONS

Based on the reports of those frequently awed, I present in the following sections how the respondents in the SAI tend to experience the twelve positive emotions from the Flourishing Factor Test in Chapter 6. I describe them in detail here because, until recently, psychology has focused more on our negative emotions than our extraordinary positive states. However, even when things were bleak, and in the aftermath of the understanding kind of awe, the participants in my study almost universally described some degree of the following emotions. I call them *elations* not because they're all experienced as exclusively happy emotions, but because they represent awe's unique blend of intense, reflective, and confusing jubilation about being fully alive in the aftermath of both the best and worst that happen to us. It's not that awe makes us feel elated with what we experience, but that it gives a strange euphoria of feeling more alive than we ever imagined we could, even if something bad makes us also feel that life is just too overwhelmingly intense to live.

Amusement

To be amused is to feel diverted and distracted from our usual conscious state and to feel entertained by the experience. My SAI interviews indicate that the more awe people have in their lives, the more likely they will have a good sense of humor, so awe and amusement seem to go hand in hand.

The expression "sense of humor" was first used in England in the 1840s but wasn't considered to be a personality trait until the 1870s.[4] People easily awed are also (as often described by their spouses) "easily amused." One spouse of a woman who seemed repeatedly in the throes of the eleventh emotion said she was "too easily tickled" and that made their friends "think she's a little on the weird side and a little childish." It's this childlike, full engagement and reaction to life that constitutes "un-*adult*-erated" awe.

The easily awed report experiencing "fits" of uncontrollable laughter, sometimes even when they say that what was inspiring their awe "wasn't really funny at all." As if they've been specially let in on some cosmic joke, their laughter is made even more uncontrollable when asked by someone who's not in on the joke, "What's so funny?"

There is a little-known but fascinating field called literary ecology that studies lessons found in great literary works relating to the evolution of human emotions. Literary ecologists have discovered that comedy isn't always farcical or funny, and humor can be a part of both the comic and tragic experience. Laughter and crying are not totally discrete responses, but as those who laugh so hard they cry or cry so hard they laugh will tell you, they exist along a continuum. The frequently awed slide easily back and forth along that continuum and right past those caught languishing somewhere in between.

I've seldom interviewed someone who laughed easily, often, and hard who didn't also cry the same way, but I have interviewed persons who cry easily yet don't laugh easily, often, and hard. The "bad trumps good" principle permeates all aspects of our emotional lives, but being open to the awe response can help decrease bad's power just enough to allow a little more good to tip the scales away from languishing, toward flourishing. Awe can make us laugh at ourselves when it exposes the absurdity of our illusion of self-importance and control, make us feel silly in comparison to its grandness, and humble us when it makes us realize that we aren't the center of the world.

The easily awed develop an awe-filled attitude. They have a propensity for the preposterous and a lowered threshold for responding intensely to novelty. However we perceive the world, awe can quickly change our views. If we can learn from our awe to be more easily amused about our certainty about how the world should or does work, we can stay off our pedestals and get on with life instead of constantly trying to control it or somehow be above its mysterious powers.

Literary ecologist Dr. Joseph Meeker writes, "Comedy is more an attitude toward life and the self, and people in awe are undergoing major changes in both of these processes."[5] Another definition of awe is that it is a sudden change of attitude about ourselves and how we've been engaging in the world, and it is in this sense that the frequently awed are easily amused.

I suspect that the frequently aweds' attributes of being easily amused and experiencing uncontrollable laughter derive from the sudden and overwhelming awareness of our inability to explain, with our usually linear rationale, the cosmic incongruities that keep influencing our existence. It seems to be a laughter of relief at the realization that we're all in this chaotic comedy of life together. It's elicited by the sudden awareness that nature has honored us by deciding to let us in on the long-standing joke, along with the idea that we're not nearly as smart, separate, or powerful as we think.

When we're awe inspired, we can't possibly take ourselves seriously in the face of the sobering magnificence we are encountering. As author Daniel Wickberg points out, our sense of humor is stimulated because we find "relief or release in self-abnegation," and "transcend a narrow rationality of circumscribed self-interest," and this seems to be another way of defining our eleventh emotion.[6]

A federal court judge was visiting Hawaii for a meeting at which I was lecturing. She was mentally and socially rigid, formal, and very judgelike when I met her, but when I asked her to describe a time she was in awe, she said, "I went to the top of Haleakala on Maui yesterday morning at sunrise. I was in total awe, and for some bizarre reason, I began to laugh so hard tears rolled from my eyes. People must have thought I was out of my mind, but I had no regard for how I looked to others and really no sense of myself. It was a frightened kind of laughing that a child might do. What I was experiencing was so overwhelming. It was a kind of laughing that a group does when a comedian points out something about our shared flawed humanness. It's like relief laughing, because you don't know what else to say or do."

Fascination

Awe is the embodiment of feeling highly interested, but it is much more than that. The sense of fascination experienced with our eleventh emotion is one of total raptness and being willingly taken

in by the magic right before our eyes. It's like the enthralled inno-
cence of a child repeatedly fooled by his uncle pretending to "take
his nose" by touching it and then showing it to him with his thumb
sticking out between his first two fingers.

I saw a little girl at the beach recently. She had been running and
screaming in delight but stopped suddenly to pick up a seashell.
She exclaimed, "Oh! Oh! Oh!" and sat down to look at it, smell it,
taste it, and listen to it. She became oblivious to all the noise and
hubbub around her and fell into complete awe of that tiny token
of the vast ocean that all the adults were looking at. She must have
played with the shell for several minutes before she stood up,
kissed it, and lovingly put it back exactly where she had found it.
She ran off to play, stopped, waved back at the shell, and splashed
into the waves to see her impatient mother yelling, "What in the
world were you doing?" What she was doing was enjoying the
throes of awe's profound fascination.

Compassion

Compassion is, literally, heartfelt sympathy. It's a sensation you
first feel primarily in your chest, with warmth spreading out to
your entire body. When we're in awe, we fall into a state of profound caring for and about what or who awes us. *Passion* literally
means "to suffer," and when we're in awe, we are so emotionally
moved that it almost hurts.

Compassion means "to suffer with": to share the physical, emotional, and spiritual dimensions of the losses and crises in life. Awe
often inspires feelings related not only to the wonderful vastness of
nature but also to the pain we and others inflict on the world
through our selfish disregard. If only for a brief moment, it makes
us feel connected and profoundly responsible, and it brings out our

custodial instincts and focuses them onto the world. If we choose
to think longer and deeper about whatever inspires our awe, these
feelings of connection can become more intense and permanent.

"Flying over the Brazilian rain forest left me in such a total state
of awe I couldn't sleep that night." These were the words of an
executive taking part in a corporate reward trip. She continued,
"The tight green canopy seemed to go on forever beneath us, and
then I saw a few brown empty spaces littered with logs. The pilot
said there was a lot of logging going on and that many trees were
dying because of global warming. As we turned out over more
expansive greenery, I began to feel a pain in my chest. I thought I
was going to have a heart attack, but it was a slow, throbbing pain
like my heart was sobbing, and I began to cry. 'What have we
done? What are we doing? What are we doing to our paradise?
Why aren't we taking care of it?' These thoughts kept running
through my head, and the more I was in awe of the forest, the
more sadness I felt. It seemed like I was dying with the forest and
felt such deep compassion for it."

Contentment

Being in awe is also a feeling of being remarkably lucky, lucky to
be alive to experience whatever or whoever inspired our awe. Awe
can make us feel overwhelmingly gratified that we've been allowed,
however briefly, to even *have* a life no matter how good or bad it
seems at the moment. With a feeling that life's endless mysteries
have just been exposed to us, it's being able to say, "That's life!"
not with a sense of surrender, but with a feeling of recommitment
to keep trying to figure it out. One SAI respondent was a ninety-
two-year-old man I met fishing on the Lake Huron shore. He
looked upset, and I asked how he was feeling. His answer revealed
the sense of contentment someone experiencing their eleventh

emotion often reports. He said, "That's life. You get to go fishing, but you can't ever know what you're going to catch, so you might as well be content with being allowed to fish."

The combination of feeling amused, fascinated, and deeply compassionate all at the same time would not seem to lead to feelings of calmness and contentment, but that's what gives our eleventh emotion its unique power. It's full of perceptual paradoxes and serves as the consciousness catalyst for a host of conflicting emotions from both sides of the Flourishing Factor Test (see Chapter 6). As a result we feel elatedly gratified and, for at least a moment, off of the hedonistic treadmill and free of the search for more or better. We haven't found *the* good life, but we've realized a good one.

A friend on whose television show I had just appeared invited me on a tour of his remarkable home and to spend the night. It was a huge mansion, stunning in both size and style. As we walked outside the next morning to wait for his chauffeur to take us to the studio, the sun was just coming up, and the dew was glistening off tips of huge old pines in the front yard that had been there long before the new home and would be there long after. My host walked to one of the trees, gently touched a branch, took a sample of the dew, and placed it on his tongue. I could see tears in his eyes as I walked to join him. He turned to me and said, "Awesome, isn't it? I feel so fulfilled when I'm out here and that all I've done has been worth it. I feel so settled, peaceful, and content to be away from all the crap and hassles, like nature is giving me a little hug to say 'nice going.' It's this place—not the huge house—that touches my heart." There were tears in his eyes when he looked back over his shoulder as we drove away, and he said, "I still taste the dew and smell that pine. In a way, it makes me feel like that house shouldn't even be here. The pines would be enough."

Gratitude

"Thanks a lot." How many times a day do we say those words, and how many times do we really feel them in our hearts and experience the wonder, thankfulness, and appreciation for life? Awe inspires deep gratitude by causing us to, as psychologist Abraham Maslow wrote, "appreciate again and again, freshly and naively, the basic goods of life with awe, pleasure, wonder, and even ecstasy, however stale these experiences may have become to others."[7] That's what awe does; it turns what has become stale into something fresh and what we have allowed to go neglected to feel new again.

When we're in awe, we experience a sense of sincere appreciation being drawn out of us. Author Gregg Easterbrook describes this primal feeling of gratitude toward those who lived before us to give us our chance to live as we do. He says this debt is to the "99 percent of Homo sapiens ever to have existed who possessed less and knew less and died much younger" than we do and to the "hundreds of generations who came before us [who] lived dire, short lives, in deprivation or hunger, in ignorance or under oppression or during war" and who at least in some measure did so in order that we might be able to live with such abundance and the freedom to savor it.[8]

Awe is an overwhelming feeling of deep gratitude not just for an object, place, person, or idea but for what the existence of these things means. As one Hawaiian elder put it as she looked out at a triple rainbow arching over the deep blue ocean, "It's at times like this I feel I have to thank God for allowing me to live awhile on his land. I want to give my most sincere thanks to my ancestors for making this home for me to visit. I wish I could hug them and tell them how much I value what they've given me."

Hope

Because whatever awes us expands our consciousness and dilates our imagination, being in awe can make us feel and think that anything is possible. It tantalizes and sometimes frightens us with nature's infinite chaotic manifestations, yet makes us eagerly anticipate what future mysteries might await us.

The hope associated with being in awe is not the kind that leads us to sacrifice this moment by looking forward to a better one later. It's not feeling that life will get better but that life couldn't be any better. It's a mindful hope that doesn't separate things into distinct categories of good and bad but instead sees good and bad in everything.[9] Instead of being the kind of hope we're supposed to have so we can be motivated to achieve our goals, it is hope inspired by a suddenly deepened faith that, no matter what we do or fail to do, there is always something remarkable about life just waiting for us to discover. It's the kind of hope we can experience only if we are totally alert and awake in the present moment and not trying desperately to find something better about tomorrow.

A fellow cancer patient who was on the unit with me visited Hawaii. She had experienced several relapses and was due for a checkup when she returned to the mainland. With her bald head covered with a scarf and her entire body covered in white clothing to prevent her weakened skin from being destroyed by the sun, she was slouched over the railing watching the dolphins playing with their handlers. She was so awed by her first dolphin sighting that she didn't respond to my greeting, so I stood quietly and waited to get her attention.

After several minutes, the frail woman looked up at me over the floral surgical mask moistened by her tears. "Awesome, just awesome," she said in a whisper. "I wish I could have felt their splashes.

I've never seen anything like it, and you know what? It really inspires a different kind of hope in me, like there's so much to life right now that isn't touched by my cancer and never will be. All the ugliness of this damned disease is overwhelmed by those happy beasts, and they make me stronger."

Serenity

It may not seem that serenity and elation go together, but there's a unique kind of serenity in those who have known and learned from awe. It's a kind of excited calmness, meaning that the person is not the model of a still and composed guru but rather of someone who emits a sense of being in a state of energetic peace with and reflection about the world and who is able to sustain and feel energized by that "peace through reflection," during both good and bad times.[10] Something about the awe-inspiring experience transforms us from anxious striving to a deeper developed sensitivity to "something much more." Those who ceaselessly strive (and who notice how the awe-inspired view life) covet it as a state of comfort, a sense of being in the world that they would like to experience. As one SAI respondent put it, "I'm stressed when I'm in awe, but I'm being stressed by the right thing at the right time. I guess you could say that I'm at peace with the idea that life doesn't ever allow you to be at peace for very long."

The post-awe version of serenity is not one associated only with being in a peaceful and calm place in which we can totally relax. It is a sense of daily being that persists no matter where we are, not a reaction that happens when we happen to be in a pristine and perfect environment.

One of the healthiest things we can do for ourselves is get a sound, sustained sleep. Those who have known regular awe in their lives tend to have mastered that skill. The easily awed are essentially "one thought" people, who don't allow their brains to dart around from idea to idea. Perhaps because of this more settled brain, they also tend to be sound sleepers. Rather than engaging in a series of random pre-sleep thoughts, they often focus on only one idea that was related to one of their awe experiences. They report sometimes experiencing awe even in their dreams.

Research shows that persons who switch between many thoughts before sleep tend to have difficulty getting to and staying asleep. These "pre-sleep thought scanners" also tend to be 25 percent less satisfied with their lives than sounder sleepers who did less random thinking before bed.[11] That's also one reason that watching television before bed and exposing ourselves to hundreds of flickering images and thoughts can make it more difficult to fall asleep. A fast-thinking brain, flitting back and forth, is a distracted brain, but our eleventh emotion happens when we are able to slow down our thinking, stop our incessant mental multitasking, and focus on one thought long enough to fully engage in something that inspires awe.

A thirty-six-year-old female hospice nurse shared her example of the serenity that comes from being in awe of life. She said, "I think the serenity that has come over me since I was in awe of watching a woman dying is different than most people mean when they use the word. I had worked with this lady for three years, and she was on the verge of death the entire time. I worked with her at our hospice. She struggled every day just to breathe. I really thought she'd have a pretty hard time passing like most of our COPD (chronic obstructive pulmonary disease) patients, but when she died and I sat beside her, holding her hand, she just passed quietly. I was in awe of what was happening, and my heart began to skip beats. She was alive one second, and her life force was just gone the next, with no struggle at all. I sat for several minutes crying and looking at her. It was frightening in some ways. Death is such a final mystery. There was some medical turmoil all around us at the moment of her death, but it was all so strangely wonderful and comforting at the same time. I don't know where her life energy went at that precise moment, but it's somewhere still, maybe all around us and maybe in me, and that's what I find so awe inspiring about it all. I think of that terrible, wonderful, quiet moment, and it focuses and comforts my mind. Other silly thoughts can't get in at those times, just that one. It gives me something to ponder, and it settles my soul before I sleep."

After a major life event like being hospitalized for a serious illness or having a heart attack, many people say they are going to find the serenity in life they realize they've missed by "reevaluating my life" and "resetting my priorities," but my interviews indicate that they seldom do this for very long. It's become a kind of urban legend that a major life setback changes us forever and that we go through a post-trauma born-again experience. Instead I've found that this seldom occurs as often as we're told it does or lasts as long as we assume. The awe of understanding is a long, time-consuming, gut-wrenching process that takes place within a person's life system, not just within the person. It's a process that demands more than an impulsive decision to "make some changes." The serenity so many of us in this hectic world seek isn't a matter of cutting back, following the prescribed steps in a self-help book, or making more time to enjoy life. It's to be found in stopping to reflect a very long time about three questions awe can invite us to think about: What's the most important thing to do? When should we do it? And with whom?

Joy

In his book *Human Nature Explored,* author George Mandler reported that when he asked people to list the characteristics of human nature, the list included greed, competition, ambition,

jealousy, violence, aggression, intelligence, and joy.[12] Reflecting
the Awe Deficiency Disorder that underlies our culture's epidemic
of languishing, Mandler writes of his findings, "It is only after some
probing that the positive side of human nature emerges in everyday discourse."[13] Assuming our "intelligence" is not in itself an
emotion, that leaves only the last in Mandler's list—"joy"—as a
positive natural human trait, but our eleventh emotion may help
balance things out by maximizing joy and helping us probe for the
positive side of our human nature and nature itself.

The joy associated with the awe response is much more than what
brightens a gloomy day. Unlike the joy we might report when we
win a game or experience a pleasant surprise, awe's joy is not transient, is never just about us, and doesn't leave us longing for more
of itself. Awe is so powerful that, at least for awhile, a little is more
than enough. It has a major life impact and is far more than a grat-
ifying by-product of something we did or purchased. It leads to the
realization that whatever success is, it's in the doing rather than in
the final accomplishment. It's realizing that joy is not an end state
but a process and a way of thinking about life and what we're doing,
rather than an emotional reward for having finally gotten there.

The unique joy that comes with awe not only feels good because it
makes us feel so much more alive, but also changes how easy it
becomes to feel good in the future. Based on the reports from the
SAI participants, the joy they felt when awed so transformed them
that it increased what psychologist Paul Meehl called our "hedonic
capacity," our inborn propensity to either be easy or more difficult
to please."[14] Perhaps because it also awakens us to how horrible life
can be, awe's power can also make us more alert to the pleasures life
offers, so that we may more easily experience them again and again.

Something about awe's combination of the experience of puzzling vastness, the nonrational fear, the "thoughts" and feelings coming from the heart and gut, and the diminished sense of self lowers our thrill threshold while at the same time raising our opinion of humankind, our *menschenbild* or general view of the nature of human beings. If we're in awe enough and accommodate its lessons, awe can result in an enhanced pride in humankind and its capacity for doing good, no matter how often it seems to do so badly. Just watching someone behaving altruistically can cause us to feel awe's warmth in our chests and goose bumps on our skin.

A SAI respondent described the joy that her awe brought her as she reacted to a natural phenomenon. She said, "Feeling the deadly cold, crystal-clear glacier water in the Canadian Rockies was scary but so awesome. My whole idea of what cold is changed. I wanted to take off all my clothes and jump in, but at least I dangled my toes in the water for a few seconds. I swear they would have frozen stiff if I left them in, but some guy walking by said so kindly that I should be very careful not to hurt myself and that water could do real damage. He didn't even know me, and he took the time to warn me. I don't know if my goose bumps were from the water or from his simple, kind gesture to a complete stranger. I began to giggle, and I felt such joy that I got up and hugged my husband and kids. Whether they knew it or not, everything and everyone around me suddenly seemed part of the whole experience. I felt like I suddenly loved everyone for taking the time to come to this magical place. It was like being given the perfect gift you never knew you wanted so much. I would like to feel that kind of joy again but not too soon, because it left me totally drained and exhausted."

Love

Of all the words used by persons reflecting back on their awe response, the word *love*—or at least phrases describing a profound loving feeling—was the one most often used. It's one of the most frequently used words in the English language and has the highest frequency of any word used in Bartlett's *Familiar Quotations*.[15] Awe's diminished sense of self in favor of a feeling of a caring, intimate connection is one of the eleventh emotion's most distinguishing and elating characteristics.

An attorney working for an environmental group was a participant in the SAI. Her report of her own awe response illustrates not only how love is associated with our eleventh emotion but how it can be inspired both by wonderful and terrible things. She described her feelings of love when she was awed by witnessing a polar bear trying to play with her three cubs.

"Oh, my God, don't make me talk about this," she said, grabbing instinctively for a tissue. Tears rolled down her cheeks even before she went into her description of her awe response, and she patted her chest to, as she put it, "tell my racing heart to be still." "I can't really describe the feelings I had," she whispered as if talking more softly would help her get through her description. "I had love and hate, both. Global warming is going to kill these magnificent animals, and I hate us for what we're doing to the planet. The mother bear looked so skinny, and her coat wasn't nearly as white as the ones I saw years ago. With all the melting of the ice and the shortened arctic winters, they just can't get enough to eat, but here was this frail and hungry mother so obviously weakened, yet still trying to romp and play with her cubs, but one wasn't playing. When I looked closer, I could see that it was dead. There just wasn't enough food for the mother to nurse all three of her cubs, but she kept nosing and shoving the cub to try to get it to play. The other cubs did too, but finally they just stopped and lay down together with the dead cub. They were all still there when we circled back a few hours later, but they and the dead cub were gone the next morning. I like to fantasize that the cub went with its family, but I know better. God, there was such love and courage in these innocent wonderful creatures, and nature has always nurtured them, but damn it, we're messing everything up. If we keep this up, you won't have any awe to research. It was all so beautifully moving that it's an image I'll hold forever in my heart. I felt chills, and then I felt sick. I began to sob so hard that the cameraman had to hold me or I think I could have fallen out of the helicopter. God, I love nature and her beasts and I love nature's love, but God, how I hate what we're doing to her and her creatures."

Pride

The sense of pride that comes with awe is not just basking in praise for something we've accomplished. It's not personal pride but a sudden feeling of being proud to be a part, however small, of such a magnificent world.

Another participant in the SAI was a Hawaiian guide at the botanical gardens up the mountains near Wailukui on Maui. He was over eighty years old, and he beamed with the loving pride he clearly had for the gorgeous plants that filled this magical place. When I asked him about the feeling of being in awe, he laughed. "This place is awe itself. Have I been in awe here? Every single day for more than fifty years, I have." With a laugh and tears in his eyes, he continued, "I smell the flowers and feel their energy, and I feel the cool dampness beneath the massive plants and trees, and I can almost hear and feel the land's energy that is always giving birth from the past to what is born here, flourishes here, and then dies here, giving its energy back to the land to create new life. I breathe in the air that this cycle makes for us, and I listen to the songs of the birds that sing to celebrate it. Sometimes, I feel like I am these gardens, and my chest feels all warm, and I get chicken skin. I have such pride that I've been allowed to be a part of and responsible for this cherished place."

Zeal

Once we've experienced awe, we often feel zeal or a spurt of energized, passionate commitment to life and an eagerness to do something to show it. SAI respondents reported that they felt not only emotionally moved but also mentally inspired to do or think in new ways. Awe elevates us, but as you will read in Chapter 8, it can cause us to sink to depths of human prejudice and bigotry. Without thoughtful accommodation, the ardor, sense of being roused to action, and motivating energy related to our eleventh emotion can come dangerously close to fanaticism and an emotional vigor that can turn to biased aggression.

A SAI respondent, a firefighter, described the zeal he felt from being in awe of a massive forest fire started by a careless camper. He said, "I felt it in every part of my being. Of course it was hot, but what caused me to be in awe was how the heat seemed to sear my soul. It was like someone I loved and who had taken care of me was on fire, and I felt the power of nature like never before. I was a part of it and trying to help it, but I saw all the living things flashing up to flames right before my eyes. I wanted to save everything I could. But I became enraged, too. I think I could have killed all the damned weekend camper wannabes who come up here and don't know what the hell they are doing." Slamming his backpack to the ground, he swore, and muttered as he walked away in tears.

Sexual Desire

There's something unique about us humans (and perhaps a few chimpanzees): We make love facing each other. Of the approximately 30 million species on Earth, only humans (and some researchers say Bonobo chimps, too, and maybe just a few other animals) engage in face-to-face lovemaking. All mammals seem to experience ecstasy from the act of mating, and their species wouldn't survive if they didn't, but humans are unique in that we are aware of what's causing it. We "know" that it's our connection with another person that causes it and that we can ignite ecstasy in another being. We know that we can literally come together to transcend the illusion of "other" and even sometimes create life itself through that connection. Sex causes us to experience the elation of knowing and experiencing beyond any question that we are the cause of intense feelings in another being, that we can weave ourselves into the total being of another person, and that he or she can do the same with us.

Many of the SAI respondents described their awe response as experiencing the sense of ecstasy and the kind of elation that comes with sexual release. One said that her awe was "like having an orgasm without the sex." In terms of the body's response to awe, she's not exaggerating. The intensity of the body's response to awe bears some resemblance to the sexual response cycle that involves what researchers described as the stages of excitement, plateau, orgasm, and resolution. Here's one SAI woman's description of her eleventh emotion, which seems to parallel the sexual response cycle. She was what she called a "storm chaser," who was talking about her close encounter with a massive tornado. "It was the anticipation, I guess, like a kind of foreplay for what was ahead. I felt tingly all over, maybe from the energy, the electricity, or the ions coming from the storm. When we got closer and that massive black spinning funnel's roar was shaking our van, I sort of froze. When the lightning flashed in the dark clouds and things started to swirl all around us, I just became lost in the whole thing. I was

totally gone and taken away by what was happening. When the
funnel moved over the top of the highway overpass we were hiding
under, I felt this huge relief and I felt drained, relieved, and
exhausted. I broke out laughing when my husband said he felt like
he was just screwed by a tornado and had a climatological climax,
but as I think about it, the whole thing did make my body feel a lot
like it does when we make love."

In conducting interviews with people who came to our clinic for
help with various sex-related issues in their lives, there were some
who experienced what one patient called POA, "post-orgasmic
awe." One husband who had learned in our clinic to stop trying to
make love to his wife and start making love with her said, "I was
totally gone, but after I finished coming, I began to shudder, quiver,
cry, and laugh all at the same time. My heart was beating like
crazy, and I had chills and goose bumps. The intensity of what I
had just shared with my wife was overwhelming. I felt such awe for
her and for our relationship. It was like I had fallen more in love
not only with her, but also with our marriage."

The twelve reactions described in this chapter constitute the
unique kind of elation associated with our eleventh emotion.
For a moment in time and even when it's something bad that
inspires our awe, our eleventh emotion seems to allow good to
trump—or at least blunt—bad. Being in awe is an opportunity
for great joy, but like all that is mysterious and powerful, if we
fail to engage in the important step of thoughtfully accommodating the awe-inspiring experiences into our lives, it can also have
awful consequences: its elation can result in desolation and, sometimes, as you will read in the next chapter, it can have devastating
consequences.

8

AWFUL AWE

"I shrieked aloud in agony, 'Either this is madness or it is Hell.'"

—THE SQUARE IN EDWIN A. ABBOTT'S FLATLAND
WHEN SEEING A THREE-DIMENSIONAL WORLD FOR THE FIRST TIME

THE DARK SIDE OF AWE

There's a terrible, dark side to awe. We saw this dark side firsthand when the United States employed what it called its "shock and awe" strategy for "liberating" Iraq. By beginning the war with a massive bombardment intended to shock the enemy and awe them into submission to the power of distant, vast, mind-boggling power (what we keep calling the "world's superpower"), we were trying to use the dangerous side of the eleventh emotion to manipulate and take control of an entire country. With little awe of our own for the cultural history or ancient religious beliefs of the place we sought to control, we used the components of awe—particularly fear and the sense of vastness and confusion—to humble rather than to inspire. We played on the same ignorant kind of awe that had led many people in Iraq to comply with the corrupt evilness of leaders, who themselves used awe's power to maintain

their control. We used the same tainted version of awe that ter-
rorists use to try to shock and scare persons into embracing those
things that inspire their awe. When we use awe for its shock value,
the terrible price of this thoughtless, single-minded kind of ignorant awe will continue to be paid for generations.

As much as it can enlighten and elevate us spiritually, mentally, and
emotionally, awe can also cause us to descend into the depths of
what is worst about humankind. Its intensity and disruption of how
we think about the world can—as it did for the square in Edwin A.
Abbott's 1984 mathematical satire and religious allegory *Flatland*—
be madness or hell on earth. In its purist and most natural form, in
which we allow it to make us think in new ways, it can lead to a
genuine enlightened joy evoked by a deeper awareness of the significance of being alive and sharing that privilege with others. But
when it is detached from the realities of the facts of our own and
others' lives, it can lead to an artificial exuberance that obstructs the
real and necessary unhappiness that, in turn, provides the motivation for making the changes required for a truly meaningful life.[1] At
its worst, awe—particularly the ignorant or awe-lite kind—can
result in egotistical, aggressive self-righteousness and obedient deference. Under these circumstances, awe creates barriers between us
and causes people to compliantly do the bidding of immoral leaders
who promise protection from "the others."

When we fail to accommodate what inspires our awe by not thinking
long enough, slowly enough, and hard enough about our experiences,
awe's fear, diminished sense of self, and dilation of the imagination by
the vastness we encounter get the best of us rather than make us better. Instead of having our consciousness broadened by awe's assur-
ance that we can never know all the answers, it becomes constricted
because we believe an authority figure has found the answer for us
and that we don't have to do any more deep thinking for ourselves.

When enough of us allow someone to capitalize on, and manipulate, the power of our eleventh emotion, it also has the potential to be a force that, by resulting in millions of narrower minds, can contribute to the destruction of all that inspires an awe of understanding in the first place. You have read how being in awe can lead to a creative consciousness that enlightens us and makes us want to protect, nurture, and enhance the world, but awe without thoughtfulness can do just the opposite. It can cause us to think that we've finally "seen the light" or to be blinded by the glare of celebrity, power, or authority and proceed with our own or someone else's unfounded confidence and undeserved self-esteem to do stupidly selfish, destructive things. Awe can leave us in a hyper-aroused state of compliant zealotry that renders us easily led by false prophets or comforted by false prophecies. It can awaken a profound love for the world and everyone in it, but without the accommodative rational thinking that gives our eleventh emotion its transformative powers, it can also stir up the irrationally vicious, xenophobic hatred for those who don't "get" the "it" we think or someone who awes us has discovered. If enough of us experience true reflective awe frequently enough, it has the potential to lead entire civilizations to new awe-inspired heights of knowledge, forgiveness, and tolerant wisdom, but when millions allow themselves to be led by those who corrupt the features that give awe its power, it can and has caused the fall of a civilization.

ATHENIAN AWE

One of the first examples of awe's dark side taking down an entire culture can be found in the decline and fall of the center of the Greek culture. Although there are always many complex causes for the demise of any culture, awe was a major one in bringing down Athens, Greece. According to Thucydides, an Athenian general who served in the fifth-century war (between the Peloponnesian League led by Sparta and the Delian League led by Athens), awe may have contributed to the defeat of the Athenians, from which they never recovered.

Thucydides is considered by many to be the first historiographer to present factual details of events rather than moralistic descriptions of interventions by the gods. His *The History of the Peloponnesian War* is the most accurate account of that war. In it he describes in detail the second phase of the war during which the Athenian army had achieved a major strategic victory by being able to conquer and blockade the Sicilian city of Syracuse.[2] After laying siege to the city for two years and achieving their goals there, the Athenians prepared to pull out victoriously and move on to other objectives. Just as they were preparing to sound the signal to depart, something awe inspiring happened that would change their minds and the history of the world: a total lunar eclipse.

What a sight that 413 B.C.E. eclipse must have been. With none of the ambient glow of bright city lights, this was a time in history when dark was pitch-black. At night it was almost impossible to see the ground beneath your feet or a person standing next to you, so the rising of the moon was as much anticipated and relied upon then as the light of a sun rising is today. While ancient civilizations could sometimes predict an eclipse, they couldn't explain them, and their overwhelming mysteriousness led to all the features of the awe response. As the white moon began to gradually turn black, the Athenians experienced full-fledged awe, and what took place next illustrates what can happen when the most important aspect of our eleventh emotion—the thinking part—is neglected, and only the fear, sense of overwhelming vastness, and feelings of powerlessness remain.

Awe's role as our most transformative emotion derives from its capacity to inspire a deep and slow refection that allows us to accommodate what has happened, think in entirely new ways, and develop new explanatory systems. It's the mental afterglow or post-awe increased mental awareness through which we contemplate the meaning of what has just happened that results in a more creative consciousness beyond shock and impulsive actions. Without accommodation, awe can become a superstitious portent supporting our preconceived fears, biases, and narrow self-protective and self-enhancing view of the world. When this happens, being "awe struck" becomes being "awe stuck," in the sense that we stop thinking creatively and start reacting automatically. Instead of our consciousness becoming dilated, it becomes constricted, intolerant, and territorial.

When we're awe stuck, we become prone to the fear-driven, irrational thinking and actions that almost always get us (and the world) in big trouble. Awe's fear component dominates, and its usual diminishing of the self is corrupted into being consumed with enhancing or saving it, or turning it over to those ready to exploit it. Instead of being an eye-opener, awe becomes a mind-closer, and that's what happened to the awed Athenians. Their awe excited them, but they failed to help it enlighten them. They immediately assimilated the cosmic event into their preconceived superstitious views of nature and considered the eclipse to be a bad omen, signaling that now must not be the right time to depart Syracuse.

It wasn't the darkness of the night that led to the Athenians' fateful decision but their failure to use their awe to inspire enlightened thinking. Their nonaccommodating, awe-driven decision to completely alter their plans and to remain in the city allowed time for the Syracusans to break the Athenians' siege and destroy its army and naval fleet. That major defeat would result in the overthrow of

Athens' unique democracy and eventually the end of what had been the birthplace of Greek civilization.

RAGE, RATIONALITY, AND RELIGION

As I write these words, millions of people are being slaughtered by the cruelty of awe-inspired war. Although nonrational, faith-driven religious or reverent awe can result in our most altruistic and loving behaviors, some who experience it convert their eleventh emotion to aggression and atrocities aimed at cleansing the world of those in awe of a different power. It becomes a fear-driven, irrational, protective self-absorption, through which they become increasingly limited to their own worldview and progressively more intolerant of other explanatory systems.

Awe-inspired murder is taking place right now as people in awe of a belief, a religious or theocratic system, or of a tyrannical leader are fighting to defend or impose upon others that which inspires their awe. The zeal that can result from being in the kind of intense awe associated with a religious belief is being distorted into a fanaticism that, in turn, leads to a feeling of having the "moral obligation" to wage "holy war" (the ultimate oxymoronic phrase) in order to annihilate innocent "infidels," so named because they are viewed as ignorant heathens who have fallen in awe of the wrong god, guru, or belief.

Although religion has historically been a major example of awe gone wrong or the only catalyst for war and violence, it isn't the only one. The "bad trumps good" principle sees to it that we humans are perfectly capable of indiscriminate violence we manage to defend with all sorts of rationales that don't include the will of God. Just a few days before the Allah-awe-inspired attacks on New York City's twin towers, two men in Sacramento shot and killed several people in order to satisfy their need for what they said was "personal revenge" and retribution against those who didn't think as they thought. They killed not in the name of God or religious zealotry but were motivated by the zeal of their own personal rage and need to get even. Aside from mental illness and the motive to take what someone else has, feeling that someone has somehow diminished our self-esteem is the most frequent cause of violence. Along with racial bigotry and class hatred, many of our world's worst atrocities have been attributable not to religion but to these aspects of the worst about us. The power of awe that reenergizes and brings out the best in us also lends the energy behind the actions that show what's worst about us.

FROM ZEAL TO ZEALOTRY

Awe always shakes us out of our apathy and, if we think carefully about it, results in creative enthusiasm, passion, and a sense of urgency for a more connected and meaningful life, manifesting itself as healthy zeal. Nonreflective or nonaccommodative awe, however, can result in the zealotry shown by blind faith in and excessive fervor for a cause or a person who elicits our eleventh emotion. When someone is a zealot, he or she can't conceive how anyone could see the world and explain its mysteries differently than that person does. In awe of our own or an authority figure's ideas or beliefs, the zealot thinks that way is not only the right way but the *only* way . . . and it's not too far to the next step of trying to impose that way on others who are not similarly awed.

It may be that the "bad trumps good" principle has an even more sinister version in the form of "terrible trumps decency" or "killing trumps kindness" or "bigotry trumps acceptance." Being in understanding awe can make us feel that, in the final analysis, we are all one, and there really are no "others." But ignorant awe is going on when, as I so often see them do when my crippled son Scott walks past them, people gawk at what they see only as an "other"—as different from them as a third dimension was to Abbott's square. They are fascinated only by difference, and the fear and confusion of this sort of awe overwhelms the need for understanding that gives awe its true power of transcendence.

There is some evidence that we may have a genetic tendency to not only reject or distance ourselves from what we see as an "other," but also even to kill anything that is seen as an "other." Our primate chimpanzee relatives sometimes suddenly attack and kill other chimpanzees for no other apparent reason than that they are "others" who aren't of the violent chimp's clan. Healthy awe derived from contemplative processing of what awes us never leads to an enhanced sense of "other." Instead, it results in a profoundly deepened awareness of the fact of our ultimate connection with everyone and everything. However, the intensity of awe-inspired religious fanaticism that we see in the reddened, sweaty, enraged faces of the zealots in the streets, screaming death to some other group, is much too often associated with and motivated by a religious belief fueled by the thoughtless, irrational reverent awe that sees all "nonbelievers" as dangerous "others."

The only possible way we can be cruel to, or harm, another person is to think of that person as "other" yet our most precise sciences like mathematical cosmology prove that in the final analysis, there is no "other." After about 400 years of our contemplation of the 13.7-billion-year-old universe, science has gone from thinking of

the universe as "other stuff" somewhere "out there" to the realization that we were given birth by and are still a part of that
"stuff." As cosmologist Brian Swimme puts it, "We learned that
what we thought was other turned out to be 'mother.'"[3] He suggests
that we can become more aware of the illusion of "other" by "walking in starlight" and contemplating that the stars we're looking at
created the elements in our body and, that in a quite literal sense,
we are really stars looking up at ourselves.

There's a major difference between having zeal and being a zealot.
Because healthy awe results in a much more open-minded and
dynamic consciousness that causes us to see many new ways, this
kind of awe never leads to unquestionably and steadfastly going
along with one way or seeing persons who don't go along with that
way as "other." In fact, it leads to the exact opposite, by eliciting
new and puzzling options and ways of thinking and being in the
world, and new understandings of how others are being in the
world with and as a part of us. The zeal that derives from reflective
awe leads to high-level excitement and eagerness to learn more,
not to accepting one view and a persistent search for vindication
for that view. It results in a drive for connection, not separation,
and for "figuring out" more than "following."

It's easy to see when awe has rendered someone thoughtless
instead of more thoughtful. The inflammatory and vitriolic language of conservative commentators who label the liberal philosophy "godless" and liberals as "pin-headed treasonous traitors,"
along with the cruel, derisive mocking by those who call themselves liberals of what they see as the "over-godly, Bible-thumping,
loony, religious right" are examples of the intolerance of the awe
stuck and their tendency to quickly identify what they see as "the
other" rather than the "us." The dark side of awe results from the
rock logic that leads to assimilation and not the more fluid logic of

accommodation that is essential for awe to be a positive influence on us and the world.[4]

When a leader of a nation is in nonreflective awe of his own religious-political view, believing he knows what everyone most certainly wants, needs, and must have, no matter their historical or cultural heritage, he can become sincerely and unalterably confident that "the others" are trying to kill his people, whom he is sure are in awe of the same things he is! All other sources of awe are "other" and, therefore, must be defended against or destroyed. He fails to see that enemies' hatred might be aimed not at what he and those who follow him believe and hold in awe, but what they do—in other words, against policies more than people, and against actions more than ideas. Sociopathic zealots are so in awe of their own religious-political views or compliant with someone else's that they do, in fact, kill just because others are "other" and not similarly awed. And when this happens, the broader issues are masked by the constricted imagination that comes with thoughtless awe. When that happens, no flip-flopping is allowed, and everyone must stay the one and only course.

How did we do it? How did we make awe so awful? How did we take the combination of two of our most magnificent human qualities—our capacity to believe in a Creator or a creative unifying power, and our capacity to be in awe of what has been created—and corrupt this eleventh emotion into such a negative force in the world? The answer is that if we take the time and pay attention, being in awe is easy. The problem arises when awe arouses us but doesn't necessarily inform us. Our reverent fear and awe's sense of powerlessness can easily be transformed to evil when we haven't taken sufficient time to accommodate awe into our own lives.

THE MEANNESS OF THE CLOSED MIND

The continuing conflict between persons claiming exclusive knowledge of God's way and certainty regarding which group they think constitutes an "other" enemy (also in awe, but of the wrong god or belief system) derives at least in part from our eleventh emotion's vulnerability to corruption. Instead of the wonderful, freeing openness of reflective awe, nonaccommodative awe causes our minds to be closed and defensively mean-spirited. The unthinking and thus unaccommodating religious-turned-territorial awe experienced by some believers in Judaism, Christianity, or Islam continues to make it extremely difficult to resolve the long history of conflict between these groups. Maybe if we can better understand the awe response and learn how to lovingly and creatively direct the fear, the sense of overwhelming vastness, the diminished sense of self, and the mind-boggling confusion that make the awe response our most powerful emotion, we can discover some new ways in which we could diminish whatever part awe's dark side plays in today's versions of carnage committed in the name of God.

I don't claim to have the knowledge to explore or question the moral legitimacy of the basic theological claims and authority at the core of the religious conflicts that persist today, but I do think that unless we include an understanding of our powerful eleventh emotion and the awe-turned-fanaticism factor that contributes to them, we're not likely to make the progress that is so sorely needed to stop the madness and end the senseless bloodshed.

One example of awe's most awful side took place in a small village in the hills of southwestern Uganda. It was in this beautiful place that the ugly side of religious awe took another terrible toll. Nine-hundred and twenty-four members of a religious cult called the

Movement for the Restoration of the Ten Commandments of God
were murdered by their own leaders. Many, including women and
children, were burned alive in a church while banging in horror on
doors nailed shut by six of the cult's leaders, just before the building was intentionally set ablaze. The leaders who perpetrated this
atrocity claimed to be in direct contact with the Virgin Mary, had
predicted the coming of the end of the world, and had awed their
followers into turning over their worldly goods to them. The leaders' prophecy of the end of the world had not come true, and this
led to cult members' demanding a return of the possessions they
had surrendered. This combined with the leaders' unrelenting
greed and pure pathology played a major role in this horrific carnage. However, the power of the awe response, which the leaders
exploited through their visions, along with their ability to inspire
and manipulate awe from the followers they eventually slaughtered, provided much of terrible negative energy for one of the
world's worst mass murders.

How can awe become so awful? How can butchery take place "in
the name of God"? How can we be in awe of a Supreme Being and
be so awful to that Being's creations? How does reverence become
rage? How does awe for the God we believe in turn into a motive
for murdering those who aren't in awe of our image of God? How
can awe of God lead us to do such ungodly things? These things
happen because, like any of our other ten basic emotions, awe can
become pathological. Those who go through life primarily with
awe lite, or under the influence of the ignorant version of awe that
leads to fascination but not new and deeper thinking, can become
easy targets for brainwashing by evil sociopaths—people like
Charles Manson and cult leaders who work their evil under the
guise of religion.

After my years of studying awe, I personally have no faith in faith, at least as so many people are using this word these days. *Faith* has come to mean a blind, trusting acceptance of a belief, usually one into which we were indoctrinated as children when we were the most vulnerable and most prone to being ignorantly awed. When people ask me whether I'm "a person of faith," they are usually asking whether I unquestionably believe in the idea or being they hold in such awe. To save the time and avoid being proselytized, I usually answer yes, because my own awe experiences have taught me to have faith that there is much, much more to this world than I or perhaps anyone can understand. For me, Einstein's words capture the kind of faith my awe inspires. He wrote, "I don't try to imagine a personal God; it suffices to stand in awe at the structure of the world, insofar as it allows our inadequate sense to appreciate."⁵ That's the kind of faith that the understanding kind of awe inspires, but somehow we have come to believe and teach our children that blind faith itself is a virtue, but it's not.

Author Richard Dawkins writes, "Faith is an evil precisely because it requires no justification and brooks no argument."⁶ The awe of understanding inspires more questioning and deepens our faith that there's so much more to be understood, but those who experience ignorant awe channel whatever inspires it into a preset unquestioned faith. The awe of understanding can sometimes lead to acceptance of an established belief system or embracing a specific religion. But without the awe-inspired questioning mind, there's a danger of what awe can do to those who are easily brainwashed by evil sociopaths. These sociopaths make others believe they have already done all their thinking for everyone, so they embrace megalomaniac gurus who hide behind the guise of religion to achieve their selfish ends.

Killing in the name of faith in the one right god is certainly nothing new. It's been going on throughout history—through the

religious Crusades, the Inquisition of the Middle Ages, the blood-
bath of the Jewish Holocaust, and the "racial cleansing" in various
parts of today's world. But why hasn't religious or reverent awe
been a consistently motivating force in helping us *solve* our inhu-
manity toward one another rather a force that too often *inflames*
it? Why does intense religious awe become a cause of, rather than
the solution to, the cruelty in the world? Maybe it's because we've
allowed our capacity to be in awe to be manipulated by mad "mes-
siahs," who create God in their own image or make their image
that of a god. Maybe the contrast between the unnerving, diminished sense of self that comes from being in awe and the arrogant,
self-confident certainty conveyed by those in the grips of their own
non-reflective, nonaccommodative awe makes us want to feel as
comfortably certain as they are.

As pointed out in the introduction to this book, being in awe
doesn't necessarily make us feel great, but it does make us greatly
feel. When we're highly emotionalized, we may be easy prey for
those who know how to spot someone who is open, vulnerable, and
searching for answers. Maybe, when awe causes us to look for
meaning in dying stars or immortal cancer cells and to go in search
of "something more" (such as a higher authority exerting some
control over this seeming chaos), there are those who know how to
give us what we want so they can get what they want. Maybe there
are those who know how to give us a god to comfort us and save us.
Maybe there are natural-born awe-manipulators who know how to
capitalize on what psychologists call the "authority gradient."

THE DANGER OF ONE-WAY AWE

The authority gradient means that we tend to defer to, be impressed by, and even awed by those persons whom we see as "above" us in some way. A key difference between the awe of understanding and the awe of ignorance is that the latter is one way only. It's an awe experienced simply because a person is perceived to be above and somehow distant from us, and is therefore automatically better, smarter, and more deserving of our deference or even our awe. The understanding kind of awe, on the other hand, goes both ways. It's inspired not only by status and appearing to be better, prettier, smarter, more famous, and more powerful than we are, but also by those persons we think are beneath us on the social hierarchy.

Judges sit on high benches looking down on their courts. They wear black robes, and people stand when they enter and leave. Executives sit behind huge desks in massive offices with impressive artwork, along with pictures of themselves with other people higher up the social scale and more famous than they are, and evidence of their accomplishments hang everywhere. These strategies are aimed at our eleventh emotion, and it seems to be more easily elicited by those who are above us than by those socially below us. How sad it is that we so often restrict our awe by thinking of "up" or "above" as more awe inspiring than "down" or "below." Fortunately, there are millions of people who experience their eleventh emotion both ways and who are as easily awe inspired by the courageous struggles of the socially disadvantaged as they are by the stars, celebrities, and others who have learned to manipulate the distance and fear that come with awe.

One of psychology's most famous studies illustrated the impact of the authority gradient. Stanley Milgram's research on compliance to authority in social situations was conducted at Yale University in 1961.[7] It took place at a time when, as we are still today, people were struggling to understand how the horror of the Holocaust could have happened and so many people could be led to do such dreadful things. Using a shock machine (which, unbeknownst to the participants, really didn't administer shocks), volunteers for the study often administered what they thought were lethal electric jolts to complete strangers, who were faking cries of agony and experiencing what the shockers were fooled into thinking could be damaging or potentially lethal shocks.

Milgram's famous study offers insights about how even mild awe for a higher-up who is in a position and a situation where everyone else seems to go along with that belief unquestionably can cause us to do immoral things, even harming fellow human beings. Using Milgram's sham electric shock generator, two-thirds of men and women in his study obediently (and, as they reported later, against their own moral better judgment) "electrocuted" another person. The contrived experimental situation was under the control of a white lab-coated experimenter, who simply told the subjects to keep administering increasingly strong "shocks" to persons they couldn't see in another room. Participants thought they were acting as teachers, giving shocks for wrong answers in a learning experiment. There was no real electricity involved other than at the start of the study, when a very small forty-five-volt battery jolt was given to the shockers (called the "teachers"). Throughout the rest of the study, the "students" in the other room were acting as if they were being shocked by pounding on the wall and screaming when a shock was administered by the "teacher."

Ninety percent of the subjects administered at least one or more shocks even after the "victim" had pounded on the wall in clear distress. Despite the evidence that someone was suffering, the power of awe for authority was overwhelming. This form of "up

only" ignorant awe can result in a passive compliance and dangerously blind faith, in this case, yielding to the authority figure
clothed in his symbolic white lab coat, who was assumed by his
status to have done all the thinking necessary for everyone.
Participants' awe had placed them low on the authority gradient,
so they relegated themselves to a subservient status that led them
to be willing to do terrible things. Sadly, there are too many examples
in the world where the "terrible things" have been real.

Would you do it? Just because one of the "uppers" on the authority gradient told you to, would your ignorant or thoughtlessly reactive version of the awe response cause you to shock and keep
shocking a person who was pounding on the wall in agony and
then strangely fell silent? Most of us would say we wouldn't, but we
would be wrong. Even a little of our eleventh emotion can make us
vulnerable to manipulation. When psychologists asked students
who knew about the famous Milgram studies if they would have
"gone along" and electrocuted another human being, they said
they would defy the authority figure.[8] Yet most who consider themselves immune to manipulated awe will, according to the research,
go along with someone high on the authority gradient.

The difference between the awe of ignorance and the awe of
understanding has profound personal and social consequences,
and knowing the difference is essential if our awe response is to be
healthy, healing, and connecting in its impact.

LETHAL AWE

The deadly consequences of upward-oriented, thoughtless, compliant, toxic awe are reflected in the finding that co-pilots on the

low end of the authority gradient in the cockpit can fall under the
awe spell of their pilot. They fail to question his or her judgment
to such an extent that it has been estimated that as many as one
in five of the crashes of airplanes can be traced back to cockpit
voice recordings that show the co-pilot's reluctance to speak up
and question the judgment of the pilot.[9] The impact of being in awe
of an authority figure or a situation in which one feels or is made
to feel very low on the authority gradient is so strong that a co-
pilot could be willing to sacrifice himself or herself and all the
other crew and passengers rather than going against the awe gradient imposed by unquestioned authority. Being aware of awe's
authority gradient is important not only in the cockpit, but also
when we choose a self-help book, follow the advice of a life guru,
or decide to comply with any leaders' directions.

Pop psychologists might say that the co-pilots must have suffered
from "low self-esteem" or an "inferiority complex" imposed by
some childhood deprivation or trauma, but that only gives a label
and not an explanation. Even if we do have the dreaded "low self-
esteem" or feel inferior for some alleged dysfunctional family reason, it's ultimately the dark side of our eleventh emotion that
causes us to give in, go along, and react compliantly rather than
fully experience, think, and act based on reflection. It's not increasing our self-esteem or trying to feel more superior that will help us
act more socially responsibly and caringly; it's learning to resist
ignorant awe and being open to the awe of understanding, free of
the barriers of being socially above and below.

My interviews indicate that the awe of understanding is almost
always in reaction to nature or processes like a fuller awareness of
our own senses, a strong emotion, giving birth, loss, illness, healing, dying, suffering, loving, and other manifestations of profound
connection or disconnection from "something more." Based on

what I've learned, true, thoughtful awe for another person also happens, but not because that person is perceived as somehow above us. Instead, the reverse seems true. Our awe of understanding derives from a deep and profound sense of connection and sameness with that person as being part of the same world and sharing our same struggle in that world.

Whenever I want to point out the toxic potential of being in thoughtless awe, particularly as it is manifested in the sometimes lethal hesitancy to challenge persons of authority or to speak up in awe-inspiring situations that cause us to slip down on the authority gradient, I describe and show pictures of the 1993 crash of Northwest Airlines Flight 5719 in Minnesota. The pilot had descended the plane much too steeply and missed the runway. The cockpit voice recorder revealed that the co-pilot knew that the plane was at much too high of an altitude for the pilot's descent but had only meekly warned, "Just . . . you just gonna stay up as long as you can?" As the plane was tearing through the treetops and up to the final moments before final fatal impact, the co-pilot continued to deferentially respond to the pilot's commands.

Our eleventh emotion is easily activated in situations as exciting, power-surrendering, and frightening as flying and the hierarchical nature of the cockpit, but there are many other examples of awe-inspired deference that lead to a lethal hesitancy to act. The trappings that inspire awe are used in the military as means of discipline, and a little ignorant awe is essential in the war business where long, deep reflection can result in disaster. Striking the balance between reactive and reflective awe, however, is still a challenge the military must face. Our military is now studying what it calls the "trans-cockpit authority gradient" as it related to the differing ranks between pilots and co-pilots. It is finding that significant difference in rank between pilot and co-pilot, the esteem (awe) in which a co-pilot holds the pilot, and the resultant cockpit timidity of the co-pilot can be detrimental to aviation safety.

CELEBRITY AWE

Awe always diminishes our sense of self. That's what so wonderfully freeing, exciting, and confusing about our eleventh emotion, but it doesn't have to diminish our thinking and willingness to assert ourselves based on our reflection about what inspires our awe: Why? So what? Now what? When it comes to persons who inspire our awe, it's our responsibility to ask why and whether they really deserve it.

Followers whose awe of a person or idea had rendered them low on the authority gradient were in total compliant awe of Jim Jones as they followed his command and drank lethal juice at the massacre in Jonestown. Millions were awed by the waving flags, shouting chants, and thundering nationalistic music Hitler used to convince and intimidate a nation and nearly the whole world. Kim Jong-il of North Korea uses awe to manipulate his people by presenting thousands of marchers moving in perfect unison in the name of his glorification. The people of Iran comply with President Mahmoud Ahmadinejad, who uses radical religious views as the basis for his call for the total destruction of Israel and what he calls the "Zionist stain of shame." In addition to the social, economic, religious, and political factors that contribute to these disastrous circumstances, our failure to use our awe response's capacity to make us more creative thinkers contributes its share to this deadly motivational mixture.

When tyrants use the characteristics of awe to trick and control us, they are capitalizing on the authority gradient factor, appealing to assimilation's "rock" logic of "I'm right, you're wrong" thinking, or tapping into our chimpanzee fear and hatred of anything our defensive brain sees as "other." As a result we become mentally isolated and create artificial mental boundaries between people, ideas, and beliefs we ourselves create.[10] In effect, we become awed by our own intense reaction and lose track of what or who inspired it. We become turned on, but not tuned in, to clear, rational reflection.

Whenever our awe response results in a sense of separation rather than deeper and more profound connection, it's the dark side of awe that goes to work and will have toxic consequences. The long list of tyrants in the world could never have exerted their will upon us, had we thought long and hard enough about how and why they were exerting their power. Whether awe results in enlightened surrender to a higher wisdom or yielding to the characteristics of a leader, awe for people, things, events, or ideas depends on whether we sit down, shut up, reflect long and hard, and are willing to alter our explanatory systems and question our most basic beliefs.

COLUMBUS AND KIM JONG-IL

By using the power of the vastness, fear, and diminished sense of self that comes with the awe response, despotic leaders manipulate their people by awing them into submission. To inspire awe and hold his people down on the authority gradient, Kim Jong-il of North Korea claims divine birth and magical gifts like writing a book a day and scoring eighteen holes-in-one in a single game of golf. In order to perpetuate his image as a divine, distant, mystical being, he stays aloof from his people and always higher up by wearing elevated shoes and standing on huge stages that require the masses to constantly look up while he looks down upon them. Even the ubiquitous posters and portraits proclaiming his unbelievable exploits are hung high. At the rare times he appears in person, it's always at a distance and as if he were a demigod so that he elicits shocked awe, the unthinking version of our eleventh emotion.

Christopher Columbus used this same toxic power of awe in much the same way as the likes of Kim Jong-il. As a means of controlling a group of indigenous persons whose kindness and charity he regularly abused, he managed to use the cosmic coincidence of a lunar eclipse that occurred on the leap-year date of February 29 in 1504 to trick them into compliance with his needs.

Columbus had been marooned for months on the island of Jamaica. As he and his crews awaited rescue, the natives on the tiny island had regularly brought Columbus and his crew food and provisions, but Columbus's arrogant lack of appreciation caused the natives to stop their assistance. Facing starvation, Columbus used awe's toxicity as a ploy to get back the food he needed. He consulted his shipboard almanac and saw that a lunar eclipse was due. He gathered the native chiefs and warned them that God would punish them if they did not continue to supply him and his crew with food. He said that as an omen of God's intent to punish them, he would take the Moon from them. After dramatically presenting his awe-inspiring prediction and with the flare of a king leaving his court, Columbus turned with his colorful robes blowing in the wind and disappeared into his cabin on board the ship. He had used the fear component of awe, the part that leads to shock more than inspiration, to achieve his selfish goals.

The natives had been pushed even further down the authority gradient, so when just as this apparent Italian demigod had predicted, the Moon began to disappear, they fell to the bottom. Here was a man who was able to know the will of God, and they had offended him. They began to shout and beg for Columbus to do something to restore the Moon, but he calculatedly remained in his cabin until just the right moment, before suddenly appearing to announce that he had just learned that God was prepared to withdraw his punishment of the natives if they agreed to continue supplying him and his crew with everything they needed. Like the co-pilots who gave up their own lives and those who drank a poisonous potion, the native chiefs immediately went along, and right on cue, the Moon started emerging from the dark shadow, leaving the natives in total awe of Columbus's power. From that moment until several months later, when rescue finally arrived, the Jamaican natives gave Columbus everything he asked for. With Columbus's darkening of the Moon, history had provided another example of the dark side of awe and the manipulation of our eleventh emotion.

CATALYST FOR A NEW CONSCIOUSNESS

To make awe truly and positively inspiring, we have to be up to its challenge to think harder, deeper, and longer about why and how we live. We have to be cautious if our awe makes us feel very happy when there is little in our life that seems to merit it. We have to see if we might not be able to experience our own version of the awe that others have that seems to have so powerfully controlled their lives. We have to be willing to realize how little we and anyone else know and how little we will ever know, while at the same time remaining mentally invigorated enough to keep trying to know more and more. We have to realize the principle that dumb people, because they don't know they don't know, tend to think they know much more than they do, while smart people, because they always want to know more, probably actually know more than they think.

In 2003, in one of the first of the very few scientific attempts to describe the awe response, psychologists Dacher Keltner and Jonathan Haidt wrote, "Theorists agree that awe involves being in the presence of something powerful, along with an associated feeling of submission. Awe also involves a difficulty in comprehension, along with associated feelings of confusion, surprise, and wonder."[11] This uniquely vulnerable state is conducive for mental and spiritual development but also makes for fertile ground for falling under the spell of those who would try to close our minds and capitalize on awe's feelings of fear and of submission. If we become mentally bankrupt, we fall into the hands of receivers—in this case, those who would use awe to control us and the world. They're the ones who offer to complete awe's cycle by doing its hardest part for us. They offer to do—or to already have done—all of our thinking for us, by providing their own biased, self-serving cognitive map. This enticing proposition allows us to not have to keep trying to draw and redraw our own maps. It seems to be the nature of tyrants that they can convince so many that they know so much, and the nature of those who live under tyranny is to be too easily ignorantly awed by these false prophets.

THE CHOICE OF A LIFETIME

In a famous Hindu epic, Arjuna is the reluctant hero of the story. To boost his courage to go to war, he is given a special "cosmic eye" by Krishna, who is believed to be a manifestation of the god Vishnu. Krishna is trying to persuade Arjuna to lead his forces into a cataclysmic battle between feuding branches of a royal family, each trying to be in control of the kingdom. Awe is often used as a means of intimation, when there is a difference of ideologies or conflicting claims of control of territory. By giving Arjuna the magical eye, Krishna hopes not only to provide him with a new vision, but also to shock and incite Arjuna into fighting for Krishna's side. The eye allows Arjuna to see God and the universe as they truly are, and the experience for Arjuna is, as Krishna knew it would be, mind-boggling. Depending on whether they choose to be awe inspired and think, or become awe stuck and close their minds, mind-boggled people are ready to learn or be led.

The epic describes Arjuna's fear and amazement at what he sees, as he falls into a state of total awe. He is completely stunned by the images that fill his mind, feels the hair on his neck standing on end, and is confused as he struggles to make some sense of what he sees so intensely for the first time. Elevated to heights he never imagined possible, yet at the same time in a vulnerable state of dread and confusion, he offers what my own research and the few others who have studied awe would consider to be a good definition of the state of awe. He says, "Things never seen before have I seen, and ecstatic is my joy; yet fear and trembling perturb my mind."[12] Based on my interviews of persons who have known awe in their lives, this description captures what awe feels like and the wonderful confusion it causes that can inspire creative new ways of thinking, but what happens next in this epic illustrates the serious downside to awe.

Arjuna is deeply moved and truly awe inspired by what he has been allowed to see and the power of the god who made this cosmic vision possible, but it's the power of the fear and trembling that this awe induces that seems to get the better of him. Instead of thinking and reflecting about the meaning of all that his cosmic eye provides as new ways to experience and think about the world, Arjuna becomes so afraid and confused by it all that he becomes totally submissive to the will of Krishna and the ideas and positions he holds in the battle for control of a kingdom. Arjuna's awe causes him to slide down the authority gradient to a state of compliance. He falls to the ground and submits totally and completely to the wishes of the man who was so skilled in inducing and using awe to inspire Arjuna to fight. Arjuna complies with all of Krishna's commands, agrees to lead Krishna's army into battle, and to comply when Krishna tells him, "Do works for Me, make Me your highest goal, be loyal-in-love to Me, cut off all [other] attachments."[13] For the remainder of the epic story, Arjuna does Krishna's biddings.

It's not difficult to think of parallels of the lessons of this Hindu epic and being "awed into submission" in the pious-politics of our modern world. Author Max Weber describes how being in awe has not only psychological, but also profound sociological consequences.[14] He says that charismatic leaders can bring about revolution "from the inside" by changing people, who then go on to change the societies and the world in which they live. History is full of examples of awe-inspiring leaders who changed the world by changing millions of people by influencing their eleventh emotion "from the inside out." Jesus, Buddha, Gandhi, King, and Mandela are just a few examples of positive change, but there are more than enough examples such as the likes of Stalin, Hussein, and bin Laden who have led from the dark side of awe.

Because the vastness that inspires awe disturbs our comfortable consciousness, makes us feel small in comparison to the physical or personal power of what we perceive, and challenges us to develop a more creative way of thinking about our lives and the world, our eleventh emotion always involves fear and confusion. As you have read, these two states can lead to profound insights or incitement to irrational actions. When we're afraid, puzzled, and greatly impressed all at the same time, we're vulnerable and often fail to take the time to think slowly. Awe can literally scare the wits out of us, meaning that it can cause us to fail to use our intellect to reason in a broad context about whatever has stirred our consciousness. It can deaden or awaken us. It can lead to mass murder or great acts of caring. Ultimately, it could even destroy or save the planet. The choice is ours, and it's the choice of our lifetime.

YOUR AWE-INSPIRED LIFE

"All the efforts of the human mind cannot exhaust the essence of a single fly."

—St. Thomas Aquinas

LESSONS IN AWE

"That's life." You've probably said and heard that phrase many times, perhaps most often conveyed more with a sense of helpless, pessimistic surrender to forces beyond our control than to an enlightened awareness of the remarkable mysterious process of life. As you have read, the ignorant variety of awe derives from experiencing life's fascinating mysterious ways without doing a lot of long new thinking or mind changing. This awe lite still inspires us and intensifies our lives, but it doesn't inform us. It's a quick emotional pick-me-up (and sometimes a bring-me-down) free of the hassle of deep reflection or reconsideration about such ideas as why are we here, how did we get here, and what's most impor-tant in my life. The awe of understanding is different, and those who experience it are more likely to say, "That's life?" with a tone of questioning in their voice.

When I refer to ignorant awe, I'm focusing on its root word *ignore*. Awe lite allows us the intensity of being in awe without the effort, and often pain, of paying full, deep, reflective attention. It allows us to go about our often-languishing life, ignoring much of the mystery of life and staying within the range of our preestablished explanatory system. We still feel inspired, but not moved to try to know more about what we may never know. With the awe of understanding comes the challenge of a mind forever opened and seldom at final peace and closure.

You have read several stories from my study of the awe response as reported by SAI respondents. In my analysis of them I've found several commonalities that, particularly for those who choose (or feel they have had thrust upon them) the harder, more understanding kind of awe, might be of some help in their endless, but always remarkable, journey. I share some of these commonalities in this chapter, but if you already have a lot of awe lite in your life and that's enough for you, you may find what you're about to read bothersome. If your mind is made up about the meaning of life, and you have ready answers that serve you when remarkably good and bad things happen to you, you may not be willing to try to learn about how an awe of understanding can open it more. However, if you would like to see how those who experience understanding awe do it and grow with it, you may find some suggestions for how you can make that kind of awe more a part of your life and use it to help you as you deal with whatever life has in store that will surely, sooner or later, leave you in awe. Understanding awe's newly awakened and broadened consciousness allows no room for ignoring. It draws you into the full, uncensored experiences of life that inspire awe and intensifies and broadens your attention. It causes you to realize the undeniable truth that life's blessings and catastrophes are—if we don't ignore

them once we've been awed by them—too enormous to be managed alone, and life's wonders in whatever form they are presented
to us are too vast to be fully savored in isolation. The awe of understanding can be experienced alone, but it results in the undeniable
urge to share what happened and talk about it with someone else.

If we look deeply and long enough to be in awe of an event, a person, or an occurrence in nature and think deeply enough about
what nature seems to be telling us through its unique creations,
most persons in understanding awe told me that they came up
with the same lesson: Life is the way it's supposed to be and has to
be. That's life, but awe offers the opportunity to reflect why this is,
so what, and now what?

The awe of understanding invites us to live more often in the challenging but exciting state, the awareness that there is the "something
more" we're looking for, that there's always pain involved when we
find it, that "something more" is much too much for us to ever completely comprehend, and that we flourish most when we retain our
excitement for life and all that comes with it by continually opening
ourselves to those things that expand our imagination, stretch our
understanding, and increase our sense of infinite connection.

IT'S OKAY THAT IT'S NOT OKAY

Many of the SAI respondents told me that at the core of our
eleventh emotion is a comforting feeling that things are as they
should be even when they so desperately wished that they weren't
that way. There's the sense that, despite the pain, the world and
we are okay together, or at least that it's okay that everything is not
perfectly okay. As my friend Kewena told me about performing

hula, "We never get it perfectly right because we're not supposed to. Things always are, have to be, and must be not totally perfect. Totally perfect would be an end, and all nature and life is an unending process, and that's what makes it so awesome."

If you decide to have more awe in your life, you will have to be willing to take on and think deeply about your role in the process as an imperfect being in an imperfect world that keeps teasing us with its imperfect grandeur. That we were given the gift of being in awe indicates that there are forces at work that seem to want us to keep trying to know more about life, and that fact alone was awe inspiring to many of the SAI participants. For them, when they said, "That's life," it was as if they were just given a remarkably difficult, troubling, but fascinating puzzle to keep trying to solve, and they were awe inspired by being given that gift.

Awe makes us aware that we and everything else are made to exist in a constant state of imperfection, one that causes us to live with a respectful dread and delight about life. It's a way that we suddenly feel that we've been given the opportunity to "get right with the world," even when what's happening in our world seems to be going so wrong. The lesson to be learned from understanding awe is that the purpose of life isn't to be happy but just "to be" and to accept the gift of being allowed to at least try to figure out the why of why we are.

If you want to be happy all the time, awe is not for you. It's too upsetting and causes too much uncertainty. It can cause sadness and the spiritual guilt of realizing that we failed to relish the good in life when we had the chance. We can be awed by the profound sense of "never will be" that comes with a terrible loss, but if we open our minds and hearts to be awed more, often right now in the present moment of our existence, the memories we create will ultimately heal us when we hurt, sustain us when we suffer, inspire us when we think we can't go on, and offer solace when the awe of loss hits us in our hearts.

One of the SAI respondents wrote of her awe response, "I think awe is not feeling really great, but it is *really* feeling. Once you get past the excitement and fear and start thinking about what just happened to you, awe is a kind of sudden sense of making up with nature, and feeling that things are okay again between you and the world. It's a kind of parent-child relationship, and awe sort of puts you in your place. You feel that you've been allowed back home again. It feels that things are suddenly more right than you ever imagined, but you feel sort of sad too. You can't help thinking that you've missed so many opportunities to be awed before."

We can go through life in the languishing state described earlier by blindly being washed over by waves of detail and striving for a perfection that will never be attained. We can be so focused on doing and getting that we end up ignoring so much of the world and all we experience is an occasional awe lite. We can live under the influence of stress-induced hormonal highs. These provide an artificial happiness that prevents the necessary pain of living from acquiring the critical mass necessary for introducing the changes in our lives to make living more legitimately and meaningfully happy. We can continue on, denying or despairing over the inevitable physical separation that awaits us all, or we can stop to become more fully aware of the magnificence around us that offers lessons of the infinite connection echoed in yesterday's legends and resonating in the mountains, forests, oceans—or the face of someone we suddenly realized that we love beyond description.

The challenge in trying to lead an awe-inspired life is that it regularly exposes us to *the* fact of life. Like the beautiful rose with picky thorns on its stem, life's remarkable essence always masks a pain hidden somewhere inside its beauty. The more we have to love, the more we have to lose. The more we care, the more we are sure to grieve. As one SAI respondent wrote, "The thing about awe is that you really, really get into appreciating life so much that you live so intensely that any pain seems worse, particularly the pain of losing your life or the ones who make your life so awesome." A common theme running through the reports from the SAI participants is summarized by poet Kahlil Gibran's words, "Your pain is the cracking of the shell that encloses your understanding."[1] So if you are considering a life with more understanding awe, get ready to feel more deeply than you thought anyone ever could and then, by life's rules, to hurt more profoundly than you feel anyone ever should. Again, that's life.

DEATH OF THE HOMUNCULUS

Is describing awe as "an experience of such profound connection that the sense of self is totally lost" merely psychobabble, or can being awe inspired really cause the brain to lose all sense of its self and cause the imagination to expand? Can we be so emotionally caught up by something that changes take place within us? And do those changes cause who we are as individuals to become totally "lost in the moment," so that we are no longer concerned with the "what's in it for me" question? New research from neuroscience says yes.

It used to be assumed that the brain contains an area that acts something like a self-homunculus or "observer," which exists in the prefrontal cortex and "watches" what's going on in other parts of the brain, like the sensory cortex in the rear of the brain where our perceptions are being registered. The interaction between these areas was, and still is, seen by many scientists as equivalent to our subjective awareness of our world and what we experience as the self experiencing the world. But findings by neurobiologists Ilan Goldberg and his colleagues at the Weizmann Institute of Science in Rehovot, Israel, illustrate how our eleventh emotion might happen neurologically.[2]

Using advanced brain-scanning techniques, Goldberg's team observed changes in the brains of subjects either experiencing intense sensory (perceptual) stimulation or engaging in deep self-introspection. They were surprised to see two distinct neural patterns in each state. During self-focus, brain areas involved in perception (sensory cortex) were suppressed, and during intense perceptual focus, the regions related to self, concern, and reflection (prefrontal cortex) were suppressed. In the context of awe, this may indicate that the more we are focused on our selves, the less likely it is that our perceptual centers will be alert and open to awe-inspiring events. Conversely, when we allow ourselves to be swept up by the external world, we can lose ourselves, get "in the zone," and experience the full intensity of our eleventh emotion.

AWAKENING THE SILENT SELF

To lead a life full of awe, trying to quiet the self-center of our brain is not enough. Just telling ourselves we want to "be more connected" is insufficient to result in a more awe-inspired life. The eleventh emotion happens when you use all of your brains (the ones in your head, your heart, and your gut) to become more aware of what your entire body is sensing that inspires awe. You have to try to be more sensitive to the subtle signals from the world and processed by your entire body—signals that are constantly coming in but are going unrecognized by a brain that is busy being consumed with thoughts about the self and the now to help, improve, and assert it.

But, again, a warning about awe. This extreme sensitivity carries with it not only the ecstasy of being more fully alive, but also the full and deep agony that comes from living so fully and intensely. For many, ignorant awe's brief, passing high allows them to continue to languish along without the struggle and pain of lengthy reflection and whole heart, mind, and body reactions to dealing with unsolvable issues like love and death. For these people, "wow" may be enough.

Research indicates that we have our awake self that is busy with day-to-day survival and also a more silent self constantly bombarded with stimulation collected by our basic senses that usually escape our attention. It's when these much more subtle signals are picked up by our silent self that awe happens. We're seeing, hearing, smelling, and feeling much more than we're aware of and, if we're willing to put our awake self to sleep for awhile, our silent self might be able to arouse our eleventh emotion. In other words, it's not the limits of our five basic senses that set the parameters for being in awe but our awake self's numbness that causes us to miss out on so many awe-filled opportunities.

British poet and author William Blake pointed out that "man's perceptions are not bounded by organs of perception; he perceives far more than sense (tho' ever so acute) can discover."[3] There is fascinating research that shows that we are aware, at least on some level, of signals sent from the super-sensitivity of our basic senses.

What if, by making a simple change in our consciousness and our view of ourselves, we could actually increase our visual acuity? What if we've been missing out on what our senses are experiencing because of our brain's limited self-image? What if images are coming into our brain sight unseen, and we could improve our sense of vision and be able to see things we couldn't see before just by altering who and how we think we are? Imagine how much more often we might be in awe of the world if we were more often seeing what our eyes are.

SIGHTS UNSEEN

Science shows that we have an awake self dealing primarily with a very narrow range of what our senses are bringing to us and a silent self that is receiving all sorts of wonderful signals we don't perceive. There is evidence that, if we become less consumed with our awake, alert, constantly striving-to-survive-and-succeed self, we can come to see much more than we ever imagined. It seems that the only thing preventing us from being more in awe of our lives is quite literally our "self." An intriguing study by Harvard psychologist Ellen Langer suggests just that, and that we'd be awed if we really saw what we've been seeing.[4]

Langer's research shows that our visual acuity is affected by how we decide to view ourselves. She asked research subjects to "become" air force pilots for an afternoon. They were told to wear the uniform of a pilot and were given the chance to fly a jet airplane in a flight simulator. Everything was made as real as possible, and subjects were asked to really get into the part and not just go through the motions. They were instructed to act just like pilots and imagine possessing the skills and attributes of fighter pilots, including excellent vision and manual dexterity. Before piloting the imaginary plane and before the simulation had been explained, each participant was given a physical exam, including an eye test. What happened next provides evidence that "believing is seeing" and that what we choose to believe about ourselves directly affects not only what we will see, but also how well we can.

During the flight simulation, the participants were asked to read the markings on the wings of another plane that could be seen by looking out of the simulator's cockpit window. The markings were actually letters equivalent to those on the eye chart used to measure the subjects' vision. As if given a new pair of glasses, nearly half of the pilots-for-a-day showed measurably significant improvement in their visual acuity. The pilots who did not show an increase in their visual acuity were motivated to enjoy the experience but were not told to totally immerse themselves in the role and try to "become" a pilot.

The implications of Langer's study are stunning—one might even say awe inspiring. If how we elect to think and feel about ourselves actually alters how well one of our most important physical senses (that is, sight) operates and makes it more sensitive, we have evidence that what we think about ourselves is crucial in determining what information gets through to us.

When a loved one dies, many of us regret that we didn't "see" more of that person and drink in his or her image when we had the chance. Langer's and others' research indicates that we may have seen more of them than we know and can see much more of the people we love right now if we become more alert to signals from our silent selves. Busy, self-focused people, intently absorbed in multitasking, may have less to be awed by because they "see" less than those who see themselves as inseparable from the world and as beings ripe for awe-inspiring experiences.

TOO SELF-CONSCIOUS TO BE FULLY CONSCIOUS

The more self-conscious we are, the less fully conscious we seem able to be. The more we think about who we are and try to defend the boundaries established by what psychologist Cordelia Fine calls our "vain brain," the more we shut out the subtle perceptions of things like a tiny flower that may lead to awe.[5] When we focus on ourselves, we sometimes fail to see what we could "see" or sense if we were less constrained by being so self-conscious. A very old classic study illustrates this point.[6]

In a study in 1898, researchers showed subjects cards on which were printed a single number or letter. The cards were placed so far away from the participants that they could not read them. When asked to read the cards, the frustrated subjects complained that they couldn't see anything at all on the cards. However, when asked to name the characters anyway, they were correct much more than they would have been by just guessing and pure chance, which is exactly what the participants in the study said they were doing. The researchers summarized their findings by writing that we have "within us a secondary subwaking self that perceives things which the primary waking self is unable to get at."[7]

There is abundant evidence of a neglected "sub-awake" self that sees, hears, and senses things our dominating awake selves fail to perceive. It may be that we are awed when signals from the silent self suddenly "break though," and we see as we have never seen and hear as we have never heard.

It's not just our visual sense that is picking up signals we don't perceive. Years before the study on the numbered cards another study was conducted that showed that even though subjects said they could not detect very subtle differences between two nearly identical weights, they were actually right almost 70 percent of the time when they took a guess.[8] Summarizing their findings, the researchers wrote that the detection of stimuli beyond the awareness of the awake self should "be fully studied by psychology and assiduously cultivated by everyman." It is this cultivating of a more open, broad, and creative consciousness that helps us lead a more awe-inspired life.

Based on my interviews of persons who had known many awe experiences, I suspect that the being in awe relates in some way to sensations from the sub-awake self that senses what we never imagined we could. It's this self that seems to see with a vision we never knew we had and to hear by listening in ways we never knew we could. One more study illustrates this power of perception beyond the awareness of our narrow self-concept.

Viennese neuropsychologist Dr. Otto Pötzl was working with casualties of the First World War. He examined several soldiers who had suffered gunshot wounds to their occipital lobe in the back of each of their brain's cerebral hemispheres. He was awed by what he discovered.[9] The soldiers had been severely wounded in their primary vision centers and were totally blind, yet they kept staring at pictures they could not possibly see. They reported "seeing" images their brains could not have detected. Dr. Pötzl decided to see if he could replicate this finding in persons without damage to their visual center.

Using healthy volunteers with no brain damage, Pötzl flashed a detailed picture for one one-hundredth of a second before their eyes, and then asked them what they had seen. Often with frustration, the subjects protested that the image had been presented much too fast for anyone to see anything, but they were told to go home and try to recall the details of the dreams they might have that night. They returned the next day to relate their dreams and draw any elements of their dreams that they could remember. When the drawings were objectively analyzed, they contained many fragments and associations that unmistakably related to the original flashed pictures.

One reason that our dreams can often contain bizarre images is that our awake selves were too busy to know what they were seeing until they went to sleep. Your brain's awake self has a whole set of tendencies and preferences based on defending and enhancing your awake self, but your silent (or what researchers describe as your "sub-awake") self is free of such limits. When you quiet, or at least ignore, your brain's awake self, it can't exercise its influence and censorship.

Because it isn't hampered by the busy and selective consciousness of the brain's awake self, the brain's sub-awake self is free of the biases and inhibitions of that self and has more direct channels for connecting with what is awe inspiring about the world around us. If we can get past our selfish selves, there seems to be a much broader and richer database from which to be awed.

We can at least begin to get past our limiting sense of self by resisting the easier path of ignoring those awe-inspiring events and people who might totally mess up our explanatory system. We often harbor a fear that if we lose ourselves by fully engaging in all that life offers, we will stop working and do nothing but sit on the shore and be in awe of sunsets, but I found that persons who were most regularly in awe were able to focus on their work and be as productive as the chronically multitasking who delude themselves in thinking they can do many things well at once.

Ultimately, people lose their sense of self by paying intense, full, prolonged attention to the world around them and by allowing themselves to stop for a long time to think about whatever it was about these experiences that inspired awe. We can become less self-focused by trying less to experience life and putting in the mental effort of being aware that we are experiencing life. It's when we're most engaged in life itself and with someone with whom we share life that we can lose all awareness of time, place, and self—a state psychologists call "flow."[10]

One of the simplest things you can try to "de-self" yourself is to make a tape recording of your discussions with the people around you. Try doing that at dinnertime with your family or when you're just talking with your spouse. Play back the tape and count the number of personal pronouns you use (I, me, mine) compared to collective nouns (us, we, ours). If you are high on the self side, make an effort to balance back to more "us." Doing so can help focus your attention where awe is usually found, in that rare place where the self isn't the center of attention.

THE SELF AT PLAY

More evidence of unrecognized sources of stimulation for our eleventh emotion comes from studies of patients with a condition called "blind sight." It's a condition in which damage in one tiny part of the visual area of the cerebral cortex results in patients being left with a black hole or blind spot in a part of the visual field. I experienced this black hole when I had a retinal detachment, and I panicked when one part of the world I was seeing went entirely black. Even though there is no way these patients could have the conscious experience of seeing light or an object in that blind spot, they do, in fact, react to stimuli presented in this spot, but only under one certain condition. Instead of being asked to actually see something they can't possibly see, they have to feel they are playing a guessing game.

Psychologist Lawrence Weiskrantz at Oxford University flashed lights in various areas of the visual fields of patients with damage to their brains in the visual area. When the lights fell in the area of the patients' blind spots, as expected, they couldn't see them.[11] However, when Weiskrantz encouraged them to take part in a make-believe game by pointing at lights they didn't see "just for the fun of it," they pointed accurately to lights in their blind spots as if they could actually see them. They could not only point to the flashes of light, but, although they couldn't verbally report what they were seeing, they could distinguish between the unseeable simple shapes like circles and crosses through simple gestures that indicated the "invisible" shapes.

Perhaps because of the dominance of the awake self, the blind-sighted patients were able to "see" only when they were "playing." Our egotistical striving self doesn't have much time for silliness and playing around, but if we elect to lead more awe-inspired lives by taking ourselves less seriously, we are going to have to consider a more playful approach to daily living.

Genuine play is characterized by a lack of a sense of either self or goal, and a lack of both are states conducive to falling in awe. Author James P. Carse describes what he calls "infinite play," in which "the only purpose of the game is to prevent it from coming to an end, and to keep everyone in play."[12] When winning or self-enhancement or personal power is not the objective, play can help open the mind to all sorts of weird possibilities. Unlike earnest golfers focused on the hole, you might be able to be aware of where you are playing and with whom, both possible sources of awe. It may seem a long way from experiencing awe, but a small step to being more available to it might be to just to play catch or hit a tennis ball going back and forth over the net as long as possible. At least it's a lot easier to come to appreciate life when we're not so busy trying to win at it.

ONE WORLD, TWO SELVES

Cambridge psychologist Tony Marcel has also done interesting work on the issue of the two "selves" involved in being awe inspired.[13] He presented subjects with very weak flashes of light that were almost impossible to see. He asked them to indicate when they saw a light by either blinking their eyes, pressing a button, or by saying, "Yes, I see the light." Through their blinking signal, the subjects accurately saw many more of the subtle flashes than when they tried to give a verbal response. In terms of accuracy, button-pushing was somewhere in between blinking and verbally responding. When the subjects were asked to respond by both blinking and verbally responding, the eyes often accurately said "yes" while the voice incorrectly said "no." By very carefully measuring the time between the light flash and report, Marcel excluded the possibility that simple reflex blinking was taking place.

Marcel's work and that of other researchers challenges the idea that we have one self or level of consciousness with which we perceive our world. It seems that a response more closely linked to our automatic, unconscious system may be more sensitive than our normal, awake self-consciousness and that all of our brains are more perceptive than just the head brain, dictated by its self-concept part.

The more the awake self is involved in our daily lives, the less sensitive to our world we actually seem to be. The less separately or selfishly we view our world, the more likely we are able to be awed by sensations that our awake self never imagined, and that may be why being in awe can be so frighteningly mind-boggling. All of a sudden, we feel, see, hear, smell, and touch in ways we never imagined we could. It's as if a part of us that has gone long neglected is given freedom to feel, and that's essential for our eleventh emotion.

Psychologist Nicholas Humphrey has looked at the research supporting the idea that we have an awake and a less-awake self with which we perceive our world.[14] He speculates that the less self-conscious we are, the more our unawake self is able to respond to our world. His own work with monkeys who had their striate cortex (their brain's primary visual center) removed is that they "saw what couldn't be seen" much better and more easily than humans who had this same degree of brain damage. The monkeys seemed entirely comfortable with their blind sight because they weren't limited by clinging to one view of themselves. The idea of seeing what they couldn't possibly see didn't stop their monkey play, because they didn't have the dominating sense of one self telling them to "get real and grow up."

Humphrey suggests that humans who had their visual centers destroyed but still experienced blind sight tended to be stunned by the experience because of their highly developed sense of self. The experience didn't seem to be their own, they didn't understand what was going on, and their ever-skeptical and cynical awake self denied the possibility of seeing what can't be seen. I found very few high-level cynics among the frequently awed; so, on some level, their eleventh emotion seems to help them transcend their highly honed cynical self.

In an important side issue in Humphrey's research, he noticed that one of his visually impaired but blind-sighted monkeys became unable to see in that way when she was frightened or in pain. He says, "It was as though anything which drew attention to her self [the awake self alerted by the pain] undermined her ability to use unconscious percepts [the unawake self]."[15] This finding has implications for pain management and the possibility that getting our minds off ourselves might help diminish the brain's experience of pain because its self-center is distracted from what's going on.

If we want to lead an awe-inspired life, we have to be less self-focused, more concerned about connection than competition, and willing to think longer and harder when awe alerts us to wonders we never knew we were seeing, hearing, smelling, tasting, and feeling. We have to take ourselves a lot less seriously and take opportunities to be alive much more intensely and attentively. We can also help lower our awe threshold with a lot more playing and laughing and allowing ourselves to get totally lost in whatever we're doing and with whom.

Languishing can be described as looking so hard for the "good" life that we can't see and appreciate life itself. Flourishing is learning to be in awe when we say, "That's life," even when things aren't going the way we wish. Awe is our emotion for experiencing all of life, not just one up or down part of it, and it's more likely to happen when we get past the currently popular idea that the secret to life is to have high self-esteem, to maintain a positive attitude, and to think hard enough that the power of our intentions will ultimately cause life to yield to us and give us whatever we want or think we need. People in understanding awe eventually learn that it is life itself that decides that.

Awe leads to the discovery that the real secret we've been looking for is that there are so many wonderful secrets we will never know and that something is allowing us the chance to profoundly and sometimes painfully realize and fully experience that fact. The real secret, then, isn't to be found in getting the life we want but in being able to be in awe of the life we have and learn through all the wonderful and terrible things it gives us. My son's statement when he described the impact of his cerebral palsy sums up what an awe-filled life is like: "Dad, my life isn't very good, but it's certainly incredible. That's life."

10

LEFT IN AWE

"The man who has known pure joy, if only for a moment, is the only man for whom affliction is something devastating."

— SIMONE WEIL

FOREVER STILLED

My son Scott killed himself last night. In the most agonizing moment of our lives, my wife and I found him lying on his bed, and for the first time in his painful thirty-five-year life he was completely still. Since the moment of his birth, whether awake or asleep, his cerebral palsy had caused the left side of his body to shake and spasm so painfully that walking was difficult, and his awkward gait became a target for staring and mocking by those who knew only the ignorant "isn't that interesting" version of awe. That kind of awe lite derives from being a distant observer who sees those who appear different as a "distant other." Perhaps many people are so detached from their lives that they could see only a broken being who disturbed their preconceived notion of how things are supposed to be or challenged their comfort zone that they or someone they loved could be handed such a life-long challenge. In a sense, my son died because not enough people could be in understanding awe of him and of the gifts he offered about how to thrive through adversity.

A brief lack of oxygen at birth had damaged a part of Scott's brain that is no larger than the head of pin, yet it left his mouth slightly twisted to one side and his lips quivering so severely that speaking was always a struggle. He was almost always impatiently asked to repeat what he said or even whether he was intoxicated, and the failure of others to be in understanding awe that could have expanded their view of life was a constant source of embarrassment to Scott, which eventually caused him to write, "I can see no way out." He really meant he could see no way in.

Now as he lay in total silence, his lips were finally still, never again to help him say, "Hi, guys? What's up?" or "Is there anything I can do to help you?" or "What's for dinner?" His voice will never allow us to hear the loving smile that somehow resonated in it. As we saw him lying there, we knew we would not only yearn forever to hear his voice just one more time but that he had so much more to say that he would never say, and we had so much more left to say to him that he would never hear. He would never know that I long ago planned to brag about him as an example of a person who lived in and inspired awe and to dedicate this book to him.

As I write now about our loss of our son and for reasons I don't understand, the words of French philosopher Simone Weil have just come to my mind. I only vaguely remember reading about her almost forty years ago in my one and only philosophy class, but I suddenly recall verbatim that she wrote, "Difficult as it is to really listen to someone in affliction, it is just as difficult for him to know that compassion is listening to him."[1] Did Scott know the depth of our loving awe for him? Does he—can he—know in some way now? Is there any way to tell him? Questions like those are the nagging consequences of being thrust into a state of understanding awe that we will now be in forever.

FROZEN OUT

As I took my son in my arms that last night, the warmth I had felt from his body from the first time I held him against my heart in the neonatal intensive care unit had vanished, and I began to sob uncontrollably. Now that Scott is gone, I still feel the terrible coldness of Scott's body on that worst night of my life, and it's as if some of the warmth of my own spirit left with his. I wonder where the warmth of my son's loving spirit went, but I am so thankful that we spent so many of our moments in loving awe of and with him. I also wonder why so many people never took the time to be in awe of such a wise spirit.

It's our eleventh emotion that is most significant at this time of our grief. It results in an irresistible need to know and learn more about Scott, about life, and about death. As much as I hate what we're going through, we know that the intensity of our awe and grief stems from our reverence for our son and the fact that it is because he was so much worth loving that he is worth such intense grieving.

I've learned that—far beyond awe lite—there exist levels of awe that we can never imagine until something about the mysteries of life inspires them. As you have read, awe doesn't always make you feel good or happy, but if you let it and don't just let the moment pass, it makes you feel like no other emotion can. I can't help thinking how Scott must have felt so frozen out of much of life because of the chilling isolation others imposed upon him, and I wonder if my constant chill is Scott's imprint upon my soul teaching me to embrace others and life to find my warmth.

If we allow it to, awe causes us to ask questions that probably have no answer. I sob when I think that I treated Scott as an independent adult; perhaps he needed me to hold him more, to offer him warm shelter against the cold world in which he was forced to live, and I am inspired to connect more profoundly than ever with my wife, the rest of my family, and others around me. As I wrote in the pages I finished before Scott left us, the awe of understanding always diminishes our sense of self and makes us question ourselves, and I am experiencing the sting of this most difficult aspect of the awe response. It's not easy or happy, but it is the most intensely alive time of my life.

In the painfully continuing process of my dreadful awe of understanding that our horrid loss has imposed on—and inspired within—my wife and me, Weil's words keep coming to my mind. They never did before, and I'm not sure why they keep doing so now, but the awe of understanding often leads to new insights and seemingly bizarre synchronicities that demand our attention and effort to understand them. Weil wrote, "Affliction is anonymous. It deprives its victims of their personality and makes them into things. It is indifferent and it is the coolness of this indifference— a metallic coldness—that freezes all those it touches right to the depths of their souls. They will never find warmth again. They will never believe any more that they are anyone."[2] Despite his loving courage, it may have been this feeling of being totally depersonalized that facilitated our son's decision to no longer find any sense or value in trying to remain a living person. Difficult, unanswerable questions like these come with being in awe.

Scientists know that there is no such thing as "cold," only the absence of warmth. The refrigerators and the air conditioning that cool our homes work because they remove heat; cold happens because the warmth is gone. Was it Weil's "metallic coldness"—the hard, harsh coldness Scott sensed from some people who denied him of their warmth—that led to his seeking the uncertain shelter of "a better place"—maybe a warmer, more accepting place—that he mentioned in his last note? These are more questions that our eleventh emotion demands we try to answer.

A DE-IGNITED LIFE

The completed manuscript for this book had already been sent to my editor long before my writing of this final chapter. I thought I had described our eleventh emotion as well as I could, but the kind of awe I'm having now makes me realize how much more I am about to learn about the full spectrum of awe that comes with a grief as intense as the love we had for our son. The problem with being in awe is that the physical loss of the object that inspired that awe sends your consciousness reeling, and the reality of death slams home the tenuous brevity of life.

I hope the prior chapters have not made awe seem only like a short-lived, wonderful, uplifting, fascinating experience, although it can certainly often include such reactions. However, if that's all it is, it's only awe lite and an ignorant awe in the sense that it does not lead to a powerful and often painful dilation of the consciousness and stretching of the soul that my wife and I are going through now. Perhaps the most profound lesson we've learned from our awe for what's happened so far is that it is not grief so much as yearning that dominates so much of our thinking. For what are we yearning? Do we not still have Scott? How can we access what it is that we so urgently yearn for? To us these are awesome questions that give us so much to think about that we have less time to just cry and take more time to talk and think together.

Before Scott died I wrote in the introduction to this book that I was in awe of him, and I used my relationship with him at his troubled birth to try to describe what awe feels like. I was looking forward to surprising him with this book and am so deeply saddened now that he will never read what I said about him, but somehow I think he knows beyond words.

I am now writing while in one of the most intense, deep, painful aspects of awe, the kind that comes only with the end of a life. I'm constantly pondering why Scott ended his life, and I have all of the most severe manifestations of the awe response—awe's puzzling state of fear, need to understand what seems incomprehensible, and nagging inspiration to learn how to be in awe of my son on new levels I never thought I would have to seek. More now than ever, I know that it's our eleventh emotion that's been provided to us to deal with the full overwhelming implications of the phrase, "That's life." Just when I was learning more about being in awe of my son's courage to live in the face of his challenges, I'm left in the most profound awe of trying to understand why he lives no more and what that means on so many levels.

Someone who read this last chapter asked me, "What's the payoff? What good is awe when things are so terrible?" That's the thing about awe: There is no "payoff." It's a process—I've suggested the most intense of all human processes—and that in itself is enough for me. I quoted cosmologist Brian Swimme when I wrote the first pages of this book, his view of awe as being "stunned by the magnificence of where we find ourselves."[3] That's exactly how awe feels to my wife and me right now, totally, unavoidably immersed in the full spectrum of life and death. As we watch others languishing around us in their busy, intense lives, we wonder if they will ever know the awe we feel and that our awe for our son acts as a guide even at this most terrible of times.

In the interview from which I took his quote, Swimme speaks about the idea of "igniting life" and feeling brought to life by awareness of our ultimate connection with the stars and the cosmos. But Swimme says nothing about the awe of "de-ignition" of life and what someone as brilliant and loving as Scott could be thinking or feeling when he gives up his gift of being created by those forces and decides to de-create himself. Our awe has left us to dwell on this appalling mystery for the rest of our lives, even as some of the spark that ignited our own lives seems to have been snuffed out.

AWE'S ACHES

You have read about awe's powerful impact on our bodies, and I'm experiencing it as I write these words. My shoulders still throb with pain from my futile minutes of attempted CPR (cardiopulmonary resuscitation). I can literally feel death, and it boggles my mind. That's the challenge of awe; it's often easier to be awed and move on than to be awed and think about the meaning of the experience forever. My awe causes me to be drawn mentally to where Scott died and at the same time repulsed and frightened by it, which is characteristic of the contradictory nature of our eleventh emotion.

In Chapter 1, I asked you to imagine a choice between an awe-filled

life and one that would be much easier and less upsettingly challenging. I know that beyond trying to lower our awe threshold, we
really don't often have that choice. We're given the life we're given.
Popular-psychology bromides aside, we actually have relatively
little control over the most important and difficult things that happen in our lives. Right now I often wish I had had the choice of a
simpler, easier life with children without impairments, much less
awe, and just a little awe lite once in a while. I have that thought
for only a moment because I know on some level that our life with
Scott was so awe inspiring that he left us in undeniable awe. I
know when I look deeper into my consciousness for some meaning, any meaning, that lurking just beneath the good things of life
lurks the horror that can come with the chaos that is life.

You have read that awe is not something that always makes us
happy or provides the answers we seek and that bad always trumps
good. I'm learning that firsthand, however, it is the very essence of
fully living through all that life gives and takes from us that makes
life awe inspiring. I'm in awe of our loss and all the mysteries of it,
and even though I must keep trying, I know there won't be "closure" or "getting past" what's happened. If I can stay in awe of
what's happening, I won't expect answers. I don't want there to be.
If I am to go on living and retain any hope for future awe in my life,
Scott's death has to result in more "openture" than closure. I want
to yearn, grieve, and cry for our son for the rest of my life and keep
learning about the awe he inspired in us. The awe of understanding doesn't promise the answers that will "put trauma behind us."
Unlike a bout of severe anger, sadness, or joy, awe changes us forever, and this most horrid, intense awe will surely cause me to
search forever for answers I will never find but must keep seeking.
The awe that Scott inspired in me leaves me no other choice but
to keep trying to understand and recall the awe-filled moments we

so often shared and what they mean now. I remember the lesson from my son when in his usual wry wit he once said, "Dad, if my life were a fish, I'd throw it back in. I'm not all that impressed with the fish I caught, but it sure is one hell of a fish, isn't it? I guess you have to take the fish you have and try to figure out why you got it and what it means."

As understanding awe does, my awe also causes as much regret for what would never again be as for what could or might be, that I must think about and relate with my son in ways and on levels that leave me in awe. While it isn't often discussed in popular grief counseling, I'm learning that awe is one of—if not the only—emotion that helps us learn not only to survive through crises, but in a very difficult and strange way, thrive through them. Even though I wrote most of this book before I lost my son, this event has validated much of what I said. Awe, the deep kind of understanding version, is the one emotion that can help us keep looking for meaning even when the search seems so endless. We can be in awe of life, go through the emotions, and have a little awe lite once in awhile, or cling to our prior explanatory system when awe rocks our world. These are choices we all can make, and as for me, it's the energy of awe as a powerful emotion that is somehow helping me find at least some energy to keep trying to understand Scott's life and death. I feel a deep sense of honor at being allowed to take part in this sacred process, and I am in awe of it.

A GRIEVING AWE

My whole body is in a total state of upheaval. I have goose bumps during the day for reasons I don't understand, and I'm often exhausted and agitated at the same time, all manifestations of our eleventh emotion. My heart skips beats and flutters, and an occasional tear drips out of my eye as if my body knows I'm sad even when I'm distracted from my depression. Sometimes I suddenly begin to cry, but there is no specific thought or feeling eliciting my tears, so something within me aroused by the awe response seems to know and feel more or differently than I think and challenges me to keep looking for whatever that is.

I sleep but never fully feel rested and want to binge on junk food even though I can't taste it. I'm confused, overwhelmed, and feeling lost, and all of these reactions are the same ones involved in varying degrees with both depression and the awe response. Even in situations less traumatic than ours right now, awe is often colored by a sense of sadness and even depression. Remember, the research shows that depressed people tend to be more in touch with reality than their denying counterparts, and I've never been more in touch with real life in my life or felt such value for life. The difference between disabling reactive clinical depression and the awe response is that as terrible as this time is for my wife and me, we have never felt more alive and never wanted to cling to life more. We want to live long so we grieve long and keep thinking about Scott and his life with us. Feeling this way isn't feeling "good," but it is feeling more intensely alive than we could have ever imagined. Depression often involves a nagging sense of giving up, but my awe for my son spurs me on to never give up trying to understand what has happened.

I feel more alive than I've ever felt; yet because of awe's diminishing the sense of the importance of the sense of self, I feel closer to and more welcoming of death than I ever have—both feelings associated with our eleventh emotion. My unrelenting grief has left me in a state of the most dreadful awe of my life and—as true awe does—has urged on my search for understanding that I likely will never find.

The awe of understanding described in this book offers no "payoff" in the form of final answers or feeling better about life. Perhaps the greatest challenge to living a life in true awe is to be able to savor the opportunity to take part in the excitement of the search for answers and feel inspired that there is so much we can never know. Persons who feel they already "have the answers" don't need awe to keep them going, only faith in the answers they already have or that someone else imposed on them. I am not comforted now by certainty, but I am vitally involved in finding meaning, manageability, and comprehensibility in the unavoidable and strangely awe-inspiring fact and agonizing fear of death.

The depth of my confused suffering at my son's loss of his life is as mysteriously awe inspiring as the fact that my son had fought his way to life when he was born. I'm in the most profound awe of my life, not only because of my son's existence but because of existence itself and what its "end" means. The fact that a beautiful awe-inspiring flower finally withers does not mean that its blooming was in vain or the beauty it shared has been lost, but it does mean that we can never again be in exactly the same awe of that same flower in that same way and must keep looking for new ways to reflect on the cycle of life.

Our Hawaiian family will honor Scott soon with a hula, praise of his life, and music in his honor. They will freely talk about Scott's life and death and their search for meaning in both. One of the Hawaiians said, "The only difference between an Hawaiian wedding and an Hawaiian funeral is that there's one less dancer. We have to learn more about the dancer, his dance, and our dance. None of us gets our way, but 'the way' is what must inspire our awe and need to understand."

AWE'S TRANSFORMATION

As I struggle to negotiate my awe of understanding, the good memories are not enough to touch the grief, and as of this writing, the agony of "no more" still far exceeds any appreciation for what "once was." I know that awe will help us transcend from the bothersome feeling of "no more" to being in awe of "what once was," but I also know my wife and I will have the hard work of accommodating the lessons of Scott's life and death to get to that better place.

Just as Scott struggled as a baby to stay alive defined who I was then, his death now defines all I will ever be. I'm not a psychologist, an author, a lecturer, nor, at least not for now, a husband or father to my living son. I'm the dad of a son who died too soon. I have been transformed by the awe of my loss. That's what the awe of understanding's intensity can do to us if we elect to pursue it; it changes us forever, and it changes how we think and feel about ourselves, the world, and our place in it. Unless we cling to the selfish orientation to life of, "What's in this for me?" or "What am I getting from this transformation?" awe helps us learn that our joy and wisdom are to be found between us and not within us. Remembering Scott forever and talking about our awe for him together will never reduce our yearning for him, but, over time, it will ease our grief.

THE NECESSITY AND CHANCE OF AFFLICTION

I don't know why, among all the other possible names and sources of reflection and for learning from my awe, the French philosopher

Weil keeps coming to my mind. It just did again. Is that you, Scott, trying to tell and teach me something, or is it another death delusion associated with the denial dimension of grief that hopes the departed can communicate with us? Is it just a coincidence that Weil herself, like Scott, suffered from excruciating migraine headaches and very poor physical coordination that, combined with her brilliant mind, resulted in her being seen as "other" and so often rejected and excluded in her own life? As I read more about her and her physical condition, is it possible that Weil herself suffered from a mild form of cerebral palsy? I can't say for sure, but when I read that at age thirty-four, one year younger than my son, she ended her own life, I felt the goose bumps and frightening thrill of another awe response.

Weil wrote about the kind of suffering Scott experienced that led to his taking his own life as something only those souls that seem least deserving of it seem to experience. She said it was unimaginable suffering that transcended the mind, body, and physical or mental anguish to "scourge the very soul." She said that affliction is associated with two characteristics of life itself—necessity and chance. She taught that affliction and the terrible in life, what I called in this book the "bad trumps good" principle, is necessary because it is hardwired into existence itself and, therefore, is inescapable. We can curse it or try to deny it, but "that's life." She added, however, that affliction is also a matter of chance because chance, too, is a built-in part of nature. Weil wrote that we don't suffer because of the traditional Christian theodicy of some kind of divine atonement or paying for our sins. We suffer because we are alive. People don't kill themselves because they don't want to live. Everyone wants to live. They end their own lives because they don't want to suffer anymore, and who among us can assess the level and meaning of the suffering of another being?

The affliction that so plagued my dear son was so unjust because it was chance. Scott was a cosmological statistical victim of both the necessity and chance of life's necessary suffering. All of us are victims of these forces and will experience them in our own unique ways. We can either choose a life of understanding awe that draws us into the endless struggle to understand life or spend our days in ignorant awe, passingly interested in the new, the better, and the "other."

Weil also pointed out that it is the person who has known pure joy, if only for a brief moment in life, for whom affliction becomes so devastating. She wrote, "Joy is the overwhelming consciousness of reality."[4] Had I not been in profound awe, I wonder if Weil's wisdom would have ever come to my mind? A life of awe, however difficult, as was the one my son led, must be full of that kind of joy, because for when all is said and done, Scott was more fully, painfully, magnificently immersed and conscious of life's good and bad realities than anyone I have ever known. He lived his life in awe as a sensitive, perhaps hypersensitive, person and saw life in ways my wife and I are going to continue forever to try to understand more fully. It's the effort, not success at finding final answers, that will sustain us. It's the interminable pain that motivates our search that leads to new awe for our son every day, the dread that always comes with our eleventh emotion. Scott had a sufficient awe of understanding to trust in the boundless mysteries of the universe, to end his life here, and to go there where his note said he was "sure we will all be in a better place together again." Those words leave us much to ponder about life itself.

As I struggle through my awe of understanding, I hope my son has found the comforting joy of that mysterious silence and is somewhere, somehow still in as much awe as we are in awe of him. Because of our awe, we've seen signs lately that Scott's essence, energy, or whatever word you may want to use is all around us. I hope that, without the agonizing pain my wife and I are enduring through our awe, what you've read about our eleventh emotion in this book will leave you in awe throughout your life, no matter what challenges it holds in store for you. Whether or not you agree with all you read, I hope you will take what you learn here about awe as a warning not to approach the end of your life, or the end of a loved one's life, with the feeling that you have not yet fully lived and loved by choosing to be in as much awe of the persons you love and of life itself as possible.

You have read about the unavoidable evolutionary principle that "bad trumps good." In my fascination with awe's power, I've probably overaccentuated the positive sides of awe throughout this manuscript, and that's the side people often prefer to talk about. I've probably overemphasized the kind of awe that is inspired by nature and events, but ultimately it's our awe for people, our connection with them, the moments of awe we share with them, and life's unavoidable processes that may be the highest and ultimately most painful and instructive kind of awe of all.

The thrill of being in awe for the good things in our lives can be the most elevated of all human emotions, but the awe we feel at the worst times can cause us to feel lower than we imagined possible. That's life and, I suggest, that's what our eleventh emotion is for— to help us negotiate, fully engage with, and learn to value and savor (whether good or bad) all that life offers, and to discover what those offerings suggest about life's ultimate meaning. Awe can teach us that the only real negative emotion is a stuck emotion, one that thoughtlessly dominates our lives.

My own awe and the awe of those you have read about in this book have taught me that we need to lower our awe threshold so that we accumulate as many memories as we can. We can have them stored away to help us when awe causes us to realize—as it eventually does—the unavoidable and sometimes horrid impact of the reality of the downsides of the phrase "that's life" and the unavoidable, overpowering reality of the "never wills."

Perhaps the best news I can share with you, even at this most difficult time when I am in the most intense awe of my life, is that allowing ourselves to fully experience awe seems to be capable of preparing us to find meaning and manageability in any crisis and of exposing new vistas for flourishing with those we love.

Don't wait! It always amazes me that millions seem consumed with spending their days trying to prolong their lives rather than being in awe of them. Every day, be on the constant lookout for people, places, things, and ideas that inspire awe. At the end of the day, write down an awe-inspiring experience and what about it you would like to reflect on. By doing so, you're less likely to die before having fully lived, a fate we know our son did not suffer. And, as Scott was fond of saying, you may not end up having what has increasingly become defined for us as "the good life," but I guarantee that you'll end up with a remarkable one.

ENDNOTES

INTRODUCTION

1 Adams, D. *The Salmon of Doubt.* London: Pan, 2003, p. 99.

2 For a description of this relatively newly recognized psychological dysfunction, see Cushman, P. "Why the Self Is Empty: Toward a Historically Situated Psychology." *American Psychologist,* Volume 45, 1990, pp. 599–611. See also Levy, S. T. "Psychoanalytic Perspectives on Emptiness." *Journal of the American Psychoanalytic Association,* Volume 32, 1984, pp. 387–404. See also Keyes, C. L. M. "The Mental Health Continuum: From Languishing to Flourishing in Life." *Journal of Health and Social Behavior,* Volume 43, 2002, pp. 207–222.

CHAPTER ONE

1 Haldane, J. B. S. *Possible Worlds.* New York: Transaction Publishers, 2001.

2 Dawkins, R. *Unweaving the Rainbow.* London: Penguin, 1998.

3 Dawkins, R. *The God Delusion.* Boston: Houghton Mifflin Company, 2006, p. 361. Although this is a book describing the science behind atheism, it is full of awe-inspiring examples of what can inspire awe in those with open enough minds and hearts to contemplate the fact that there is no limit to what is left to learn about life and its meaning.

4 This concept of "existential anguish" was developed by philosopher Paul Tillich and is similar to the thinking of Søren Kierkegaard and Sigmund Freud and their views on our primary fear. For a description of Tillich's philosophy in this regard and a critical analysis of it, see Hook, S. "The Atheism of Paul Tillich." In Hook, S. (Editor). *Religious Experience and Truth: A Symposium.* New York: New York University Press, 1961.

5 Kant, I. *Foundations of the Metaphysics of Morals.* Beck, L. W. (Translator). Indianapolis, Indiana: Bobbs-Merrill, 1785–1959.

6 Grand, S. *Creation: Life and How to Make It.* London: Weidenfeld & Nicolson, 2000.

7 For an excellent scientific discussion of emotion, see Plutchik, R. *Emotions and Life: Perspectives from Psychology, Biology, and Evolution.* Washington, D.C.: American Psychological Association, 2003.

8 Cattell, R. B. *Personality and Motivation Structure and Measurement.* New York: Harcourt Brace Jovanovich, 1957.

9 Izard developed the "differential emotions theory" that suggests that we don't learn our emotions but the cues that elicit them and that they evolved as response mechanisms that can take place without "thinking." See Izard, C. E. *The Psychology of Emotions.* New York: Plenum Press, 2001.

10 Adams, D. *The Salmon of Doubt.* London: Pan, 2003, p. 99.

11 For a description of the important distinction between experience and awareness as related to happiness and perception, see Gilbert, D. *Stumbling on Happiness.* New York: Knopf, 2006, pp. 58–63.

12 For a discussion of the issue of "experiencing what we are experiencing," see Schooler, J. W. "Re-Representing Consciousness:

Dissociations Between Consciousness and Meta-Consciousness."
Trends in Cognitive Science, Volume 6, 2002, pp. 339–344.

CHAPTER TWO

1 More than twenty years ago, psychologist Aaron Antonovsky
referred to the importance of what he called a "sense of coher-
ence" in our life. He said it had three components: comprehensibility, or the ability to make sense and find some order in what
is happening to us; manageability, or the discovery of one's
resources for dealing with the chaos of life; and meaning, referring to learning how life makes sense emotionally. Awe can lead
to all three of these skills. See Antonovsky, A. *Unraveling the
Mystery of Health.* San Francisco: Jossey-Bass Publishers, 1987.

2 Gilbert, D. *Stumbling on Happiness.* New York: Alfred A.
Knopf, 2006, p. 65.

3 These dimensions of awe were described by the Awe Inspiring
Experiences study group centered at UCLA. See http://www.
bec.ucla.edu/BECSpeakerSeries.htm.

4 Masson, J. M., and McCarthy, S. *When Elephants Weep: The
Emotional Lives of Animals.* New York: Delacorte Press, 1995.

5 As quoted in Masson, J. M. *Dogs Never Lie About Love.* New
York: Three Rivers Press, 1997, p. 1.

6 Psychologist Steven Coren has done extensive studies of dogs. He
found that they only lack the language, math, and music intelligences but show the other four of the "basic seven" including the
spatial, kinesthetic, intrapersonal, and interpersonal intelligences. See Coren, S. *The Intelligence of Dogs: Canine
Consciousness and Capabilities.* New York: Free Press, 1994.

7 As quoted in Masson, J. M. *Dogs Never Lie About Love.* New York: Three Rivers Press, 1997, p. i.

8 As quoted in Wright, R. *The Moral Animal.* New York: Pantheon, 1994, p. 364.

9 Zohar, D. and Marshall, I. *SQ: Connecting with Our Spiritual Intelligence.* New York: Bloomsbury, 2000, p. 148.

10 As quoted in Heschel, A. *God in Search of Man.* New York: Straus and Giroux, 1955.

11 Ibid.

12 See for example Ramachandran, V. S. and Blakeslee, S. *Phantoms in the Brain.* London: Fourth Estate, 1998.

13 Newberg, A., D'Aquili, E., and Rause, V. *Why God Won't Go Away.* New York: Ballantine Books, 2001.

14 I highly recommend the work of psychologist Jonathan Haidt, who has written extensively on ways in which we can learn from ancient wisdom and its most basic teachings in order to bridge the gap between the secular and religious and liberal and conservative thinking. See Haidt, J. *The Happiness Hypothesis: Finding Modern Truth in Ancient Wisdom.* New York: Basic Books, 2006. Haidt is a pioneer in the study of awe.

15 Emerson, R. W. "Nature." In Whicher, S. (Editor). *Selections from Ralph Waldo Emerson.* Boston: Houghton Mifflin, 1960, p. 24.

16 There might be something about my living in Hawaii that relates to this belief system. The Hawaiian culture is pantheistic and sees the divine in every thing and person. Years ago, I read a book by physicist Harold J. Morowitz, which he had written on his sailboat moored just off Lahaina, Maui. He also referred to himself as a pantheist in the tradition of Giordano Bruno, who preceded

Spinoza and asserted the view that God existed in nature and not above in heaven. Bruno was burned for his views, and Spinoza excommunicated, so the issue of our beliefs about divinity can get us into a lot of trouble and reflects the downside of awe when we fail to come to grips with the challenges it presents us to reflect deeply and maybe even change our mind. See Morowitz, H. J. *Cosmic Joy and Local Pain: Musings of a Mystic Scientist.* New York: Charles Scribner's Sons, 1987.

17 Several love letters written by Einstein have recently been released. It turns out the twice-married Albert also had many extramarital affairs, and his letters reveal his impulsive, romantic side. In one, he writes, "Gravity can't explain why we fall in love." Renn, J., Shulman, R., and Smith, F. *Albert Einstein/Mileva Marcic: The Love Letters.* New Jersey: Princeton University Press, 2000.

CHAPTER THREE

1 See an interview of Brian Swimme by Carol Ludwig and Bob Gardenhire "Igniting: An Interview with Brian Swimme." In *Presence,* Volume 8, Number 1, March, 2007, pp. 45–52.

2 For a fascinating and carefully researched discussion of the dangers of the unrelenting push for happiness, see physician Ronald Dworkin's *Artificial Happiness: The Dark Side of the New Happy Class.* New York: Carroll & Graf, 2006.

3 Kramer, P. *Listening to Prozac.* New York: Penguin, 1993.

4 The phrase "pleasure police" was used by author David Shaw to describe the health establishment's persistent nagging and threats that almost anything that feels or tastes good isn't good for us. I'm using the phrase with a reverse meaning to describe

the current "feel good and by happy or else" culture. See Shaw, D. *The Pleasure Police.* New York: Doubleday, 1996.

5 Stevens, W. *The Necessary Angel: Essays on Reality and Imagination.* New York: Vintage Press, 1965, p. 26.

6 See, for example, Bonanno, G. A., Rennicke, C., and Dekel, S. "Self-Enhancement Among High-Exposure Survivors of the September 11 Terrorist Attack: Resilience or Social Maladjustment?" *Journal of Personality and Social Psychology,* Volume 88, 2005, pp. 984–998.

7 I report the research on "post-traumatic growth" and thriving through trauma in my book *The Beethoven Factor: The New Positive Psychology of Happiness, Hardiness, Healing, Hope.* Charlottesville, VA: Hampton Roads, 2003.

8 Ibid. See also Aspinwall, L. G., and Staudinger, U. M. *A Psychology of Human Strengths.* Washington: American Psychological Association, 2003.

9 Ryff, C. D., and Singer, B. "The Contours of Positive Human Health." *Psychological Inquiry,* Volume 9, 1998, pp. 1–28. See also, Ryff, C. D., and Singer, B. "Flourishing Under Fire: Resilience as a Prototype of Challenged Thriving." In Keyes, C. L. M., and Haidt, J. (Editors). *Flourishing: Positive Psychology and the Life Well-Lived.* Washington: American Psychological Association, 2003, pp. 15–36.

10 Stevens, W. op. cit. p. 30.

11 Actor Alan Alda's *Never Have Your Dog Stuffed: And Other Things I've Learned* (New York: Random House, 2005) discusses the necessity of "letting go" and the more profound legitimate feelings that come with deep, full, natural grieving.

12 Davidson, R. J. "Affective Style and Affective Disorders: Perspectives from Affective Neuroscience." *Cognition and Emotion,* Volume 12, 1998, pp. 307–330.

13 See Kagan, J. *Galen's Prophecy: Temperament in Human Nature.* New York: Basic Books, 1994.

14 Burke, E. *A Philosophical Inquiry into the Origin of Our Ideas of the Sublime and the Beautiful.* Boulton, J. T. (Editor). Notre Dame, IN: University of Notre Dame Press, 1958.

15 One was an unpublished manuscript at the University of Wisconsin by D. R. Lowe and D. Keltner written in 1997. Another was an unpublished paper by student R. Kayer with his faculty mentor D. Keltner at the University of California, Berkeley, titled "The Mechanism and Function of Awe: A Cognitive Enhancement Theory," written in 1998. The most comprehensive review of the topic was by J. Haidt and D. Keltner in their paper "Approaching Awe, a Moral, Spiritual, and Aesthetic Emotion." *Cognition and Emotion,* Volume 17, 2003, pp. 297–314. As I did in my review of the literature for this book three years later, I learned they also found scientific psychology had essentially ignored awe as a basic human emotion.

16 One of the three scientifically oriented articles ever written about "awe" and the first to suggest the concepts of "vastness" and "accommodation" was by D. Keltner and J. Haidt. "Approaching Awe, a Moral, Spiritual,, and Aesthetic Emotion." op. cit.

17 The term *accommodation* was used by psychologist Jean Piaget to describe how children learn to mentally "fit in" new experiences in their life that don't make sense to them when they're first encountered. See J. Piaget and B. Inhelder, *The Psychology of the Child.* Weaver, H. (Translator). New York: Basic Books, 1969. (Original work published in 1966.)

18 Acts 9:3–7.

CHAPTER FOUR

1 Bechara, A., Damasio, H., and Damasio, A. R. "Emotion, Decision Making and the Orbitofrontal Cortex." *Cerebral Cortex,* Volume 10, 2000, pp. 295–307.

2 For an excellent review of the science of emotion, see Plutchik, R. *Emotions and Life: Perspectives from Psychology, Biology, and Evolution.* Washington: American Psychological Association, 2003.

3 Ibid., p. xvii.

4 See Gladwell, M. *Blink: The Power of Thinking Without Thinking.* Boston: Little Brown, 2005, p. 23.

5 For examples of approaches to understanding human emotion, I highly recommend Daniel Goleman's book *Destructive Emotions: How Can We Overcome Them?* New York: Bantam Books, 2004.

6 See entry 2 in the *Oxford English Dictionary.* Oxford, England: Oxford University Press, 2002.

7 For an example of some of these definitions and theories, see Strongman, K. *The Psychology of Emotion.* New York: Wiley, 1987.

8 For an example of the many approaches to a "basic emotions list," see Kemper, J. D. "How Many Emotions Are There? Wedding the Social and Autonomic Components." *American Journal of Sociology,* Volume 93, 1987.

9 James, W. "What Is an Emotion?" *Mind,* 1884, Volume 19, pp. 188–205.

10 For a fascinating discussion of the ideas of second-century physician Galen, who speculated that humans had nine emotional temperaments that resulted from various mixtures

of hot/cold and dry/moist "humors," see Kagan, J. *Galen's Prophecy.* New York: Basic Books, 1994.

11 James, W. *The Principles of Psychology,* Volume 2. New York: Holt, p. 1066.

12 The view that some of our emotions "just happen to us" before we mentally label them is suggested by psychologist Robert Zajonc. He argues that our emotional reactions can be quicker than our interpretation of them, and some of the SAI participants also described this kind of awe response. See Zajonc, R. "Emotions." In Gilbert, D., et al. (Editors), *The Handbook of Social Psychology,* 4th Edition. New York: McGraw-Hill, 1998.

13 This idea of embracing our present life without the promise of another one later is discussed in Dawkins, R. *Unweaving the Rainbow.* London: Penguin, 1998.

14 For the most concise and accurate description of "the language of emotions" and the search for the meaning and impact in our life, see Plutchik, R. *Emotions and Life: Perspectives from Psychology, Biology, and Evolution.* Washington: American Psychological Association, 2003. Although like most scientists in this field, he does not include awe in his index or on his lists of emotions, I highly recommend his book not only as a text for college courses in human emotion but for laypersons interested in learning more about the science of emotion.

15 Justman, S. *Fool's Paradise: The Unreal World of Pop Psychology.* Chicago: Ivan R. Dee, 2005, p. 5.

16 Kaminer, W. *I'm Dysfunctional, You're Dysfunctional: The Recovery Movement and Other Self-Help Fashions.* New York: Vintage Books, 1993, p. 30.

17 Ibid., p. 31.

18 Goleman, D. *Emotional Intelligence: Why It Can Matter More Than IQ.* New York: Bantam, 1995, p. 181.

19 Sommers, C. H., and Satel, S. *One Nation Under Therapy: How the Helping Culture Is Eroding Self-Reliance.* New York: St. Martin's Press, 2005, pp. 110–114. I also address the issue of the current pop psychology unchurched religion of inner awareness in my book *The Last Self-Help Book You'll Ever Need.* New York: Basic Books, 2005.

CHAPTER FIVE

1 Byrne, R. *The Secret.* New York: Atria Books, 2006.

2 As quoted in Adler, J. "Decoding the Secret." *Newsweek,* March 5, 2007, p. 53.

3 Dawkins, R. *The God Delusion.* Boston: Houghton Mifflin, 2006, p. 355.

4 Ibid.

5 This idea is elaborated by physicist Steven Grand in his book *What Is Good? The Best Way to Live.* London: Weidenfeld & Nicholson, 2000.

6 Einstein, A. "Religion and Science." In *Ideas and Opinions.* New York: Crown Publishers, 1954, p. 36.

7 From James, W. *Psychology: Briefer Course.* New York: Holt, 1890.

8 Childre, D., and Martin, H. *The HeartMath Solution.* New York: HarperSanFrancisco, 1999, p. 6.

9 The concept of "emergent property" is described in Minsky, M. *The Society of Mind.* New York: Simon & Schuster, 1985.

10 Crick, F. *The Astonishing Hypothesis.* New York: Simon & Schuster, 1994, p. 3.

11 Darwin, C. *The Expression of the Emotions in Man and Animals.* Chicago: University of Chicago Press, 1963. (Originally published in 1872.)

12 Frysinger, R. C., and Harper, R. M. "Cardiac and Respiratory Correlations with Unit Discharge in Epileptic Human Temporal Lobe." *Epilepsia,* Volume 31, 1990, pp. 162–171.

13 Lessmeier, T. J., et al. "Unrecognized Paroxysmal Supraventricular Tachycardia: Potential for Misdiagnosis as Panic Disorder." *Archives of Internal Medicine,* Volume 175, 1997, pp. 537–543.

14 The "yips" as caused by the heart is discussed at http://www.pgaonline.com/improve/features/mentalgame/improve_heartmath062904.cfm.

15 Carter, C. S. "Neuroendocrine Perspectives on Social Attachment and Love." *Psychoneuroendocrinology,* Volume 23, 1998, pp. 779–818.

16 This unpublished study is described in Jonathan Haidt's outstanding book *The Happiness Hypothesis.* New York: Basic Books, 2006, pp. 97–98.

17 Elevation as a positive emotion is described in ibid., p. 193–200.

18 Newberg, A., et al. *Why God Won't Go Away.* New York: Ballantine Books, 2001, p. 42.

CHAPTER SIX

1 For a complete description of languishing and its demographics, see Keyes, C. L. M. "The Mental Health Continuum: From Languishing to Flourishing in Life." *Journal of Health and Social Behavior,* Volume 43, 2002, pp. 207–222.

2 For a discussion of languishing, see Cushman, P. "Why the Self Is Empty: Toward a Historically Situated Psychology." *American Psychologist,* Volume 45, 1990, pp. 599–611.

3 For a discussion of this issue, see Pearsall, P. *The Last Self-Help Book You'll Ever Need.* New York: Basic Books, 2005. See also Hillmann, J., and M. Ventura. *We've Had a Hundred Years of Psychotherapy—and the World's Getting Worse.* New York: HarperSanFrancisco, 1992. See also Pearsall, P. *500 Therapies: Discovering a Science of Daily Living.* New York: W. W. Norton, 2008.

4 Easterbrook, G. *The Progress Paradox: How Life Gets Better While People Feel Worse.* New York: Random House, 2003, p. xxi.

5 For an interesting discussion of the Aristotelian origins of the concept of flourishing and the concept of flourishing in a geopolitical context, see Richard H. Trowbridge's 2003 online article "The Flourishing Earth." At www.animadversions respectingtheFC.doc.

6 Pogge, T. W. "Human Flourishing and Universal Justice." In Paul, E. F., et al. (Editors). *Human Flourishing.* New York: Cambridge University Press, 1999, p. 333.

7 Fredrickson, B. L., et al. "The Ongoing Effect of Positive Emotions." *Motivation and Emotion,* Volume 24, 2000, pp. 237–258.

8 Davidson, R. J., et al. "Alterations in Brain and Immune

Function Produced by Mindfulness Meditation." *Psychosomatic Medicine,* Volume 65, 2003, pp. 564–570.

9 Cohen, S., et al. "Emotional Style and Susceptibility to the Common Cold." *Psychosomatic Medicine,* Volume 65, 2003, pp. 652–657.

10 An important and fascinating study of resilience after the terrorist attacks on the United States on September 11, 2001, showed that positive emotional states like those associated with the awe response related to more resilience and sense of meaning, manageability, and comprehensibility in the face of terrible crises. See Fredrickson, B. L., et al. "What Good Are Positive Emotions in Crises? A Prospective Study of Resilience and Emotions Following the Terrorist Attacks on the United States on September 11, 2001." *Journal of Personality and Social Psychology,* Volume 84, 2001, pp. 365–376.

11 Steptoe, A., Wardle, J., and Marmot, M. "Positive Affect and Health-Related Neuroendocrine, Cardiovascular, and Inflammatory Processes." *Proceedings of the National Academy of Sciences,* Volume 102, 2005, pp. 6508–6512.

12 This finding is from research by G. V. Ostir and his colleagues who showed that the effects of emotional states like awe reduce the chances of stroke in older adults. See Ostir, G. V., et al. "The Associations Between Emotional Well-Being and the Incidence of Stroke in Older Adults." *Psychosomatic Medicine,* Volume 63, 2001, pp. 210–215.

13 For example, see Ostir, G. V., et al. "Emotional Well-Being Predicts Subsequent Functional Independence and Survival." *Journal of the American Geriatrics Society,* Volume 48, 2000, pp. 473–478.

14 Gill, K. M., et al. "Daily Mood and Stress Predict Pain, Health Care Use, and Work Activity in African American Adults with Sickle-Cell Disease." *Health Psychology,* Volume 23, 2004, pp. 267–274.

15 I develop this point in my book *The Beethoven Factor: The New Positive Psychology of Hardiness, Happiness, Healing, and Hope.* Charlottesville, VA: Hampton Roads Publishers, 2003.

16 This definition is based on the research of C. L. M. Keyes, a pioneer in the emerging field of positive psychology. See Keyes, C. L. M. "The Mental Health Continuum: From Languishing to Flourishing in Life." *Journal of Health and Social Behavior,* Volume 43, 2002, pp. 207–222.

17 This position stems from the "Broaden and Build" theory of emotion proposed by Barbara Fredrickson at the University of Michigan and her colleagues. See Fredrickson, B. L. "What Good Are Positive Emotions?" *Review of General Psychology,* Volume 2, 1998, pp. 300–319.

18 Fredrickson, B. L., and M. F. Losada. "Positive Affect and the Complex Dynamics of Human Flourishing." *American Psychologist,* Volume 60, 2005, p. 679.

19 As quoted in Norem, J. K. *The Positive Power of Negative Thinking.* New York: Basic Books, 2001, p. 159. This book is one of the best, most scientifically based, and highly readable sources of a discussion of the crucial role of negative thinking and defensive pessimism.

20 The importance of negativity to flourishing is discussed in Schwartz, R. M., et al. "Optimal and Normal Affect Balance in Psychotherapy of Major Depression: Evaluation of the Balanced States of Mind Model." *Behavioral and Cognitive Psychotherapy,* Volume 30, 2002, pp. 439–450.

21 Eckman, P., et al. "The Duchenne Smile: Emotional Expression and Brain Physiology." *Journal of Personality and Social Psychology,* Volume 58, 1990, pp. 342–353.

22 Rosenberg, E. L. "Linkages Between Facial Expressions of Anger and Transient Myocardial Ischemia in Men with Coronary Artery Disease." *Emotion,* Volume 1, 2001, pp. 107–115.

23 For a description of this effect, see Lorenz, E. N. *The Essence of Chaos.* Seattle: University of Washington Press, 1993.

24 Fredrickson, B. L., and M. F. Losada. "Positive Affect and the Complex Dynamics of Human Flourishing." *American Psychologist,* Volume 60, 2005, p. 683.

CHAPTER SEVEN

1 This finding was described in a study by Kahneman, D., and A. Tversky. "Prospect Theory: An Analysis of Decisions Under Risk." *Econometrica,* Volume 47, 1979, pp. 263–291.

2 Rozin, P., and Royzman, E. B. "Negativity Bias, Negativity Dominance, and Contagion." *Personality and Social Psychology Review,* Volume 5, 2001, pp. 296–320.

3 Franklin, B. *Poor Richard's Almanack,* Mount Vernon, NY: Peter Pauper Press, 1980, reprint form 17331–758, p. 26.

4 For the most comprehensive review of the history of the concept of "a sense of humor," see Wickberg, D. *The Senses of Humor: Self and Laughter in Modern America.* Ithaca, NY: Cornell University Press, 1998.

5 Meeker, J. *The Comedy of Survival.* Tucson, AZ: The University of Arizona Press, 1997, p. 12.

6 Wickberg, op. cit.

7 Maslow, A. H. *Motivation and Personality,* 3rd Edition. New York: Harper and Row, p. 136.

8 Easterbrook, G. *The Progress Paradox.* New York: Random House, 2004, p. 238.

9 For a discussion of "mindful" hoping, see Langer, E. *Mindfulness.* Reading, MA: Addison-Wesley, 1989.

10 Roberts, K. T., and Messenger, T. C. "The Terminally Ill: Serenity Nursing Interventions for Hospice Clients." *Journal of Gerontological Nursing,* Volume 11, 1994, pp. 17–22.

11 Khalek, A., Al-Meshaan, A. O., and Al-Shatti, A. "Themes of Presleep Thoughts." *Journal of Social Sciences,* Volume 23, 1995, p. 63.

12 Mandler, G. *Human Nature Explored.* New York: Oxford University Press, 1997, p. 4.

13 Ibid, p. 5.

14 Meehl, P. E. "Hedonic Capacity: Some Conjectures." *Bulletin of the Menninger Clinic,* Volume 39, 1975, pp. 2953–3007.

15 As reported by Berscheid, E. "The Human's Greatest Strength: Other Humans." In Aspinwall, L. G., and Staudinger, U. M. *A Psychology of Human Strengths.* Washington: American Psychological Association, 2003, p. 43.

CHAPTER 8

1 For a fascinating discussion of "artificial happiness," see Dworkin, R. W. *Artificial Happiness: The Dark Side of the New Happy Class.* New York: Carroll & Graf, 2006. Just as I completed the manuscript for this book, I discovered this wonderful book and its caution about falsely inducing happiness as a panacea for the widespread discontent that requires focus on what is really causing our displeasure, related to the reflective awe discovered in this book.

2 Thucydides. *The History of the Peloponnesian War.* Crowley, R. (Translator), New York: Barnes and Noble Books, 2006.

3 As quoted in Ludwig, C., and Gardinhire, B. "Igniting Life: An Interview with Brian Swimme." *Presence,* Volume 8, Number 1, March, 2007, p. 46.

4 *"Rock"* and *"Water" logic* are terms introduced by Edward de Bono. See his book *I Am Right, You Are Wrong: From This to New Renaissance: From Rock Logic to Water Logic.* New York: Viking, 1991. For a discussion of the adversarial competitive approach to life characteristic of toxic awe, see Kohn, A. *No Contest: The Case Against Competition.* Boston: Houghton Mifflin, 1986.

5 As quoted in Dawkins, R. *The God Delusion.* Boston: Houghton Mifflin Company, 2006, p. 10.

6 Ibid, p. 308.

7 Milgram, S. "Behavioral Study of Obedience." *Journal of Abnormal & Social Psychology,* Volume 67, 1963, pp. 371–378.

8 Geher, G., et al. "Self and Other Obedience Estimates: Biases and Moderators." *Journal of Social Psychology,* Volume 142, 2002, pp. 677–689.

9 Tarnow, E. "Self-destructive Obedience in the Airplane Cockpit and the Concept of Obedience Optimization." In Blass, T. and Mahway, N. J. (Editors). *Obedience to Authority: Current Perspectives on the Milgram Paradigm.* New York: Erlbaum Associates, pp. 111–123.

10 de Bono, Edward. op. cit.

11 One of the first and most comprehensive and well-documented presentations of the topic of awe appears in Keltner, D., and Haidt, J. "Approaching Awe, a Moral, Spiritual, and Aesthetic Emotion." *Cognition and Emotion,* Volume 17, 2003, pp. 297–314. I came across this article as I was collecting my interviews on awe, and I have employed many of their insights and examples in this book.

12 *Bhagavadgita.* Archer, R. C. (Translator). London: Oxford University Press, 1969, II:45.

13 *The Bhagavad-Gita.* Zachner, R. C. (Editor and translator). Oxford: Clarendon Press, 1969, p. 45.

14 Weber, M. *Economy and Society: An Outline of Interpretive Sociology.* In Roth, G., and Wittich, C. (Editors). Berkeley, CA: University of California Press, 1978, p. 1117.

CHAPTER NINE

1 Gibran, K. *The Prophet.* New York: Knopf, 1968, p. 52.

2 Goldberg, I. I., Harel, M., and Malach, R., "When the Brain Loses Its Self: Prefrontal Inactivation during Sensorimotor Processing." *Neuron,* Volume 50, April, 2006, pp. 329–339.

3 Blake, W. *The Complete Poetry and Prose of William Blake.* New York: Knopf, 1982.

4 Langer, E., et al. "Believing Is Seeing." Unpublished paper, Harvard University, referred to in Ellen Langer's book *Mindfulness: Choice and Control in Everyday Life*. London: Harvill, 1991.

5 For a description of how the brain distorts and biases our perceptions to protect our self-esteem, see Fine, C. *A Mind of Its Own: How Your Brain Distorts and Deceives*. New York: W. W. Norton, 2006.

6 Sidis, B. *The Psychology of Suggestion*. New York: Appleton, 1898, as quoted in Merikle, P. M., and Reingold, E. M. "Measuring Unconscious Perceptual Processes." In Bornstein, R. F., and Pittman, T. S. (Editors). *Perception Without Awareness: Cognitive, Clinical, and Social Perspectives*. New York: Guilford Press, 1992.

7 Ibid., p. 10.

8 Pierce, C. S., and Jastrow, J. "On Small Differences in Sensation." *Memoirs of the National Academy of Science*, Volume 3, 1884, pp. 75–83. As quoted by Kihlstrom, J. F., et al. "Implicit Perception." In Bornstein, R. F., and Pittman, T. S. (Editors). *Perception Without Awareness: Cognitive, Clinical, and Social Perspectives*. New York: Guilford Press, 1992.

9 This study is described in the fascinating book by Guy Claxton that deals with what he calls our "undermind" that senses what our fast thinking and intention-driven brain fails to sense or know that we sense. See Claxton, G. *Hare Brain, Tortoise Mind*. Hopewell, NJ: Ecco Press, 1997.

10 This selfless state is described in Csikszentmihalyi, M. *Flow: The Psychology of Optimal Experience*. New York: HarperCollins, 1991.

11 The so-called "blind sight" studies are reviewed in Lawrence Weiskrantz's book *Blindsight: A Case Study and Its Implications*. Oxford, UK: Clarendon, 1986.

12 Carse, J. P. *Finite and Infinite Games: A Vision of Life as Play and Possibility*. New York: Ballantine Books, 1986, p. 8.

13 Marcel, A. J. "Slippage in the Unity of Consciousness." (CIBA Symposium 174). Chichester, UK: John Wiley & Sons, 1993.

14 For an example of this idea, see Humphrey, N. *Leaps of Faith*. New York: Anchor Books, 1993.

15 As quoted in Claxton, G. *Hare Brain, Tortoise Mind,* p. 128.

CHAPTER TEN

1 The quotes from Simone Weil in this chapter are presented mostly from my own memory and very old lecture notes. I read her work in my one philosophy class forty years ago at the University of Michigan, but for some reason they are resonating now. See also Weil, S. *Gravity and Grace*. New York: Routledge, 1998.

2 Ibid., p. 52.

3 Ludwig, C., and Gardenhire, B. "Igniting Life: An Interview with Brian Swimme." *Presence,* Volume 8, Number 1, March, 2007, p. 51.

4 Weil, op. cit., p. 73.

INDEX

Abbott, Edwin A., 196

accommodation
  characteristics of, 86–87, 109
  logic of, 203–204
  mental, 160, 192, 199

Adams, Douglas, 19

Addie's gift, 83–84, 137–138

admiration, 99, 131

adulthood, characteristics of, 40–44

afferent neurological connections,
  132. see also brain

agnosticism, 110

Ahmadinejad, Mahmoud, 214

aloha, 84

altruism, 83–84, 137–138, 189

amusement, 166, 177–179. see also
  humor

amygdala, 132. see also brain

anger, 92, 153–154, 162, 170

animals
  chimpanzees, 192–193, 202, 215
  dogs, 45–46, 88
  elephants, 45
  emotion in, 44–45, 98, 131
  monkeys (research), 233,
    239–240

anxiety, 10–11, 21, 133, 152, 161

approach-avoidance system, 162–163

Aristotle, 151

Arjuna, 218–220

Aron, Raymond, 161

arousal system (SAM), 139–141

a-Santa-ists, 42–44, 56. see also
  Santa-ists

atheism, 110

Athenians, 197–200

authority gradient, 208–216, 220

autonomic nervous system, 136–137.
  see also nervous system

awake self, 235

awareness and experience, 24–26

awe deficiency disorder (ADD),
  145–146, 188

awe diaries, 32, 36–38, 110

awe-inspired life, 21, 23, 26–29,
  227–228. see also flourishing; languishing; life

awe-inspired war, 200–201

awe-inspiring leaders, 220

awe lite, 19–22, 23, 87–88, 223–224,
  243

awe of understanding, 109, 223–225

awe response. see also brain; physiological aspects of awe response
  accommodation and, 86–87, 109,
    160, 199, 203–204
  experiential aspects of, 24–26
  facial expressions of, 100, 131
  God, closeness to and, 22, 36–38

heart and, 53–54, 132–134, 137
in-between areas, 113, 148–149
as innate, 105
as natural, 44–48, 54
as observable, 35–36
scientific description of, 218
supernatural, 50–52
twelve characteristics of, 129–143
vastness and, 86–89
awesome, definition of, 147–148
awe stories (SAI participants)
anticipatory fear, 37–38
awe-inspired life, 228
being alive, 28
being okay, 227
being uplifted, 137–138
body first, 132
children, 81–84
compassion, 123–124, 180–181
connective consciousness, 143
contentment, 181–182
death, 186–187
excited calm, 141
facial expression, 100
happiness, 161
healing, 153–154
heart first, 133
joy, 188–189
love, 190–191
necessary losses, 71–72
negative emotion, 162–163, 168
overwhelming awe, 4, 140
pride, 191–192
serenity, 185–187
sexual response, 136–137, 139,
192–194
spiritual awareness, 75
zeal, 192
awe struck, 199–200
awful awe, 195–221

bad trumps good
as obstacle in life, 67, 171–176,
178
principle of, 76, 105, 255, 257
violence and, 200–202
Bard, Philip, 107–109
Bartlett's Familiar Quotations, 190
basal tears, 142
Bechara, Antoine, 93
Beethoven Factor, The (Pearsall), 70
behaviorism, 97–98
Blake, William, 230
blind sight, 234–240
blind spots, 236–237
body. see brain; nervous system;
physiological aspects of awe
response
Bohr, Niels, 118
bombshell, 14–16
Bootes supervoid, 57. see also cosmos
brain
afferent neurological connections
and, 132
amygdala, 132
awake self, 235
cranial nerves, 134
deep self-introspection and, 229
egotistical demands of, 24–25
frontal brain symmetry, 154
God spots in, 51, 54–56
occipital lobe, 234
orientation association area, 55
posterior superior parietal lobe,
55–56
prefrontal cortex, 228–229
quantum physics and, 121–122,
125–126
sensory cortex, 229

sub-awake self, 233, 235
temporal lobes of, 54
three brains, idea of, 134–135,
    229–230
vain brain, 233
breathlessness, 35, 141–142
broaden and build theory of emotion,
    159–160
Bruno, Giordano, 59
Buddha, 61, 90
Buddhism, 11, 61, 90
Burke, Edmund, 74–75
butterfly effect, 164–165
Byrne, Rhonda, 115–116

cancer, 68–71, 76–80, 112, 157–158,
    169–171
Cannon, Walter, 107–109
Cannon-Bard theory of emotion,
    107–109
card-drawing study, 93–94, 97
cardioendocrinology, 53
cardiology, 53
cardiovascular system, 155
Carse, James P., 237
celebrity, awe and, 87–88, 214–215
central nervous system (CNS), 28,
    134. see also brain; nervous
    system
chakras, 53
Childre, Doc, 123
children
    awe and, 38–40, 42–44,
        81–84, 131
    with cancer, 77–78
    fascination and, 179–180
    mothers and, 135–136

chimpanzees, 192–193, 202, 215
Chopra, Deepak, 115
Christianity, 90, 205, 206, 255
Churchland, Patricia, 128–129
Columbus, Christopher, 215–217
compassion, 123–124, 166, 180–181
connective consciousness, 122–123,
    142–143, 225
consciousness
    change in, 35, 217–221
    connective, 122–123, 142–143,
        225
    consumer, 147
    cosmic, 54
    explanation of, 124–128
    feeling-emotion-consciousness
    cycle, 92
    fixedness and, 125–126
    qualities of, 9, 10, 38, 54, 73
    science and, 126–129
    self-consciousness, 233–236
    stimulation of, 84–86
    thin slicing, 97
consolation, awe and, 119–120
consumer consciousness, 147
contentment, 166, 181–182
Copernican revolution, 11–13
Copernicus, Nicolas, 11–13
co-pilots, 211–214
cortisol, 140, 155
cosmetic psychopharmacology, 64
cosmic consciousness, 54
cosmos, 5–9, 12, 57, 202–203, 249.
    see also lunar eclipse
Cranch, Christopher, 98
Cranial Nerve #10, 134
cranial nerves, 134. see also brain

Crick, Francis, 126–128, 143
crying, 142
cults, 205–206, 214

Dalai Lama, 88
dark energy, 8
dark matter, 7, 8
Darwin, Charles, 52–53, 98, 100, 120, 131
Dawkins, Richard, 10, 120–122, 207
death, 49, 76–78, 186–187, 243–253
delusion, 115–117
diaries, awe, 32, 36–38, 110
Dickinson, Emily, 110–111
diminished awe, 40–44
divinity, 31–36, 98–99, 110. *see also* God; Higher Power
DNA, 10, 127, 128
dogs, 45–46, 88
Dogs Never Lie about Love (Masson), 45
dread, 138. *see also* fear
dreams, 234–235
Dyer, Wayne, 115

Easterbrook, Gregg, 149, 183
eclipse, lunar, 198–199, 216–217
ecstasy, 192–194
ego, 24–25, 49
Einstein, Albert, 58–59, 122, 150
elation, twelve types of, 176–194
elephants, 45
elevation, sense of, 137–138
eleventh emotion (awe). *see also* awe response; emotions

awesome and, 147–148
case for, 17–18, 91–114
dangers of, 195–197
death, idea of and, 76–78
defintions of, 98–99
qualities of, 107–111
questions about, 46–52
three brains, idea of, 134
emergent property, 124–126
Emerson, Ralph Waldo, 57
emotional health, 96, 111–112
Emotional Intelligence (Goleman), 112
emotions, 91–114. *see also* eleventh emotion (awe); negative emotions; positive emotions; sexual desire; twelve elations
in animals, 44–45, 98, 131
characteristics of, 101–106
expression of, 94–96, 100, 107–108, 131, 160
factor analysis of, 17–18
feeling-emotion-consciousness cycle, 92
gut feelings, 40, 47
healthy, 96, 111–112
studies of, 93–94, 101–102, 176, 135-136
tears, 142
ten basic, 17–18, 46, 48, 99–100, 148–149
theories of, 52–53, 97–98, 100, 107–109, 159–160
energy cardiology, 53
enlightenment illusionment, 120
enteric nervous system (ENS), 28, 134, 135. *see also* brain; nervous system
entitlement, sense of, 119
eudaimonia, 151

experience and awareness, 24–26

Expression of the Emotions in Man and Animals (Darwin), 98, 131

facial expressions, awe and, 100, 131

factor analysis of emotions, 17–18

faith, 1, 3–4, 56–59, 206–208. *see also* God; religion

fascination, 166, 179–180

fear
  anticipatory, 31, 35, 37–38
  awe response and, 131, 163, 195–196, 219–220
  of death, 49, 76–78, 253
  of divine being, 98–99
  in dogs, 46
  dread, 138
  as innate, 105
  manipulation by, 214–217
  nonrational, 157–158, 170, 189, 199–200, 204
  rational, 157–158, 162
  of unknown, 84–86

feeling-emotion-consciousness cycle, 92

feelings, 40, 47, 134–135. *see also* emotions

fight or flight response, 107–108, 160

Fine, Cordelia, 233

fixedness, 125–126

Flatland (Abbott), 196

flight simulation research, 231–232

flourishing, 145–168. *see also* languishing
  acceptance and, 240
  definition of, 150–152
  emotions and, 159–160, 164–165
  healing/health and, 153–156

test, flourishing factor, 166–168, 175–176, 182

flow, 235–236

focal dystonia, 133

fourth chakra, 53

Franklin, Benjamin, 102, 174

Fredrickson, Barbara, 159–160, 164–165

Freud, Sigmund, 95

frontal brain symmetry, 154 *see also* brain

genetics, 72–73, 124–128

Gibran, Kahlil, 228

Gilbert, Daniel, 34

God. *see also* religion
  existence of, 54–59
  God spots, 51, 54–56
  in Hindu tradition, 218–220
  pantheism, 58–59
  proximity to, 22, 36–38

God spots, 51, 54–56

Goldberg, Ilan, 229

Goleman, Daniel, 112

Grand, Steve, 14–16, 18

gratitude, 166, 183

Greek culture, 197–200

grief, 88–89, 251–254

growth, stress-induced (SIG), 32, 69

gut feelings, 40, 47, 134–135. *see also* emotions

Haidt, Jonathan, 135–137, 218

Haldane, J.B.S., 4–5

Halevi, Yehuda, 53–54

happiness, 61–69
  awe lite and, 21, 23
  genetics and, 72–73
  illusion of, 64–66
  incidence of in U.S., 149
  pursuit of, 115–117, 159, 161,
    226–227
  tyranny of, 67
Hawaiians
  aloha, 84
  celebration, 253
  culture, 34
  gratitude, 183
  ihihia, 130
  na`au, 27–28
  Pele, 72, 135
healing/health, 96, 111–112,
  153–156, 172–173
heart
  awe response and, 40, 53–54,
    132–134, 137
  hormones and, 155
  physiology of, 53, 132–133, 155
  yips and, 133
heart chakra, 53
hedonic capacity, 188
heredity. see genetics
hierarchies, 209–214
Higher Power, 36, 55, 57–59,
  110–111. see also divinity; God
Hindu tradition
  chakras, 53
  epic, 218–220
  prayer-dance, 100
History of the Peloponnesian War
  (Thucydides), 196
Hitler, 214
holy war, 200–201
homunculus, 128, 228–229

hope, 166, 184–185
horan, 25
hormones, 132, 135–140, 142, 155,
  227
Hugo, Victor, 29
human genome project, 128
Human Nature Explored (Mandler),
  187–188
humor, 88, 177–179
Humphrey, Nicholas, 239–240

Ibn Paquda, Bahya, 53
ignorant awe, 84–86, 223–224, 230
ihihia, 130
imagination, 71, 73–75, 80–81, 84–86
immediate awe, 107–108
immune system, 47, 63, 135, 140,
  154–155
in-between areas
  altered consciousness, 35
  awe response and, 113, 148–149
  languishing and, 145
  in life, 22–24
indigenous science, 33–35
infinite play, 237–238
Iraq, 195–196
Islam, 205
Israel, 214
Izard, Carroll, 17–18

James, William, 101–102, 107,
  122–123
James-Lange theory of emotions,
  107–109
Jerome, Saint 95
Jones, Jim, 214

Jonestown, 214

joy, 166, 187–189, 256

Judaism, 205

Justman, Stewart, 111

Kaminer, Wendy, 112

Kant, Immanuel, 11, 12, 13, 16

Keller, Helen, 4

Keltner, Dacher, 218

Kim Jong-il, 138, 214, 215–216

King Kong (film), 84–86

Kramer, Peter, 64

Krishna, 218–220

lactation study, 135–136

Lange, Carl, 107

Langer, Ellen, 231–232

languishing. see also awe-lite;
    flourishing
    artificial happiness and, 227
    characteristics of, 110, 113–114,
        145–151, 156
    emotions and, 159–160
    as epidemic, 116–117

laughter, 88, 177–179

life. *see also* awe stories (SAI partici-
    pants); flourishing; languishing
    awe-inspired, 21, 23, 26–29,
        227–228
    in-between areas of, 22–24
    meaning in, 1–2, 4, 9–14, 31
    obstacles in, 67, 171–176, 178

lightning, 102–103

Listening to Prozac (Kramer), 64

literary ecology, 177–179

longevity, 155–156

love, 45–46, 135–136, 150, 166,
    189–191

lunar eclipse, 198–199, 216–217

Mandler, George, 187–188

manganese, 142

Manson, Charles, 206

Marcel, Tony, 238

Marshall, Ian, 53

Martin, Howard, 123

Maslow, Abraham, 129, 183

Masson, Jeffrey Moussaieff, 45

McDougall, William, 129

McGraw, Phil, 115

Meehl, Paul, 188

Meeker, Joseph, 178

memory trace awe, 109

Mencken, H.L., 101

menschenbild, 189

middle-worlders, 121–122

Milgram, Stanley, 209–211

Miller, Neal, 103

mindfulness, 25–26, 153–154

monkeys (research), 233, 239–240

mothers, 135–136

mysticism, 2, 49, 50–55

na`au, 27–28

natural awe, 44–48

negative emotions. *see also* emotions;
    fear; positive emotions
    anger, 92, 153–154, 162, 170
    anxiety, 10–11, 21, 133, 152, 161
    expression of, 100, 131
    grief, 88–89, 251–254

list of, 167–168
sadness, 2, 88–89, 162
toxic, 160–161, 195–217
negativity, necessary, 160–164
neonatal awe, 38–40
nervous system, 28, 134–137. *see also* brain; neuroscience
autonomic, 136–137
central (CNS), 28, 134
enteric (ENS), 28, 134, 135
neurohormones, 132, 135, 139
neurons, 55, 124, 126, 134
parasympathetic, 136–137
sympathetic, 136–137
neurohormones, 132, 135, 139. *see also* brain; nervous system
neurons, 55, 124, 126, 134. *see also* brain; nervous system
neuroscience, 53, 126–128, 132–134, 154, 228–230
Newberg, Andrew, 140–141
nonrational fear, 157–158, 170, 189, 199–200, 204
nonreflective awe, 203–204

occipital lobe, 234. *see also* brain
often-awed, 155–156
open-ture, 3
optimism, 65, 161, 168
orgasm, 136–137. *see also* sexual desire
orientation association area (OAA), 55. *see also* brain
otherness, 202–203
other worlds, 117–118, 121
Otto, Rudolf, 20
overwhelming awe, 227
oxytocin, 135

pain, 68–71, 75, 157–159
panic disorder, 133
pantheism, 58–59
parallel universes, 118
parasympathetic-adrenal-cortical (PAC) neuro-hormonal system, 139–141
parasympathetic nervous system, 136–137. *see also* nervous system
Paul, Saint 90
Pearsall, Scott
death of, 243–253
as different, 74, 202, 243, 244
parental bond with, 158–159
resilience of, 68–69, 70, 241, 243–244
Pele, 72, 135
perception, studies of, 233–234
pessimism, 65, 168
physiological aspects of awe response. *see also* brain
breathlessness, 35, 141–142
gut feelings, 134–135
healing/health, 153–156
heart, 53, 132–133, 155
hormones, 132, 135–140, 142, 155, 227
immune system, 47, 154–155
observable, 35–36
research of, 102–109
pickle game, 23–24
pleasure paradox, 69–70
Plutnick, Robert, 95–96
pneumogastric nerve (vagus nerve), 134, 135
Pogge, Thomas, 151
Pollyanna, 174–176

Pollyanna (Porter), 175

popular (pop) psychology. *see also*
self-help movement
awe lite and, 21
gurus of, 23, 115–116
happiness and, 66, 68, 149
independent self, loss of 49
labeling and, 212
techniques and, 111–112, 157

popular culture, 9, 40, 65, 66–67,
116

Porter, Eleanor, 175

positive emotions. *see also* emotions;
happiness; negative emotions
compassion, 123–124, 180–181
contentment, 181–182
elation, 176–194
facial expressions of, 131
fascination, 179–180
flourishing and, 159–160,
164–166
gratitude, 183
healthy, 96, 111–112
hope, 184–185
joy, 187–189, 256
list of, 166
love, 45–46, 135–136, 150,
189–191
pride, 191–192
serenity, 185–187
sympathy, 179–180
zeal, 192, 203

positive psychology, 23, 159–160,
164–165

positive thinking, 20, 115–116,
161–164

positivity, 161–164

"Possible Worlds" (Haldane), 4–5

posterior superior parietal lobe,
55–56

Pötzl, Otto, 234–235

power of attraction, 116

prefrontal cortex, 228–229. *see also*
brain

pride, 166, 191–192

prodigious stimulus, awe as, 80–81

prolactin, 142

Prozac, 64

psychic experiences, 50–51

psychology. *see also* popular (pop)
psychology
authority, studies of, 209–211
behaviorism, 97–98
cognitive, 98
emotion, studies of, 101–102, 176
perception, studies of, 233–234
positive, 23, 159–160, 164–165

psychopharmacology, cosmetic, 64

Publishers Weekly, 116–117

quantum physics, 117–118, 121–122,
124–126

rational fear, 157–158, 162

reflective awe, 108–109

reflex tears, 142

relaxing system (PAC), 139–141

religion, 200–208. *see also* agnosti-
cism; atheism; divinity; faith;
God; Higher Power
Buddhism, 11, 61, 90
Christianity, 90, 205, 206, 255
fanaticism and, 200–208, 214
Hinduism, 100, 218–220
Islam, 205
Judaism, 205
pantheism, 58–59

religious awe, 55, 90
religious fanaticism, 200–208, 214
Robbins, Tony, 115
Ryff, Carol, 70

sadness, 2, 88–89, 162
Santa-ists, 40–44, 56. see also a-
    Santa-ists
Satel, Sally, 113
Schachter, Stanley, 108–109
schadenfreudian experience, 64
Scott, author's son. see Pearsall,
    Scott
Secret, The (Byrne), 115–116
self
    awake, 233
    deep introspection and, 229
    de-selfing, 236
    esteem, 46, 212
    sense of, 25–26, 112, 119,
        228–229, 235–236
    silent, 229–231, 235
    sub-awake, 233, 235
    two selves, 238–239
self-consciousness, 233–236
self-esteem, 46, 212
self-help movement, 49, 148–150,
    161
selfishness, 82–83
sense of elevation, 137–138
sense of entitlement, 119
sense of humor, 88, 177–179
sense of self
    entitlement, 119
    involvement with, 38
    loss of, 228–229, 235–236
    state of awe and, 25–26, 112

senses, five basic, 51, 132
sensory cortex, 229. see also brain
separateness, 122, 123–124, 150
serenity, 166, 185–187
sexual desire, 135–137, 139, 192–194
sighers, 32, 78–79
sight, 231–240
silent self, 229–231, 235
Silvers, Jen, 135–136
Singer, Burton, 70
sixth sense, 51, 94
skin conductance test, 93–94
sleep, 185–186
sociological consequences of awe,
    220
Sommers, Christina Hoff, 113
Spinoza, 58–59
Stevens, Wallace, 67, 71
stress
    growth and, 32, 69
    hormones, 140, 155, 227
    of languishing, 110
    responses to, 24, 107–108, 155
stress-induced growth (SIG), 32, 69
Study of the Awe Inspired (SAI). see
    also awe stories (SAI participants)
    awe-lite and, 20–21
    catastrophe, 88–89
    participants in, 20–21, 32–34,
        225–228
    pleasure paradox and, 69–70
    sighers, 32, 78–79
subatomic particles, 124–125
sub-awake self, 233, 235
subliminal awe, 109
subtle energy, 51

Sun Tzu, 138

supernatural awe, 50–52

Swimme, Brian, 203, 248–249

sympathetic adrenal medullary
    system (SAM), 139–141. *see also*
    brain; nervous system

sympathetic nervous system,
    136–137. *see also* nervous system

sympathy, 179–180

T-cells, 140

tears, 142

temporal lobes, 54. see also brain

ten basic emotions, 17–18, 46, 48,
    99–100, 148–149

test, flourishing factor, 166–168,
    175–176, 182

theory of evolution, 120

thinking
    positive, 20, 115–116, 161–164
    power of negative, 65

third tear, 142

thought, 40, 129, 151, 186

three brains, 134–135, 229–230

Thucydides, 197–200

toxic awe, 195–217

toxic emotions, 160–161, 195–217

transcendental movement, 56–57, 58

trans-cockpit authority gradient,
    213–214

transformation, 109

twelve elations, 176–194

two-factor theory, 109

two selves, 238–239

tyranny, 138, 214–215, 218

understanding, awe of, 109, 223–225

United States, 138, 149, 195

vagus nerve (pneumogastric nerve),
    134, 135, 141

vain brain, 233

vastness, awe response and, 86–89

violence, bad trumps good, 200–202

Vishnu, 218

vision, 231–240

von Unruh, Fritz, 46

war, awe-inspired, 200–201

Watson, James, 127

Weber, Max, 220

Weil, Simone, 244, 246–247, 254–256

Weiskrantz, Lawrence, 237

western science, 33–35

When Elephants Weep (Masson), 45

Wickberg, Daniel, 179

Winfrey, Oprah, 135–136

wonder wrinkles, 131

yips, 133

zeal, 166, 192, 203

zealotry, 200–204

Zohar, Danah, 53